Advance Praise

"A terrific read! Exotic locations, beautiful starlets, and behind the scenes gossip - *Adventures in Filmmaking* is an insiders' look at over forty years in the movie business. And it's everything you want it to be. From sex, drugs, rock and roll in the 60's all the way to a worldwide TV phenomenon in the '10s. Peter Rowe recounts an amazing life lived large. A must read for anyone fascinated by the entertainment industry."

-Jeff Willner – Fellow, Royal Geographic Society,
CEO, Traveledge

"Whether he's balancing on the rim of an active volcano in Africa, getting lost on a glacier in B.C., or dodging the land mines buried beneath the worlds of Canadian and Hollywood production, Peter Rowe tackles each adventure in filmmaking with a fearless, single-minded determination. He takes readers on a wild ride with stories that range from gripping and hair-raising to star-studded and funny, to reveal a life fully-lived."

-Susan Feldman – Executive Producer, Literary Programming, CBC
Radio ('07-'12)

"Richly entertaining and robustly comic, *Adventures in* Filmmaking is an engaging reflection on a long career in film and television. Peter Rowe recounts his life and career in film, populated with some of the most colorful and memorable figures of fringe and mainstream cinema. This is the work of a master storyteller, one of Canada's funniest and most enduring filmmakers."

-Stephen Broomer – Lecturer, Film Department,
York University

D1417490

"There's times I thought I was having an acid flashback (somehow Rowe *remembered* the sixties). Other times I almost fell off my chair laughing. Throughout I was amazed by how much he has done and the names he has worked with, both as a filmmaker and as an adventurer. To not only survive but to flourish in the über competitive worlds of the movie and TV biz for over forty years takes talent, smarts and perseverance and he has all in abundance. He's also completely down to earth and a helluva good writer. Thoroughly entertaining. I couldn't put it down."
-Jason Schoonover – Author, Thai Gold, Communications Director, The Explorers Club (Canada), Bangkok/Saskatoon

"Admirably detailed, reliably engaging, and filled with tales of genuine adventure. Rowe recalls a range of cinematic memories from confronting the establishment with student projects to documenting the volatility of the natural world. Most importantly, he has the intelligence to recognize that emotional turmoil and physical danger can be equally thrilling."

-Josh Johnson – Director, Rewind This! – Austin, Texas

Adventures in Filmmaking

Peter Rowe

Pinewood Independent Publishing

Library and Archives Canada

Rowe, Peter, 1947–

Adventures in Filmmaking / Peter Rowe—CreateSpace Edition 1.4

ISBN 978-0-9918625-0-4

Cover Photo Montage and Himalayas photo—Peter Rowe
Shark Photo - ©J Agronick/Dreamstime
Rear Cover photo – Patrice Baillargeon

Pinewood Independent Publishing
718 Hidden Grove Lane
Mississauga L5H4L2, Canada
www.peterrowe.tv

Printed by CreateSpace—an Amazon company

Contents

An old adventurer, the story goes, returned from a lifetime of explorations of the world's distant parts to pen his memoirs of his eventful life. After laboring for years on his memoirs, he was finally happy with them, and turned them over to his wife, to proofread and respond to his work. Impatiently, he watched as she turned the pages, reading his every word. When she finally finished, he excitedly demanded, "Well, dear, what'd you think?"

"Fascinating, darling," she replied, "fascinating. Strange, though, that with such an interesting life, you never married."

Lest I fall into the same foolishness, let me not just mention, but in fact dedicate this memoir to, my wife, Carolyn.

Canadian Prime Minister Lester Pearson's wife Marion once made the droll observation that "behind every successful man is a surprised woman."

I hope that should this memoir have any success, Carolyn won't be too surprised, but, like Marion Pearson, she probably will.

Chapter 1
Volcano

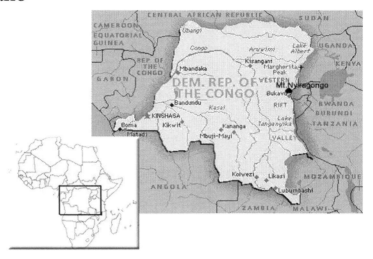

It was shortly after midnight when the wind really started to pick up. Within two hours it was really howling. Just about everyone exaggerates wind speeds, but I try not to. My partner in the venture, in a storm-battered tent beside mine, was George Kourounis—one of the world's most experienced hurricane chasers. As we were travelling light, we didn't have an anemometer with us—but we both felt there were gusts that night of hurricane force—at least seventy-five mph wind speeds. Whatever the number was, the screeching wind was flattening my tent on top of me. I felt there was a real possibility the wind could rip the tent pegs from the lava crust and hurl the tent—with me in it—into the massive, red roiling lake of molten lava below me.

We had been tent-bound now for twenty hours—trapped under nylon by pelting rain—at the peak of Mt. Nyiragongo, a massive, 11,385 foot highly active volcano that is one of the largest peaks in the Virunga mountain chain that straddles eastern Congo, southern Uganda, and northwestern Rwanda. Nyiragongo is considered one of the world's most dangerous volcanoes. It sits in a densely populated area, steaming and bubbling away right above Goma, a city of 800,000. Only four years before, it had exploded into activity, sending rivers of molten lava six feet deep flowing right through the streets of the city, killing people and trapping dozens of cars and trucks in its wake. The corrosive lava and sulphur dioxide stripped all the paint from the vehicles, and they now sit locked to the roads, taken over by kids orphaned by the AIDS epidemic, who now live in the rusting wrecks.

Getting to Nyiragongo had itself been an adventure. I'd booked our tickets a month earlier, but when we arrived at Gatwick Airport, Ethiopian Airways could not find the reservation, and told us the flight was completely overbooked. Only by making this flight could we connect in Addis Ababa with the group of Italian and Swiss climbers we were going to make the expedition with—so there was a good deal of insistent argument on our part that we had to make the plane. In the end, we did get on the flight—but not without some anxiety. As I buckled my seat belt, I watched out the window, straining to see whether our luggage was being loaded along with the rest of the passengers' bags on the luggage cart. I had my camera with me—but what about our cases of tripods, batteries, lights, and especially chargers? Without them, the camera would soon be useless.

One of the first rules of adventure filmmaking is simply that you have to have your gear with you—it has to make it through customs, not get too bashed about by baggage handlers or pot-holed roads, be able to stay dry, get charged up and keep working. Never mind high-minded semiotic cinematographic analysis, rules of thirds or exhaustive pre-shoot research. Without a fully functional camera, a platform to put it on, charged batteries, and working audio equipment you aren't even getting an image, let alone making art. And just like the shoe nail that lost the king his empire in the old proverb, every little cable, adaptor, and step-up ring is an essential

2

part of the package—and one you're not likely to be able to replace in Goma or Kigali, or even Tulsa or Honolulu.

I had been through this several times before. The year after Panasonic and JVC released the VHS format and thus created home video, I came up with what I think was the world's first "mood video". The tape was released as *Electronic Aquarium*, later re-titled *The Reef*, and has now been in distribution for over thirty years. But first, I had to shoot it. I decided to film it on San Salvador. This tiny little island in the far eastern Bahamas was Columbus's first landfall in the New World (and so the spot where he "discovered America"— even though it is over four hundred miles from the American coast— go figure). Fewer people live on the island today than likely lived on it when Columbus landed.

In 1981 the only way to get there was on little planes operated by a small airline, busted into oblivion by the US Drug Enforcement Administration seven years later, when they declared it a front for a wing of Carlos Lehder's cocaine smuggling operation. In '81, they had all my filmmaking gear (underwater gear—where one missing tiny o-ring can spell catastrophe), loaded in the belly of the small plane. Or was it loaded? I hadn't actually seen it go in.

We climbed into the six-seater in Fort Lauderdale. I exchanged glances with the diver sitting beside me after the pilot gave a short, slurred safety speech interrupted by a telltale burp. It appeared he was drunk, or else had been indulging in some of the cargo from his last flight in from the Bahamas. Still, it is generally pretty easy flying in the Bahamas, regardless of what Bermuda Triangle theorists will tell you, and three hours later he managed to plop us down on the tiny coral strip on San Salvador. After we clambered out of the plane, he opened up the side baggage compartment to let us pull out our luggage. Jam-packed with everyone's dive gear, the various bags revealed themselves. Four of my five bags were there. Where was the fifth? Soon, our inebriated captain was closing the doors, preparing to head off to get his plane filled up with fuel and himself topped up with beer for the return trip to Florida. I was frantic.

"Where is my fifth case?" I demanded. It contained the underwater housing. Without it, I would be getting an unwanted suntan, not making a film, for the next week. The next flight into the island was seven days away. He drunkenly insisted that the case could not be aboard, for perhaps ten minutes, until my frantic admonishments finally shook his addled brain and he remembered that the plane had an additional compartment in the nose cone. Sure enough, there it was. My relief was so intense I had to buy him an extra beer for his flight home.

A couple of years later, I almost had a repeat performance. I was on another tiny island—this time Truk Lagoon, a tiny speck in the middle of the vast Pacific. (Truk has now been re-named Chuuk, for some reason—probably by the same place-name-dictators that decided to re-name Bombay, Rangoon, Burma and Peking. But then it was Truk.) This time, fortunately, I had a mentor on the island who kept me out of this sort of trouble—just. I was filming throughout Micronesia, and in those days, long before Betacam, or DV, or high definition, or digital camcorders, the only format the networks would accept was 16mm film (or 35—well out of my budget). Consequently I was travelling with nineteen large cases of gear—an awkward old Arriflex BL, a back-breakingly heavy tripod, and again, a full complement of underwater camera and lights, all of which I and my assistant looked after. While on Truk, we discovered another film crew there, led by the famous underwater cinematographer Al Giddings. Al was already a legend. By then he had shot the underwater sequences for *Jaws*, *The Deep* and lots of other films, and within a few years he would go on to shoot the underwater material for James Cameron's *The Abyss*, and *Titanic*. He was also a very nice, friendly guy. His friendliness, I think, was encouraged by two other factors. First, I decided to profile him for the film I was making, and second, I think he developed the hots for my pretty assistant. We worked together for about a week. We were then both going to pack

4

up and leave, heading on the same flight for Guam and Saipan, where there was more filming to be done.

Giddings had been making a most remarkable film on Truk—a 360-degree underwater film on the shipwrecks of the lagoon, filmed with a collection of six underwater housed 35mm cameras mounted in a circular ring, with the cameraman—either Giddings or his pal, the equally legendary Chuck Nicklin—operating from inside the massive set-up. So when it came time to move, you can imagine they had a lot of gear. Forty-eight cases, as it turned out. So that would be sixty-seven pieces of luggage between the two of us. The rest of the plane was no doubt going to be filled with world travelers, island-collectors, and divers—none of whom travel very light. The morning of the flight, Giddings spotted me in the hotel café.

"You flying with us today?" he said.

"Yes."

"Here's what you have to do. Get to the airport early, get on the runway and sit beside the plane until you see every piece of your gear go onboard."

Best travel advice I ever received. When we got out to the airport (absurdly funky, with a grass roof on the open air, one-room "terminal"), I discovered how important his advice was. Also on the island, also planning to get on the plane, were a team of scientists and collectors for the Tokyo Aquarium. Their baggage consisted of twenty-eight large, heavy, portable aquariums filled with colorful fish they had plucked off the Truk reefs for display in Japan. Now, among the three of us, we had ninety-five cases to be loaded on the plane. And then there were the rest of the passengers' bags to squeeze on.

The luggage-handling department consisted of one skinny kid in filthy shorts and a Detroit Lions t-shirt that soon became so sweat-soaked in the ninety-degree heat that he abandoned it on the side of one of the carts. Giddings watched and counted every one of his cases. Taking his lead, I did the same. The Tokyo scientists shouted noisily at the kid in broken English to be careful with their precious fish. In the end, all our gear got aboard. If any bags didn't make it onto the crowded plane, they weren't any of ours. They belonged to people up above, already strapping themselves into their seats for the long flight to Guam, possibly leaving their luggage behind them.

The lesson learned on Truk was something I'd use again in future adventure filmmaking in remote parts of the world, but it really didn't help me at Gatwick, while en route to Mt. Nyiragongo. Even pre-9/11, they didn't let you wander the runways of big city airports, checking to see your luggage was aboard. Post-9/11, fuggedaboutit. So, I just had to hope for the best. We flew through the night to Addis Ababa, then on to Kigali, the capital of Rwanda. We watched anxiously as the luggage was unloaded, and finally discovered, to our relief, that all our equipment had indeed made the flights. After a long build up to this exotic shoot, I was ready to get filming. I had received the green light for my series *Angry Planet* only four months earlier, and this was just our third episode.

The goal of *Angry Planet* was to explore extreme forces of nature, but here we were dragged into extreme excesses of humanity. Rwanda had recently gone through one of the most vicious genocidal civil wars of modern times, and the evidence was still all around us. On our first day there we kicked off our jet lag and drove far out into the country to film inside a church where 5,000 Tutsis had sought sanctuary from a Hutu mob—and every one of them was slaughtered there, the floor and walls of the church a sea of red. The skulls of the victims were now lined and piled up in huge mounds—a tribute to them and a monument to their slaughter. There were once 5000 in that church. Now there were just three of us—George, me, and our Rwandan guide, and each of us was overwhelmed by this staggering memorial.

It is always a bit of a relief to get the first shot in the can (especially a first shot—first sequence—as sobering as this one). We did a bit more filming around Kigali, and then were ready to set out overland for The Democratic Republic of Congo (not to be confused, though how can you not, with The Republic of Congo, which is further to the east.) Except that our expedition leader, who organized all the non-filming logistics of the climb, was not there. A German volcanologist, living in Athens, Tom Pfeiffer, had put together a team of thirteen for the climb. There were the three of us on the filming team, two geologists—one Canadian, one American— both now living in Saudi Arabia, two Italians, two Swiss climbers, and three German volcano buffs. We were all there—but Tom was not. It turned out he had missed his flight and was stuck in Nairobi, and I (although I did not find this out until much later in the expedition) was the cause of the missed flight.

Apparently, while going over all the paperwork we had submitted on the flight down from Athens to Africa, he had discovered that I would be having my birthday while on the mountaintop. Not just any birthday, but a milestone, my sixtieth. How, though, had he learned this information? It didn't take me long to figure it out. A career of filming shark dives and avalanches and whitewater rivers and forest fires and heli-ski operations has meant I've signed dozens of liability waivers—"blood sheets", as stuntmen in Toronto and Hollywood call them—cooked up by the nervous lawyers working for the operators of these high-risk endeavors.

They usually make quite amusing reading, with your having to agree that you understand that what you are about to do is wildly dangerous and that you agree that whatever happens you will not hold them, their heirs, or, most importantly, their lawyers, responsible for whatever happens to you, whatever crazy things you may do while in their care. At the bottom, of course, you have to sign it (not literally, but certainly figuratively, in blood), and put down your birthday beside your signature. So there it was in black and white (or maybe red and white—I like to sign those documents with a red pen, just for fun, if I have one around), and so while on the plane flying down to Nairobi Tom had read this and determined that in the Kenyan capital he would pick up a bottle or two of champagne to celebrate this…not-so-momentous event (but any excuse for a party, especially one on top of an erupting volcano).

He wandered into a Duty Free in Nairobi, and mulled over his champagne-purchase decision. Was I—who he didn't know, but whose cheque to him for several thousand euros had not bounced—worthy of Dom Pérignon, or merely Charles Heidsieck? The champers would be shared by the thirteen of us, and perhaps some of our Congolese porters. Would one bottle suffice—or should he get two? And as he pondered these weighty shopping decisions, his airline called for him, heard no response, so closed the gate, and sent the plane out onto the runway. By the time he arrived at the gate, no amount of pleading could bring it back. He would have to wait another thirty hours for the next flight to Kigali.

And so, in Kigali we kept filming. It was all back-story, perhaps useful, perhaps not, but my rule is—if it moves, shoot it. Tape is cheap, and digital is even cheaper. Editors may curse you for shooting too much footage, but they'll curse you more for shooting too little. In any case, how can anyone resist filming Africa? It is so colorful, sometimes strange, sometimes beautiful, sometimes ugly, sometimes frightening, that you just want to keep capturing images of it, almost regardless of how they'll ever be used.

Eventually Tom showed up and we headed off towards Congo. There were more strange sights to see. Even as the United Nations-sanctioned war-crimes trials were going on as we were there, there were also traditional village trials of the Hutus responsible for the atrocities. These were very serious but very colorful events held in fields and courtyards not far from the roads we were passing on. They seemed to be mostly run by women—big, powerful-looking women in flowing, spotlessly clean flowery dresses. The Hutu accused were brought to this open-air justice in their bright pink jail uniforms. There were some very serious wounds being healed here. Some things you film, without asking permission. This was not one of them. We drove on.

Of course, being Africa, it was not surprising that we had vehicle problems. In the middle (it seemed) of nowhere, the problematic electrical system on one of our flotilla of vans completely stopped working. Now, in most parts of the world, the wilderness really is wild. In western Canada, our film crew was peripherally involved with a major accident on a minor road out in the wilds. After the crash it took three days before the next car came down the road (and thus was able to bring help). Stick with me—I'll tell you about it later in the book.

That's not the case in Africa. Wherever you stop, whether to fix your car or to film a shot, people soon appear from the scrub and the bushes. First boys, then little kids, then their mothers, then men. Can they help? What do you need? Soon your vehicle is surrounded by a sea of black, smiling faces, curious as to who the hell you are, and what you are doing here. Boys are sent off to bring rusty broken pliers or "spanners" to try and repair the problem.

Eventually, we got the van started again. The lights didn't work. The radio didn't work. The AC didn't work. But at least we were running again, and so we set off once more for The Congo. That was fine, until night fell, and then, of course, we had another problem. Pitch black, and no lights. I solved that by getting out a 100 watt Lowel light, designed to sit on top of the camera, hooking it up to a battery belt, and holding it out the passenger window. Sun gun lights like that are not designed to be run for long stretches, and eventually I cooked the battery. But at least we didn't die—and to my surprise, nor did we kill anyone, even though African roads become alive with pedestrians walking home in the cooler night air. Black skin, black hair, black shirts, black pants, no flashlight—and huge loads balanced on their heads. My favorite that night was a man walking with a large washing machine balanced on his noggin. At least it was a white washing machine, so we could see him.

My other favorite moment of the night was when we were stopped at one of the police/army roadblocks that are randomly ubiquitous across much of Africa. Imagine the reaction in Europe or

North America if you were stopped by the police driving at night with no working headlights, a swinging movie light hanging out the window to light your way. The Rwandan police didn't even comment on our makeshift, ridiculous lighting arrangements. They only demanded to see everyone's papers. Once they determined we didn't appear to be terrorists and had no AK-47s they could see, they waved us through. I flicked the floodlight back on, and we carried on.

Goma is the wildest, most dangerous city I've ever been in. Even people from cities like Kinshasa—no Geneva itself—are taken aback by the squalid conditions and wild-west atmosphere of Goma. A flashpoint not just in the long Congolese Civil War (the deadliest war in the world since World War II), but also in the desperate fight over coltan, the metallic black ore of central Africa, essential to the production of cell phones, and fraught with the same ethical issues as blood diamonds. Goma is a border town—one that makes Tijuana look tame by comparison. Over a million refugees from the Rwandan Genocide had streamed across the border into refugee camps ringing the city. When we were there it had the largest United Nations peacekeeping contingent anywhere on earth—and while the peacekeepers ran the airport and the refugee camps, they seemed to steer clear of trying to deal with the chaos of the city itself.

Here's how the border works. You pull up to a long lineup of vehicles trying to enter The Congo. Everyone, except the driver, piles out, grabs all their belongings, and joins an even longer line of pedestrians. While your driver takes the vehicle across, you walk across the border. I drag along my motley collection of Pelican cases, tripod tubes, camera, and camping equipment. Eventually, at a beat up desk, under the eye of numerous machine gun-toting soldiers, I'm cross-examined by an over-worked, underpaid official, who examines my papers closely. I imagine the lies that have been told here, the tears that have been shed, the stories of woe, the missing documents, the lives shattered by refusal of entry. Our own experience was no doubt trifling in comparison, but gave us a taste of the clout of officialdom. Of the twenty or so now in our party, including our Rwandan drivers and guides, nineteen of us had our papers in order. Our filming team had received our Congolese entry visas from their Ottawa embassy a month before. However one of our group, a Swiss climber, hadn't bothered. He figured he could get his visa at the border. So all of us waited for some hours in the dusty transit shack, kibitzing with Ugandan refugees while his problems were resolved. Eventually, we were all admitted into the crazy country.

What happened next was my fault—mine, and the Nikon-wielding shutterbugs I was travelling with. We'd been warned not to stick our long lenses out the open windows of our van—but how could we resist? When would we ever see such unbelievably crazy sights as this again? You don't get very good footage out the window of a bouncing van on these pothole ridden streets, but who can resist trying? I'm addicted to photography, so I feed my addiction. And there were sights to be seen, shots to be had. People are so poor in eastern Congo that they cannot afford bicycles, and so instead build themselves wooden bikes. Congolese Lance Armstrongs were riding along the street beside us in these inventive contraptions with two wooden wheels (but no gears, pedals—or steroids). Who wouldn't want to film that?

The 2006 election was approaching, and the streets were filled with posters for Joseph Kabila and his opponents. Election time is often a dangerous time to be in Africa. Soon enough, things backfired. A wild-looking character showed up wearing what appeared to be fluorescent camouflage pajamas (sounds like an oxymoron—but that *is* what his outfit looked like) He was riding a Suzuki or Yamaha 125, or a Honda Hero—something like that. He tailed us for a while, then pulled us over. It turned out he was a member of the much-feared Eastern Congolese Secret Police. He began interrogating our driver, pointing back at us—especially, I realized, at me. My long JVC HD-100, 12-120 zoom lens and matte box on the front of it, was now discreetly tucked at my feet, hidden from view. But I feared, correctly as it turned out, that it was the camera they were talking about. With a curt "Follow me!" he turned on his heel, returned to his motorbike, and led us to the headquarters of the Secret Police. We'd need to explain what we were doing there. Are you working for one of the Presidential candidates? If so, who? Our friend—or our enemy?

At the station, Mr. Pajama Man pulled in our team leader Tom, and me—owner of that big, black official looking camera, to receive our punishment. I am not a big fan of the concept that has sprung up in the past couple of years of shooting documentaries, TV shows and even features on DSLR still cameras; nevertheless there is one huge advantage to shooting on a Canon 60D. The Man can no longer tell whether you're a muckraking Michael Moore ripping hell out of the status quo or just a proud daddy ready to take snaps of junior playing on a jungle gym. Back then however, carrying a two-foot long camera covered in switches, jacks and meters—with the word "Professional" emblazoned across the top of it, that deliberate ambiguity just wasn't possible.

So the tough looking cats, some in uniforms, some, more ominously, in street clothes, along with Pajama Man, wanted to know where our filming permit was. Now, filming permits are a contentious issue for the documentary filmmaker. Like travel visas, they are a bit of a cash grab, but usually worth the hassle. If you can get them easily, efficiently, and without huge expenditure, I like to get them. National Parks, for instance, feel they have a publicly owned treasure on their hands, and they are justified in asking you to pay to take pictures of it. And they've all had issues in the past with huge commercial crews coming in, stomping around like they own the place, and ripping bushes down so some fussy director can get a different angle on the Porsche; therefore I don't object to going through all the paperwork of getting a proper filming permit.

I've also been very glad to have received filming permits in places like Pompeii, where in the midst of filming I was once attacked by a horde of uniformed Carabinieri, certain they could liven up their day by busting me for the lack of a film permit. I could see the deflation in their faces as I showed them my papers—all stamped and sealed and well defined in elegant Italian prose by the appropriate authorities. Disappointed, they handed them back wordlessly and went off to search for someone illegally feeding pigeons, or some other infraction of the local bylaws.

But there are places where permits are more hassle than they are worth. One of them is Los Angeles. In 1987 I directed a mystery thriller for a B Movie producer in Hollywood named Ronnie Hadar. Ronnie was part of the Israeli movie mafia that ran much of the Hollywood B movie scene in the 1980s, churning out straight-to-video flicks, until he eventually struck gold with that wonderfully bizarre kids franchise of the early 90's, *Mighty Morphin Power Rangers*. *Take Two* was my first feature film shot in Hollywood. Ronnie and his production manager set up an unusual, and, I thought, awkward, schedule for the shoot. Usually, on a drama, one schedules the exteriors first, leaving the interiors for the end of the schedule to act as potential cover in case the exterior days are beset with rain or bad weather. Ronnie had done the reverse. The interiors were to be shot first, the exteriors left to the last week of the short shooting schedule. "Why?" I asked him. Turned out the reason was— film permits. In the cities of Los Angeles, Hollywood, and West Hollywood, you technically require a film permit to film anywhere— even in your own bedroom (if you're mad enough to invite a full film crew into your bedroom). A film permit requires not just a daily fee to the city, but also the hiring of an off-duty police officer *and* an off-duty firefighter (four or five of each, on bigger shoots) *plus* standby paramedics and ambulances, if there are any stunts involved. And on Ronnie's bare-bones budget, the off-duty cops and firefighters would be demanding a higher hourly wage than he was paying his director. Further, the city demanded to see your entire schedule, and required that if you used these off-duties for day one, you would have to keep them for every day of your entire shoot.

Ronnie's crafty low-budget solution to this was to cram the scenes where he couldn't avoid the need for a permit—street scenes with guns and car chases on Sunset Boulevard—into the last few days of the shoot, avoiding the need for all those cops and firefighters chowing down on all the doughnuts in craft service and eating up his paltry budget for the rest of the shoot. He still had to be careful—making sure that the streets I wanted to shoot on didn't straddle two jurisdictions. Lincoln Boulevard, for instance was out, since one side of the street is Santa Monica, the other, Venice. Using it would mean two sets of police officers, two sets of firefighters. The permit hassles of Los Angeles are one of the major reasons American filmmakers came to Toronto in large numbers through the 90's. A city with an easy, one-stop permitting system is an attractive bonus.

Then there's India. If you are going to try to film in India, it's best to approach it as a giant, weird carnival of a country—unlike any place else on earth—and one that you cannot possibly handle without a local fixer to steer you through the morass of red tape, baksheesh, permits, and bribes that have become the norm there. Fortunately, I found a great one—Kartikeya Singh, and he steered us all over India for two different films, keeping us shooting in crazy situations while he ran interference from local petty officials so smoothly I barely even knew he was doing it.

However, that doesn't help you get into the country. That you have to do on your own. Go to their website—their mind-numbingly poorly designed website—and try and figure out what the rules are. Turns out they expect you to get a special filmmaking visa. Except that the local consulate has no idea how to issue such a visa—the guy who knows about it is now on leave, and his assistant is away for a month, and first you have to send the script to an official in the Ministry of the Interior in Delhi, and no, he doesn't use email—you can fax it to him, if you didn't throw your obsolete fax machine away five years ago. So you go, over and over again, to the consulate, standing in long lines with hundreds of Indian nationals anxiously waiting to renew their passports with the world's most officious—and inefficient—civil service. Fortunately, while in one of these interminable line-ups, I chanced upon…another filmmaker. He was, as the British used to say, an old India hand, having made numerous documentaries in the crazy sub-continent. He saved my sanity by giving me some advice.

"Forget about the film permit," he told me. "Just get regular tourist visas for your crew, minimize the oversized Pelican cases if you can, and tell them you're going to see the Taj Mahal."

"But what about the border?" I asked him.

He dismissed my concern with a wave of his hand.

"Chances are you'll be arriving in Delhi at four in the morning anyway—nobody's feeling too chipper—they stamp your passport and Welcome to Incredible India."

Indonesia was the same thing. My fixers there warned me to steer away from the expected film permit and come in as tourists; otherwise we'd invite a non-stop sea of red tape to be hurled at us for the entire shoot.

They were right, my Indian advisor was right, my Hollywood producer was right. So, I thought—Congo—sounds like a place where it would probably be easier to ask forgiveness than to ask permission. Unfortunately, this time I was wrong—and so here I stood in a hot, airless, secret police station, without a film permit. The whole film—maybe even the whole expedition—looked like it could implode. Of course, money can solve most problems. How much did they want to make this one go away? $1000, they told me. I laughed at them, and offered $150. They laughed at me, and came back at $500. We sawed off at $350. I handed them the bills and we were on our way. Free and clear—I thought. But it was not at all the end of the Goma hold-ups.

The first came as we approached a spot on the road to Nyiragongo where the lava from the big 2002 eruption had flowed right across the city airport's runway and continued right across the road. "Stop, stop, stop!", I shouted at the driver. I do that a lot. At first they panic, thinking it is some sort of medical emergency, or that I've dropped my watch or camera out the window, and so they come screeching to a halt on the shoulder. That's fine with me—that's what I want them to do. Soon they discover that I've seen a photo-op out the window—a troop of baboons swinging through the bush, a giant termite mound, a dust devil spinning across the veldt, a bunch of kids playing in a river—that will soon disappear. The drivers at first find this strange behaviour. They are used to passengers who just want to get from A to B as quickly as possible, roll up all the windows, complain about the heat, and maybe are willing to get out at a "scenic vista" where they'll get a shot of some distant mountains that will bore the hell out their friends and neighbours. But eventually they get used to it. They're getting paid the same whether they are driving or standing around smoking, waiting for me to get my shots of the baboon troop.

So we all piled out and I got some shots of the unusual, dramatic lava flow across the runway and highway. Of course—Africa. Other things started happening. Women passed us, with giant jumbles of firewood balanced on their heads. Urchins appeared from nowhere and quickly began assembling around us—particularly around the big guy with the big camera. Me. "You got gum, mister? You got Chiclets? Gimme money." Then, teen mothers, carrying fly-covered babies as props the way beggars at home carry squeegees or "Hungry" signs. One pleaded her case to me so passionately that I broke down, and making the classically stupid dumb traveler move, pulled out my wallet and *in full view of all the others*, gave her a small bill. (Cool money in the Congo, by the way—elephants and rhinos instead of aged queens or presidents But utterly filthy—the tattered bills look like they were printed in 1956 and have passed through about 60,000 sets of grubby hands since then.) It wouldn't be the last time I would make this dumb mistake. Two years later, in the aftermath of Hurricane Dean, I would do it on the dark, curfewed streets of Montego Bay. The events that followed that time almost killed my show host George. But you'll have to read on to find the details of that story.

At the Goma airport lava flow, my foolish move merely created pandemonium. Suddenly the crowd of boys, girls, infants, and teen mothers went wild. If that girl got a franc they might get one too. They charged at me, surrounded me, shouting "Gimme, gimme!" and "Money, money!" I panicked a bit, threw a few more

16

francs at them, and began retreating towards the van (still filming them, of course). Naturally, my retreat didn't stop things at all. Three or four boys dove into the dust and began fighting each other for the bills, ripping one of them in half. One of the boys was punched and now crying in the dirt. The rest of the crowd surged at me. George, seeing this bedlam, grabbed a camera and began filming. His shots ended up being used in the show—I think the only time I was seen in the series. Our Congolese and Rwandan guides, once alerted to the melee, charged forward to save me, grabbing sticks and beating the kids away until the mob was subdued, and retreated.

Chastened, I was glad to climb back into the van, and carry on. We had had just about enough excitement for one day—and we still had an 11,000-foot volcano to climb. We finally got to a clearing at the base of the mountain. It was quite a sight. If you've ever seen old lithographs of the early African expeditions of explorers like Burton, Speke, Stanley, or Livingston, you have an idea of it. There in the clearing stood a huge crowd of porters, waiting to carry our gear up the mountain with us. It was such a sight, I had to count them. Forty-two men and women. One would carry a tent. Another a case of cooking oil. Another a case of beer. Others a headful of firewood—for there was no fuel atop the barren peak above us. Some were ready to carry our personal bags, one to carry my camera, which he planned to carry—like everything else was carried—on his head.

But before anyone carried anything, well, they'd heard that we weren't just a climbing expedition. They'd now heard we were making a movie. That would require a different sort of fee structure. How had they heard this? They'd probably had a cell phone call from the secret police, telling them there was more financial opportunity here. The cell phone coverage in even the poorest, most remote parts of Africa—certainly in these Virunga Mountains—is better than it is in Manhattan. We were carrying a fancy satellite phone for emergencies—but it proved totally unnecessary. We could have called home—even from the peak of the seldom-climbed mountain—with a cheap cell phone and a chip from CelTel Congo—

something virtually every one of our flip-flop-clad porters, making just $10 a day, had in the hip pocket of their ragged jeans.

So how much extra did the boss want? They thought maybe $2000 for our five-day expedition would be about right. I again tried countering with $150. This time, we agreed on $500. I retreated to my luggage, and with forty or fifty sets of eyes on me, surreptitiously pulled out my rapidly diminishing emergency stash, peeled out five Ben Franklins, and went over to hand it to the boss.

"Okay, there you go. Can we get going now?" I asked. "We've got a big climb ahead of us—we're going to lose the light if we don't get going."

No, no, just wait. First, boss-man and two henchmen had to inspect the bills. They held each of them up the sun, and carefully read the dates on each. Six passed muster; four did not.

"Why not? What's wrong with them?" I asked, adopting the sucky, I'm not going to raise my voice/get riled/act perturbed/use profanity tone that one must always adopt when speaking to authorities who have power over you (that is, if you want to get anywhere with them).

The four were all pre-2004 bills. Apparently the U.S instituted some anti-counterfeiting features in 2004, and with counterfeit money being such a huge problem in central Africa, these wary customers wouldn't accept any bills dated earlier. I had to canvas through all the European climbers, seeing if they had any of the post-2004 US bills they would trade me for my spurned older ones. Eventually, I got together an approved pile of greenbacks, the highway robbery was completed, and we got the show on the road.

Only the guides and cooks (five in all) and one AK-47–toting guard were going to stay with us at the summit. The porters were just going to haul their loads to the top, set up the tents, and head back down. Most of them would return in four days, help pack up, and pick up everything we hadn't consumed, and descend the mountain with us. Within seconds of the boss man having his larceny completed and handing the order to them to go, they shouldered their heavy loads and were charging off up the trail, leaving us in their dust.

Many of the Europeans were experienced Alpine climbers, so they expected the steep but non-technical Nyiragongo to be a tough slog, but not that much of a challenge. I hoped I could keep pace with them. Filming a climb means you have to be moving faster than everyone else—trying to get ahead of the others so you can film them climbing towards you. You don't want to film bums—you want to film faces.

My technique for trying to keep up with (and stay ahead of) everyone on these third world mountain and volcano climbs is as follows: before getting to the mountain I stop at a street vendor and buy a few packages of local cigarettes. Then, once on the mountain, whenever I see what looks like a nice steep, good stretch for a photo op, I'll shout out to the guides that they should stop for a smoke break. Once they've stopped I'll hand out a cigarette to each of them, then move a few hundred yards up the mountain on my own, and get my camera ready for a good climbing shot. This cigarette ploy (officially *un*-approved by the Canadian Cancer Society) serves double duty—it gives them something to do while I get up above them, get the tripod leveled, exposure, focus, etc. set—and it also fills their lungs up with smoke, which perhaps might bring their climbing performance down to somewhere near my geezerly level. Because after I've panned them around and up the hill, I've got to pack everything up and try to catch up with these twenty-year-olds who climb the mountain twice a week.

Mountain guides around the world—from Nepal to Argentina—have adopted the Swahili expression that sounds like "poley poley", heard constantly on Mount Kilimanjaro, to remind their clients to slow down, take it easy when climbing into high altitude. They didn't have to use it much with me. I am constantly stopping, pulling out the camera, trying to tell the story. That's what adventure filmmaking is—constantly trying to develop scenarios, make things compelling—and get coverage as the story itself develops. Trying to foresee what might happen, and thus what the editor will need to set up the story, sometimes getting footage after the fact to set up an incident that has already happened. People, of course, seldom get it. They often really don't understand why you're filming things so often, from different angles, in close, far away. Haven't you got enough yet?

Fortunately, my constant companion on these *Angry Planet* adventures, host George Kourounis, did get it. He was always ready to climb a really steep part, more than once, if necessary, to do some on-camera shtick, to help get a shot set up, in short, to do whatever it took to get the show made. He attacked this big mountain with vigor, as did our climbing companions. I was even able to convince the American geologist who was climbing with us to descend into a narrow steaming hole of a fumarole that I discovered half way up the mountain. Inspired by the challenge and the opportunity to get his mug on television, he donned a climbing helmet and gas mask and went down a rope that we dropped down into the hissing fissure in the volcano. He was driven back fairly soon by the intense heat and toxic gases, but I got a nice sequence out of it that we used in the show.

Our porters stormed up the mountain like it was a short set of stairs. By early afternoon, many of them—led by the women, who seemed the fastest of the lot—had dropped their loads at the top, and were returning at a speedy clip down the mountain, ripping past our group, still plodding upward, still a long way from the summit.

So things were moving along. Some of our guides were already at the top, preparing and securing our camp. Our porters had done their work. Our film crew was slowly but surely making its way up the steep hill. The cameras were working. The volcano was smoking, but fortunately not belching any lava down on us. Was there a weak link in the operation? Perhaps two. Our camera assistant, Brian Fletcher, was a recent cancer survivor. And I, as already mentioned, was now only a day shy of sixty. People end up with nicknames on expeditions like this. My new moniker, I discovered, was "Le Vieux" (the old guy, *en français*). I'm sure I wasn't the only one wondering how Brian and "Le Vieux" would handle the big climb. We were about to find out.

While I wouldn't make any claims to be a hardcore mountain filmmaker, this wasn't my first time climbing with a camera. Back in 1974 I'd had a wild filmmaking experience in the mountains of northern British Columbia that taught me a number of valuable lessons about mountaineering. While producing a string of TV spots for the B.C. Department of Tourism, I learned of a remarkable discovery that a bush pilot had made in the remote northwest corner of B.C. Flying over the Tweedsmuir Glacier, he discovered a massively flooded river—effectively, a lake—that was not on his map. The Tweedsmuir is one of Canada's largest glaciers— seventy kilometers long, a kilometer wide, and about three hundred feet high. The area, spreading over northern BC, southwestern Yukon, and the bottom of the Alaska panhandle, is utter wilderness. Further investigation led to the realization that the huge glacier was now, as glaciologists put it, *galloping*—travelling forward at the absurd rate of up to 200 feet a day. There were two impediments—the Coastal Mountain range, and the large powerful Tatshenshini River, flowing towards the Pacific. Something had to give. At first what gave was the river, which spilled its banks, creating the huge lake. By summer, when news of the wild phenomenon got out, the glacier had slowed to a (still un-glacial) speed of about twenty feet a day. The river had fought back, and was now flowing past the glacier, undercutting its front edge and creating a spectacular show of calving massive chunks of turquoise ice from it.

I determined to film this extraordinary event. The province's catchphrase, then and now, that our photography was supposed to illustrate, is "British Columbia. Super Natural". A galloping glacier certainly qualified. I, along with my cameraman, the skilled Vancouver ace Ron Orieux, had to get up there. It wasn't easy. First we had to fly to Whitehorse, Yukon, a challenge in itself. Try telling provincial bureaucrats that in order to film their province you have to leave it and head off to another jurisdiction. From Whitehorse, a drive to remote Haines Junction, Yukon, and from there, a 150-mile, very expensive helicopter ride back into B.C., to a spot where the calving action would be peaking and thus the filming would be optimized. At this point only sixteen people in the world had seen this sight—virtually all of them government scientists. Fortunately our helicopter pilot had taken some of them in, so he knew the spot, the landing site, and the terrain.

It all sounded ideal—providing we had bright sunshine backlighting the glacier. Translucent blue giant chunks of ice sending up massive sun dappled sheets of spray as they fell into the river—it was going to look beautiful. We consulted an aviation chart to figure out which direction we would be looking—and where the sun would be. It looked perfect—as long as we got there early in the morning, when the sun would be side-lighting the glacier. That is, of course, if there was sun. This was the north. The forecast was for two days of overcast and rain. Resisting the temptation to get going, we cooled our heels in Haines Junction.

While there, being twenty-five-year olds with nothing to do, we…met two girls. The pair turned out to be glacier buffs. Glacier groupies, one might say. Who knew there was such a thing? These two were majoring in glaciers (again, who knew?) at some college in Boston—and they'd driven up to the Yukon to check some out. When they met us, I like to think, they thought they'd died and gone to glacier heaven. Not so much because the two of us were such great hunky catches, but because we had a free seat (only one, unfortunately) available on a pricey helicopter ride to see the most active, interesting glacier in the world.

In the end, the sun came out, and we piled our gear and one of our new friends aboard, and flew down to the galloping Tweedsmuir. After tracking and circling over the enormous river of blue ice, we landed on a pebble beach on the banks of the river, right below a big mountain, across from the glacier. Once we had unloaded, the helicopter took off, promising to return for the three of us at four that afternoon. As the sound of the thumping blades gradually faded into the distance, we were left alone in a land of utter silence. There wasn't another human being within one hundred fifty miles—and in fact in most directions you could travel for five hundred miles or more before you would find another person—or even a road. The silence, though, was broken by the booming cracks in the glacier and crashes as the front edges of it fell into the river. We got to work.

I strapped on the audio gear—a Uher reel-to-reel tape recorder, and a parabolic microphone, and Ron got his Éclair camera going. We stood at the edge of the beach, equipment ready, waiting for the next dramatic collapse of a five hundred by fifty foot piece of glacier into the river. Today, we'd have the camera on cache mode, knowing we could turn it on five or even ten seconds after the ice cracked, and still, through the magic of modern cameras, we'd capture it all. Back then, we had to anticipate, and hope for the best— or lose money running the film through the camera hoping something would happen. When it did happen, the giant pieces of ice would send up a tsunami of water hurtling towards us. We'd film, film, film, then grab the tripod and run at full speed up the bank, to avoid getting caught by the rushing water. Quite mad, really. Had either of us slipped into the frigid, swirling water, we would have been swept out through the icy canyon towards the Pacific. The only creature that might have saved us from an ocean voyage would have been a grizzly bear, fishing us from the shallows downstream.

Even madder was what we did next. Ron decided that with the sun moving inexorably across the sky, and with plenty of spectacular footage in the can, he wanted to shoot some "reverses" on the exploding glacier. Normally a reverse refers to the shot of the second person in a scene—a character who is looking in the opposite direction from the first character. It's hard to know exactly what a "reverse" is on a glacier—they don't teach that in film school—but he wanted to get one. There was a mountain in the way, so we just decided, willy-nilly, that we would climb over it to another vantage point down the river, so off we went. Our new girlfriend was sensible enough to stay right where she was, telling us she would see us on our return.

Ron, a west-coast kid, who'd probably been clambering up big rocks and mountains since he was eight, began climbing, carrying his precious Éclair under his arm. I—native of flat Toronto, born in Winnipeg (even flatter), a greenhorn in the mountains, a *chechako*, in the vernacular of the Yukon, with the tape recorder around my neck, parabolic mike in one hand, Ron's tripod in the other, followed.

It soon became what alpinists call a "technical" climb (steep, difficult, and scary). Both hands required. As we ascended, I did somewhat revel in the idea—almost certainly accurate—that we were probably the first human beings ever to climb this mountain. Neither cavemen nor natives nor early pioneers had much motivation to climb mountains—certainly not this one. And no sportsmen had likely ever been here. It wasn't Everest—it was just another unnamed peak in a sea of thousands of similar Coastal mountains that stretch from Alaska to California. But this one was *our* mountain. If I kicked at a stone and sent it tumbling down the hill, it was likely the first move that stone had made in its 400 million year life.

While these were interesting thoughts, mostly I focused on trying not to fall down the hill myself. Eventually, we did make it over to the other side. We filmed there. Great reverses, Ron. We recorded more glacier booms. We didn't see any grizzly bears—though some of them probably knew we were there. Then we looked at a watch. Oh-oh. We better get going back. Helicopter's going to be back at 4 p.m.

We began the return trek. Soon, we got separated on the convoluted mountain. Ron, the better, more experienced climber, moved faster, and soon was ahead of me. That was okay—you can't really get lost on a mountain—it is quite evident which way you want to go—*down*. However, there is more than one way down a hill, and so it was then that I learned for the first time a central truth about mountain climbing—it is much easier to climb up than to climb down a mountain. First of all when you're going up your eyes are leading. When you are descending you are often almost blind to where you are going, your feet searching for toeholds below you. Second, when you're ascending, if you run into problem area—a pitch that is too steep, or too slick, for instance, you can likely try and go around it. Descending, you often get trapped, finding yourself suddenly above steep difficult pieces of rock, but uncertain as to whether you should risk going down there, or climbing back up in order to search for better route elsewhere.

I started to overheat, baking with anxiety under the hot summer sun. Overheating is not good. Stick around, and I'll tell you the story of a near-fatality from overheating on one of our cave explorations. On this mountain, I wasn't about to die, but I was sure getting nervous. I looked down and in the still clear air could now see two dots moving at the bottom. Ron had made it down, and rejoined our female friend from Boston. I looked at my watch. 3:30. I kept trying to find my way down the damn hill. Everywhere I went I seemed to be finding nothing but impassable, steep cliffs. Perhaps if I had some training, some ropes, some nerve, I could have made it. Instead, I had...sweaty palms, a parabolic microphone, and a tape recorder.

At quarter to four I began to hear the distant sound that I did not want to hear. Thump/thump/thump/thump. Damn! I hoped he'd be late. Instead he's early. I had two scenarios rolling around in my addled brain. One—he would arrive with me still way up the mountain, and wait for me there, with the meter running (at 450 1974 dollars an hour), and everyone getting freaked about getting back to the Yukon before nightfall. Two—he would have to come up and somehow pluck me off the mountain with the chopper. Neither idea was very appealing.

Somehow in such situations one just rams it into fourth gear, and makes it happen. Give 'er, as they say in western Canada. Somehow I just forced myself to find a way down the steep, unforgiving mountain. In the end, I ran out onto the glacial till flats just as the Bell JetRanger was landing, jumped aboard with the others, and headed back towards the Yukon.

Did my Tweedsmuir experience help me at Nyiragongo? Yes and no. As you'll hear, my descent of the African volcano ended in another, different kind of crisis—a medical one. But for now, climbing *up* the mountain, everything was going great. George and I—and our two new best friends—two geologists on leave from their high paying jobs in the oil fields of Saudi Arabia that we'd climbed through the afternoon with—summited together, just before sunset. The pair were volcano buffs (yes, there are volcano buffs, just as there are glacier buffs), so were full of useful information about this very volatile piece of rock we were standing on.

You didn't need to be a buff to appreciate the sight we had at the top. Looking down into the massive crater, we...beheld (I think it is the only verb that does it justice) the amazing sight of the world's largest lava lake—a massive cauldron of boiling red rock, throwing chunks the size of freight cars into the air—a tempest-tossed sea of 1750° bubbling magma. Naturally, I rolled video on it.

Except that...within less than five minutes, heavy clouds blew in. We looked around, now barely able to see the tents of our campsite, perched precariously on the side of the steep hill, let alone the lava lake far below us. Proof, again, of my Rule #5 of adventure filmmaking. If you can get the shot now, *get* it now, because you never know when things are going to change and you won't be able to get it again. These few shots were hardly enough, but at least I had something in the can, unlike the amateur shutterbugs there with me, who were all wowing and zowing and, oh, we'll come back to photograph it tomorrow. As it turned out, it would be three days and nights before the clouds would clear and any more photography would be possible.

For now, I put the camera away and we all re-grouped at the camp. Everyone here? Everyone accounted for? Well, no. Everyone was there, peering through the misty darkness at each other, except our cancer-surviving Canadian compatriot, Brian. He'd last been seen struggling, well down the mountain. The tail-sweep Congolese mountain guide was also not at the top, so we had to assume the two were together. Should we go down, searching for them? Could he have had a relapse? Been injured? If we went down, would we find them—or miss them? They could take an alternate path up. Then might not we get lost ourselves on the dark, cloudy night?

In the end, we waited, and in the end, the pair showed up. He was late, and tired, but he made it. It was an accomplishment. It is always an accomplishment. The African peaks like Nyiragongo are not in the same league as the Himalayas, Andes, or Rockies—but they too can be a deceiving challenge. The greatest mountaineer of all time, Reinhold Messner, was once turned back by altitude sickness on Mount Kilimanjaro—a peak regularly summited by teenagers and octogenarians. It is a mysterious ailment, a bit like seasickness or carbon monoxide poisoning, that can hit the strong and not the weak, hit today and not tomorrow.

We had not succumbed to it. We had succeeded. We celebrated—and then, after an intense day, we slept. Little did we know that we would be sleeping for much of the next three days, trapped, tent-bound, inside our flimsy walls of nylon, as the storm swirled around us.

We made an attempt to film the next day, but it soon became obvious that it was impossible. I was well equipped with the gear needed to film in storms—indeed in hurricanes, as you'll see later, but waterproof housings and spinning glass rain deflectors are heavy. I had none of them with me at the mountaintop. By midday we gave up and returned to our sodden tents.

Our porters and guides, five of them jammed into a small bell tent, in which they slept, cooked, and stored most of the food, valiantly kept the meals coming. That night we were rousted from our tents for the evening meal. We dragged "lava bombs"—chunks of rock that had been hurled from the volcano on years previous—into a circle, and used them to either sit on or squat in front of to eat our meal. As our five cooks—French-speaking, but not exactly Michelin

Three-Star—produced the food, I received my surprise. Tom pulled out his two bottles of champagne, and everyone learned that it would be my birthday at midnight. I was toasted by all with plastic cups of the fine vintage, rapidly diluted by the pouring rain.

Within minutes the champagne was drunk, the meal eaten, the tiny damp campfire extinguished, and we were heading back to our tents. Some of our party apparently slept for hours on end. I can't do that. Six hours a night—max. But I didn't have anything to entertain myself with. Foolishly over-concerned with the backs of my porters, I had not brought any books along. I did have the camera manual, so read the thick document once, then twice, then again. Dull, boring reading. Read and re-read the troubleshooting guide, even though I was thankfully having no trouble. Couldn't perform my usual nightly rituals of cleaning the camera, as it was too dangerous. Condensation and tiny tent leaks dripped water throughout my humble abode. Better to have a dry, dirty camera than a wet, clean one. Video cameras are terribly susceptible to water damage. If only a few raindrops seep in through jacks, fittings, or ports, they can short out the circuits and virtually destroy a camera in seconds. Unfortunately, I'm an expert on the subject. That night, the camera stayed in its case, wrapped in plastic, under the tent fly, rivulets of rainwater running past it.

Finally, looking for something to do, during a brief respite of the storm, I went out for a tour around our sorry, sodden campsite. The only light coming from any of the tents was from George's, so I gave a shout—how was he doing?

Not well, it turned out. The old curse of adventure travel. Montezuma's Revenge. I have circled the (third) world with George—and know that he has a cast-iron constitution—but that night he succumbed, as most everyone eventually does, to the perils of the road less travelled. It's no surprise that our pampered western intestines can't handle the microbial attacks of the tropics. According to the London School of Hygiene and Tropical Medicine, there are 3000 different bacteria on the average person's hand, with 11% of those hands so "grossly contaminated" that they are carrying as many germs as a toilet bowl. And they did their studies in London. Imagine then what the numbers must be in Goma—or the hands of a cook at the top of Mount Nyiragongo, where there are no toilet bowls to even compare to, or sinks—or soap or water. So while travelling like this, our innards are having quite an adventure themselves—meeting all kinds of new creatures. On top of that we are popping all kinds of new drugs into ourselves out there. Malarone, just for instance, does a great job of keeping malaria at bay—but at what cost?

That's one whole paragraph I've given you on gastro-intestinal issues—and that's just about enough. I have a rule on the road—I don't tell you about my G.I problems—and I don't want to hear about yours. It is remarkable how in the more remote parts of the world one often hears tourists and travelers carrying on, to strangers, at high volume, usually at breakfast, with intimate details about the activities of their intestines. Yucch, guys. I don't want to know about it. Neither does the waiter—or that nice retired couple you just met from Des Moines.

So I didn't ask for any details. I did ask him if he had brought up any reading matter. Turns out he had. *The Hot Zone*, by Richard Preston, a terrific book about the fight against the Ebola and Marburg viruses (more microbes—is there a theme here?). George wasn't in the reading mood—so he passed the book out through the tent fly. I'd read the book a few years back, when I was pitching a TV special on bioterrorism—but I was glad to read it again. I had a long night ahead of me—and, as the storm was predicted to continue, probably another long day and night as well.

I retired to my tent, and began. I read the book once, then I read it all over again, and then, on the final night of the storm, began reading it yet again. That time, I determined to read it really slowly, so that it wouldn't "run out" before the storm did.

The first read, though, was interrupted by the wild storm. At midnight—as I mentioned on the first page of this opus, the wind really started to pick up. Soon it was not just shrieking through the lonely mountaintop campsite, but gusts were flattening my tent right against me. The tent poles were bent right down to the ground, the nylon and the guys stretched to the max, pushing the wet fabric right against my face. Claustrophobic? A little. Worrying? Yes, a lot. As the wind continued to pick up, I began to start thinking that it could actually rip the tent pegs from the ground, turn the tent into an untethered kite, and blow it…well, let's see, where would it blow it? I did happen to be less than twenty feet from the lip of the volcano's crater, and thus twenty feet from a thousand-foot fall into giant lava lake. That lake was probably being cooled down a little by the torrential rain that was falling on it—but it was still boiling at probably 1450°. All in all, it would be an unpleasant way to go.

Now, maybe you say this was paranoia. Maybe you might say that was an unrealistic fear—that surely the weight of my body, and my gear, and my big honking Sachtler & Wolf tripod, and my camera, would all prevent the tent from being sent airborne off the cliff. Perhaps you would be right—but as the howling wind again tried to smother me by blowing the tent down across my face, I decided I didn't want to take the risk. I had with me, as I usually do on these sorts of trips, a coil of seventy-five feet of light line. I determined that I would crawl out into the storm, tie that rope to the top of the tent, descend down the mountain to the end of the line, and tie it taut to a big, heavy lava bomb.

What I didn't want to do was jeopardize the rest of the expedition by getting my clothes soaking wet in the downpour. Wet clothes in a leaking wet tent can take just about forever to dry. A wet body can be dry in minutes. So I stripped everything off—everything—except for a pair of socks, and my hiking boots. You can't walk on sharp lava with bare feet. Opening the tent fly, I went out into the cold, wet tempest. With my weight now out of the tent, it was much more vulnerable to be blown away. I had to move fast. I re-set all the tent pegs, tied my line off to the windward corner of the tent, and set off, clambering down the rocky hill. I had to be careful—the rocks were slippery, and if I had slipped and fallen it is doubtful if anyone would have heard my cries for help.

30

I clambered down to a likely anchor rock, and began tying my new super-guy off to it. By now I was soaked with the cold rain—but I had the comfort of knowing there was a dry camp towel and dry clothes waiting for me back in the tent. I looked up to see a headlamp moving along the ridge. As I peered through the thick rain, I began to see who it was. George, making his way along the ridge path at the lip of the volcano, with oddly contradictory movements. He had the urgency of someone who knows he only has seconds to make it to the bathroom, and the caution of someone walking on a dark path running high above a cliff falling 1500 feet to an active lava lake—a path that is crisscrossed with the largely invisible guy-wires of fourteen tents. I wasn't going to further confuse the issue by calling to him. I silently watched as he gingerly tried to hurry along the path, around the bend to the Nyiragongo "bathroom". Let me describe it.

This most makeshift of loos had likely been built by members of the French volcano monitoring team that came to the summit every six months or so. These volcanologists had placed sensors around the mountain in order to warn the people of Goma of seismic activity in the crater. Although hidden, the sensors were eventually usually found and ripped off by thieves to sell for their scrap metal value. So the technicians would return to replace them—and on one of these trips they had built a primitive honey pot on top of the hill. It consisted of two rickety planks over a steaming fumarole. Balance on the two of them and do your thing. Don't fall off—it's a long way down. But it did have a certain appeal—the earth sending a stream of warm steam at your rear end as you squatted over it. I don't know if any Japanese have made it to the top of Nyiragongo. If one of them does he'll likely patent the thing—you know how the Japanese go for avant-garde toilet systems.

Once George was out of sight, I clambered back up the slope to my tent, climbed in, and dried off. Back to my book. There would be reading, occasional eating, and very little filming, for the next thirty-six hours. The new guy wire worked. The tent was no longer threatening to fly away, like Dorothy's Wizard of Oz farmhouse.

Finally, the storm ended, the weather cleared, and the clouds lifted. We came out from our battered tents. I scraped the mud off the tripod, and we got to work, filming one of the most spectacular and awesome sights in nature. We had a day of clear access to the volcano, and then, more importantly, since of course it photographs much better in the dark, a full night. The wild images made the difficulties all worth the trouble.

The next morning, we packed camp, and descended the mountain. This wasn't a crazy, out of control descent like my experience on the mountain beside the Tweedsmuir Glacier had been—but the steep volcano did enact its own kind of revenge on me for daring to photograph it without a film permit. It took us about six hours to hike down the mountain. My problems arose from an unlikely source: footwear.

At the Montreal Film Festival, I once heard the famous Hollywood filmmaker Roger Corman (once dubbed "the Orson Welles of Z Movies") give some advice on a directing panel. Asked by some audience member if he had some basic advice for the first-time film director, he responded with a brief but eloquent piece of wisdom: "Wear comfortable shoes."

I have always tried to follow Mr. Corman's advice, and thought I had done so on this grueling shoot—but apparently not. Later examination of my hiking boots by a podiatrist revealed that they were too small, too tight in the toe box. They were okay for climbing, but no good for descending. My feet were being punished with every step I made. By the bottom of the mountain, I discovered all my toenails had turned black. They stayed that way for the next four months, and by the time I got home my feet had developed plantar fasciitis. Google it if you wish, or else just accept that it is a wretched inflammatory affliction of the foot that hurts a lot. I limped around two more film shoots with it, but eventually got it fixed with the same cure they give racehorses—a painful but ultimately very helpful shot of cortisone into each sole.

Within four years I'd fallen in with a guy who has (I hope) solved my filmmaking footwear problems for life. Paul Hubner is a polar and alpine adventurer who also builds some of the best extreme expedition boots in the world. I filmed with him as we crossed Baffin Island by dogsled, and then on a trek through Nepal toward Mount Everest. I wore his Baffin boots; I didn't have any more problems.

On Nyiragongo, my feet were hurting, but my mind buzzed with enthusiasm, as I told George my idea for another African adventure. In his now waterlogged edition of *The Hot Zone*, I had read about an amazing place—a cave high on Mount Elgon on the Kenya/Uganda border, with two very unusual characteristics. First, it is thought to be the only cave in the world that was created by elephants. The big animals, it seems, need a huge intake of salt every day. On the savannah, where most elephants live, they can get their fix by licking it from dew-laden grass. But in the salt-less forests of Mount Elgon, where these elephants live, they found a different way. Thousands of years ago, they began digging the earth with their tusks for the mineral, and by now have created a huge cave, that they come to every few days, and enter to continue their dark quest for salt.

The second unique feature of Kitum Cave on Mount Elgon is that it appeared to be Ground Zero for a particular case of the gruesome Marburg virus disease (MVD), a close relative of Ebola virus disease. This horrible scourge, which first appeared in the 1960s near Marburg, Germany, was traced to infected grivets (Old World monkeys) that were being used to develop polio vaccines. In the 1980 case described in *The Hot Zone*, the bats that live (in the tens of thousands) in the Kitum Cave were thought to have transmitted the virus to the victim, who died a horrific death, bleeding ceaselessly from his nose and vomiting up "a stew of tarry granules mixed with fresh red arterial blood". Perfect! Let's go there. Our show was called *Angry Planet*, after all. This place sounded pretty angry.

We would, eventually, get to Kitum Cave, although only after two attempts, both aborted because of the equally angry politics and violence that swept around western Kenya during the election campaigns of 2008 and 2009. It turned out to be an extraordinary filming adventure—one that almost ended very, very badly. Spin through to Chapter Eight if you want to read about it now, or else stick with me on the signposted path through these Adventures in Filmmaking, first with a look at role of memory in movies—and memoirs.

Chapter 2
Ah, Yes, I Remember it Well (Sort of)

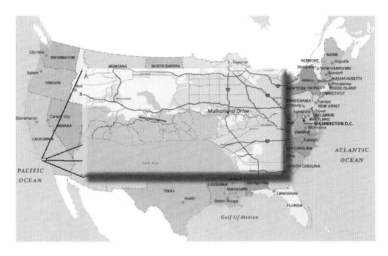

     After exploring Nyiragongo, glaciers of Patagonia, remote Pacific islands, and deep caves in western Canada and Costa Rica, I decided I ought to see if I could get membership in the Explorers Club—a unique organization based in New York with members and chapters all over the globe. Entry into the club is not easy. The word "explore" is a bit of a charged one. Some outings are better described as "adventures" or merely "travels" than the more grandiose "expeditions" or "explorations". The Explorers Club is fairly precise about their requirements for membership. In order to gain membership, you must be sponsored by two members, and must have engaged in activities beyond exotic travel—activities that usually have included some investigation and documentation of the world. I was no Buzz Aldrin or Vasco da Gama, but I had made numerous forays out into the wild world, usually with a camera, and had also filmed biographies of the lives of numerous explorers—Joshua Slocum, Étienne Brûlé, Marguerite de Roberval, and others.

Beyond that, we looked on ourselves as doing a unique new kind of exploration on *Angry Planet*—exploring not just places but moments in time. There isn't anything unique about "exploring" the beaches of Florida or North Carolina, but there is something unique about exploring them while a Category 3 hurricane is bearing down on them.

Those were some of the arguments I laid out in my application to the club. They bought into it, and awarded me membership. You know Groucho Marx's line, that he didn't want to belong to any club that would admit him as a member. Perhaps by the end of this book you'll conclude that *you* don't want to belong to any club that would allow *me* as a member.

The Explorers Club has a long and illustrious history. It was founded in 1904 by a number of prominent men of the day led by Polar explorer Adolphus Greely. Members of the club have included Roald Amundsen, Thor Heyerdahl, Jacques Piccard, Sir Edmund Hillary, and Neil Armstrong. The club headquarters is a Manhattan brownstone once owned by adventurer Lowell Thomas, and filled with stuffed polar bears, polar sledges and the like, and often, as well, with a fascinating assortment of accomplished characters.

It has also seen its share of controversy over the years. The second and third presidents of the club were Frederick Cook and Robert Peary, who both made (dubious) claims to be the first person to reach the North Pole. Club lore has it that the two presidents almost came to blows several times on the premises. Amelia Earhart never got membership, as for years the club was male-only, and in fact the club had to be dragged kicking and screaming into allowing women as late as 1981. In the 1990s there was a controversy over the strange, exotic and often endangered animal species that had been consumed at the club's annual dinner, an issue finally resolved in favor of the animals, or at least the endangered ones. The latest internecine battle, this one over club politics, and well documented by the press, was ultimately resolved in 2012. All these intriguing scraps add to the heritage and luster of this remarkable institution.

I knew my interest in adventure and exploration went back long before my entry into the Explorers Club—but only when thinking of this book did I remember that my very first foray into show business had an exploration theme.

Grade Three. Miss Brooks's classroom. No memory today of how this began—but somehow it was decided that a play would be put on for the class. A two-hander. Was it a real play—or did we write it ourselves? Or did I write it? Maybe. I do remember that the dialogue was hand-written, on a few sheets of paper. Was it copied from a book—or did we dream it up ourselves? Who knows? I *do* remember my role. The lead. The most famous, and arguably most important explorer of all time. Christopher Columbus. Importantly, for this narrative, there were long speeches. Speeches that had to be memorized.

Here's what I remember about my first theatrical venture. The front of the classroom is cleared. It now represents the poop deck of the Santa Maria. Two chairs are set up. On one of them sits my friend—was his name Bob Peters? Something like that. He is playing my first lieutenant—probably the captain of the Pinta, or some equally weighty role. We are both decked out in weird floppy hats, and wear window curtains standing in for 16th century marine finery. Each of us has a green bamboo garden stake with a small crosspiece for a handle stuck in his belt. I now doubt very much that Columbus wore a sword as he sailed across the "ocean blue", but in those days, we were all very much into weapons, and so were both armed with bamboo swords. The scenario did not require them, but in this production, they turned out to be very useful props.

I suppose Miss Brooks shushed the classroom, and then off my sidekick and I went, emoting away under our floppy captains' hats with some sort of dialogue about sailing the Atlantic and finding a New World, and the like. And then…one of us dried. Memory is tough. I don't remember now whether it was him or it was me. One of us could not remember his lines. The play ground to a halt. The two of us stared at each other, indicating with facial gestures that the other should say something. The longer it went on, of course, the more embarrassing it became. And so my goal (perhaps his as well) became not to save the play, but to try to convince my young classmates that it was *he*, not I, who had dropped the ball.

Since my facial expressions didn't seem to get him saying anything, I then determined to increase the intensity of the attack on my fellow thespian. I slowly unsheathed the bamboo sword from its makeshift scabbard, and began poking him with it, indicating, in effect—"Your turn! Say your line!" Naturally a bit peeved by this new, unscripted piece of stage business, he eventually pulled *his* sword out, and began poking back, indicating, "No, it's not! It's *your* line."

No explorer-ish dialogue came from either of our mouths. One sword poke—then another—and another. The room was quiet—except for a growing chorus of titters from the peanut gallery. Finally, Miss Brooks put us out of our misery and shut the thing down. We sheepishly got rid of our floppy hats and curtain cloaks, went back to our desks, and the class moved on, I imagine, to long division.

Any sane person would have got the message from that mortifying moment and immediately retired from performing, but instead I got the bug and joined a group known as the Toronto Children's Players. A much bigger deal than the Columbus playlet—and more conventional subject matter. Princes and dragons and that sort of nonsense, probably. My main memory of the venture involved memory (once again)—and, this time, shoplifting.

In those days Eaton's was by far the biggest retailer in Canada. In Toronto they had two big department stores—the one at Queen that has gone on to become the Eaton Centre (even though Eaton's itself is long gone), and their College Street store—a beautiful Art Deco building up Yonge at College. Eaton's College Street had on its top (seventh) floor a theatre—a big, serious stage with fly lofts, dressing rooms, giant banks of lights, a raked house with proper fixed seating, and beautiful thirties' chrome fixtures—the real McCoy. It hosted concerts and plays, evangelists and magicians, and travelogue movie presentations for fifty years. In 1976, the store was sold, and the doors of the seventh floor remained sealed for nearly thirty years. Around the turn of the current century, after a $2.5 million restoration, the space became an event venue called The Carlu for product launches, weddings, election night events, and awards shows. But back in my schooldays it was an impressive and intimidating theatre for a kid actor—and that's where we put on our annual play for five or six days every spring.

Most of the members of the Toronto Children's Players were suburban kids like me, who paid to belong and take lessons and participate. The rest, though, were a group of inner city kids who through a downtown place called the WoodGreen Community Centre got a chance (without charge) to perform with us in the plays. At that time the centre was at the corner of Queen and Degrassi Street, and if that sounds familiar it's because you've been watching those inner city Degrassi Street kids act their hearts out on TV for the last thirty years. The original *Kids of Degrassi Street* began in the WoodGreen Community Centre, and its young stars (and the stars of its various spin-offs, including its most famous alumni, Drake) are the virtual descendents of the kids who acted with me at Eaton's College Street in the late 1950s.

Of course, they were a tougher crowd than us kids from the 'burbs. After the afternoon matinee, we'd have a few hours to kill before the evening performance. Still in costume, we'd wander the aisles of the big department store, with them giving us wide-eyed suburban innocents expert lessons on all their best shoplifting tricks.

Returning to the seventh floor theater, we'd prepare for the evening production. I loved it—and I hated it. Stage fright? No, didn't have stage fright. I loved being onstage. But lines fright, memory fright, yes. Psychologists claim that the most common phobia in the world is the fear of being onstage—of speaking in public. People like me, who enjoy being onstage, find that hard to believe. As long as you have a script, or a teleprompter, or can wing it, then would you be afraid? But add memory into the mix—add the necessity to jam reams of verbiage into your head and not forget a word of it while running around and remembering your cues and hitting your marks—now you have a challenge.

The role of memory is a little-discussed but for most of us, daunting aspect to stage performance. If you doubt this, let me present you with a little showbiz memory challenge. Don't worry, I won't ask you to learn all 1438 lines that an actor playing Hamlet has to learn in order to perform that cheerful little piece of theater. No— your assignment, if you're up to it, is to learn one Bob Dylan song. Just one. Bob has published over four hundred and fifty songs—and still sings them, live, in big arenas, at an age (71 at this writing) when the old memory synapses aren't quite firing like they once used to. So—for you, just one. Go to bobdylan.com or one of the other lyric sites on the web, and have a look at, oh, let's pick..."Visions of Johanna". There are only fifty-two lines to the song. Memorize them. You'll find the chords online too—learn them as well. Words and music, ready for public performance—without an autocue. Could you do it? I couldn't.

Some people find it a breeze. Soap opera stars, for instance. I've had only a peripheral connection with the world of soap opera. In the early nineties, I was very loosely connected to the production of a big German-Canadian made soap called *Family Passions* that was shot in Toronto and played for a couple of years. In 1987, I made my first Hollywood feature, *Take Two*, which starred soap actress Robin Mattson. Robin got started in soap operas with *Guiding Light* in 1976. She's been doing it, day in, day out, pretty much ever since. She's been killed off, resurrected, had affairs, been sent to mental hospitals, murdered her cheating husbands, and spouted dozens, hundreds, thousands of pages of dialogue as Heather Webber on *General Hospital*, Delia Ryan on *Ryan's Hope*, Gina Capwell on *Santa Barbara*, Janet Green on *All My Children*, Sugar on *The Bold and the Beautiful*, Cheri Love on *As the World Turns,* and Lee on *Days of Our Lives*.

Here's what her life has been like—and how soap operas have worked, since they first began on radio, invented by Procter & Gamble in the 1930s. Every day, Monday to Friday, the cast of the soap will show up at the studio, early in the morning, their scripts—that they were given yesterday—in hand. Some of them might have as much as twenty or thirty pages of dialogue to do that day. They'll be expected to know it. They'll do a read through with the director, then a blocking rehearsal on the standing sets with the camera crew. Around noon they'll go into makeup and wardrobe, make sure they've got all those words crammed into their heads, then be all ready to shoot (no re-takes) at about two o'clock. In the fifties and sixties they used to broadcast them live—so they were shot exactly to time, in order, with music and effects mixed in live, and the actors going for broke. They still stick to those traditions, though now they have a day or so delay before broadcast, so they can tweak or repair egregious errors—but there usually aren't any. By 4 p.m. they have the episode wrapped, and, before they leave, the actors are handed a new sixty-page script they'll be expected to read and learn that evening, ready for the next morning.

So is it any wonder that with training like that Robin looked on the demands of a feature film shoot as being laughably easy? Shoot eight pages a day? Shoot four or five takes of each shot? Pshaw! What a piece of cake. I remember one day handing Robin a brand new script page at a location on Sunset Boulevard, with about four long speeches for her as part of it. She looked at it for about twenty seconds, put the page down, and immediately started a line-perfect off-book rehearsal of the scene. Soap opera actors. I recommend them. Soap training worked for Kevin Bacon, Leonardo DiCaprio, Julianne Moore, Susan Sarandon, and Brad Pitt—and lots of others. I hope some young directors might be looking for tips from this book. If so, here's one for you—use soap-trained actors. (If you can find them, that is. It's now a dying genre.)

Other actors take a different approach to lines. My pal Clark Johnson has had an interesting career. I first met him when he was a grunt in the Special Effects department, working on a film called *The*

One Thousand Dozen that I directed for the mini-series *Tales of the Klondike*. (Orson Welles was on the film as well—narrating). Clark moved on from special effects to become one of the best grips in town, then started acting. Now he's mostly a director. He's been wildly successful—his biggest film was the thriller *The Sentinel*, with him directing Michael Douglas, Kiefer Sutherland, Eva Longoria, and Kim Basinger.

I worked with Clark on two series in the early nineties—*E.N.G.* and *African Skies*. In those days, he was one of the wildest actors I knew. Clark is the brother of jazz singer Molly Johnson—and he took what seemed like an improvisational jazz-like approach to acting. It was never clear whether he had a problem remembering his lines—or whether he just found remembering them to be an impediment to real acting. Either way, he never came up with the same line twice. Shoot a new take and he'd either throw the lines out in a completely different order—or else just come up with entirely new ones. It drove the other actors—and the boom swingers and focus pullers—crazy.

This devil-may-care riffing occurred only when it came to dialogue. As well as everything else, Clark had done some work as a stuntman, and as an actor would sometimes do his own stunts. When it came to shooting action, he was all business. I once shot a big gag with him in which he was to run on cue from a transport trailer, which exploded in what we were told was the biggest movie explosion ever done to that time in Ontario. His timing was flawless; it went like clockwork. The only mishap was that the officer from the police bomb squad, assigned to the shoot to keep us all a safe distance from the explosion, parked his *own* car too close, and got a big piece of shrapnel through the roof. (Aw, gee, officer, that's too bad.)

Clark's discipline was irreproachable when it came to filming action. When it came to words, words that he had to *remember*, he was all over the map. As the director I guess I was supposed to get all stern and angry about his loose, undisciplined performing. But I learned a remarkable thing very early on. While shooting with Clark was chaotic, something amazing was revealed when you watched the rushes. Clark's naturalistic performance just exploded from the screen. His acting, regardless of how big or small his role was in the scene as written, became the focus of the drama. The editors, even though frustrated by his wild lapses in continuity from master to close up, from take to take, couldn't resist cutting constantly to him rather than to the other actors. Clark was the one who lit up the show.

Instead of being hamstrung and mentally hogtied by the issue of memory, as many actors and many amateurs thrown in front of a camera are, Clark just deftly sidestepped the problem, coming up with a Dizzy Gillespie-like solution to it that worked beautifully for him.

More typical was my experience with mountain climber Laurie Skreslet. In the early eighties I got a chance to direct the feature pilot and then the first tranche of three episodes of a CBC series called *Vanderberg*. It was a glossy, big budget show about an Alberta oil and cattle baron, played with panache by Michael Hogan. Surrounding him was a large cast of many of the hottest actors in Canada at the time—Jennifer Dale, Jan Rubes, Allan Royal, Stephen Markle, Susan Hogan, Barry Flatman, and many others. We winged between Calgary and Toronto shooting the show. As an example of the sort of dough we used to throw at TV shows back in those days, we shipped a Ferrari across the country by air, along with its owner, for our star to drive in the show. (But I am pretty certain the CBC did not pick up the tab for the $350 speeding ticket the owner got on the Deerfoot Trail, showing off his over-powered Italian beast at 140 mph to Michael).

There was a big scene in one of the episodes set at a fund-raising gala dinner. We rented the big ballroom at the Sutton Place Hotel in Toronto. All of our stars, surrounded by many extras, were in the scene—all of them decked out in formal attire and fancy gowns. While the focus of the long sequence was some dramatic interaction between the leads of the show, we also needed a keynote speaker for the event to set the scene in motion. We could have hired an actor, and given him a few fictional lines to say, but instead we decided to hire a real celebrity to do the honours. We found a recently minted overnight celebrity, Laurie Skreslet, who had just become the first Canadian to succeed in climbing Mount Everest. He would play himself, using some scripted lines that our writer Rob Forsyth came up with.

We brought him in from Calgary (perhaps he shared the flight with the returning Ferrari), and shot the scene. We filmed him doing his bit. He did all right, as I remember. Perhaps he muffed his lines once or twice, but we did a few more takes, and got through it. If he stumbled, it was not memorable to me—but as I found out later, it certainly was to *him*.

In 2012, I made a couple of films that I shot on a trek through Nepal on the trail leading to Mount Everest—the same trail, of course, that Laurie Skreslet had used thirty years earlier. One of these films documented the work that a charitable organization called the Sir Edmund Hillary Foundation was doing in Nepal. The Foundation was itself now having a black tie fund raising dinner very much like the one we had faked three decades back—this time at the Royal York Hotel. Once again, ironically, the keynote speaker was to be Laurie Skreslet. Prior to his speech, I was to show my little film about the foundation.

In the reception before the dinner, I buttonholed him, and reminded him that we had worked together back in 1982. Of course he too was amused by the coincidence, and preceded to regale me— and the others around us—with his memories of that shoot. It turned out he had found the whole process terrifying. Even though he has made dozens of public speaking appearances speaking (in his own words) about his Everest climb, the need to memorize someone else's words, and speak them on cue, was, he told us, "way scarier than climbing Everest". Everest—to this day one of the most rigorous, dangerous challenges on earth. The 1982 Canada expedition—very tough, very difficult, with lots of crazy mountain politics, bad weather, and three deaths on the Khumbu Icefall. (For all the gory details, see my buddy Keith Leckie's excellent TV mini-series, *Everest*, about the problem-filled climb.) And yet for tough-as-nails mountaineer Laurie Skreslet, memorizing and spouting lines was scarier.

If memory is a problem for young people, you can bet it gets much worse for older ones. In 1997 I had one of my best filmmaking adventures ever, writing and directing a new version of *Treasure Island* starring Jack Palance as Long John Silver. Lots of good stories, which we'll get to in Chapter Four. For now, let me tell you about Jack.

Mercurial. That's the word I use to describe Mr. Palance. Moody, if you like, but not moody in the sense of grumpy. Rather, moody in the sense of one minute up, the next minute down. You could forgive him his moods. He was an old man

Jack Palance entered showbiz as a boxer. I'm not big on boxing. Look what it did to Muhammad Ali. Did Jack's noggin get rattled a few times in those hardscrabble west Pennsylvania rings of the 1940s? How could it not? Still, he had a great life, great career, won an Oscar, and did one-armed push-ups in front of a couple of hundred million people at the 1992 Academy Awards. (Don't believe that "one billion" number that's always being tossed around. People in showbiz are all liars, with their pants on fire.) Most importantly, he was still working as a movie star when I met him at age seventy-eight. But—moody? Yes. Memory starting to go? Yes.

I learned that my producers had signed him for the part of Long John Silver while I was finishing the scripting of the old Robert Louis Stevenson chestnut—about two months before we were to shoot the film on the Isle of Man in the UK. Naturally I thought it would be a good idea to connect with him in advance, go over any script issues he might have, and try and bond with him a bit before we both got thrown into the hurly-burly of the production. I found that he was shooting a movie in—once again—Calgary. (No Ferraris were involved, so far as I know.)

So I called him up in a hotel room, following his day's shooting. It took him a minute to figure out who I was, but soon, he warmed right up. "Sure, great to talk to you. Yes, let's meet. I'm through here in three weeks. Here are my Los Angeles numbers. Come down. Call me there. We'll talk about your script. Great script. They tell me you know how to do water stuff. That's good. How we going to do this parrot business? Don't worry about it—we'll talk when you come down. Look forward to meeting you."

Phew. That was easy. So three or four weeks later, I flew to L.A. and called him up, to get a very chilly response, "Peter who? Oh yeah. Filming in England? That's not till the summer, is it? You want to talk now? How long will this take? I'm kind of busy. Alright, five minutes."

Oh, gawd, was this whole trip a bust? With trepidation, I jumped in my rental Mustang convertible, and drove out to Jack's daughter Holly's house on Mulholland Drive in the Hollywood Hills. At the time, his daughter was a Hollywood celebrity newspaper columnist, married to Roger Spottiswoode, and the pair were in England, where he was directing the latest Bond film *Tomorrow Never Dies*. Jack was babysitting their kids—his grandkids—at their house.

On arrival I immediately noticed the mercury had risen considerably. Within a few minutes I was meeting the two pre-teen grandkids, getting a house tour, and perusing a roomful of his colorful, (some might say garish) paintings. There aren't too many people in the world that have a resume that includes Oscar-winning Movie Star, Painter, published Poet, Rancher, Coal Miner, Boxer, and World War Two Bomber Pilot—but Jack was all of those. He also had a totally engaging smile, a voice that made Johnny Cash sound like a soprano, and the strength of three horses.

I still needed to get him on my side. Since kids were involved, I used one of my standard bribes—ice cream. It has become a tradition on my shoots that at some point in the proceedings I buy ice cream for everyone involved. It is usually on the last day of location surveys, when I spot a Dairy Queen or its equivalent and bring the whole caravan to a halt for an afternoon ice. Up in the Hollywood hills, I assumed there must be an ice cream shop somewhere. Regardless, I had an even better seduction tool—my Mustang convertible. I suggested the kids might be interested in a ride. They jumped at the idea, and so off we went on the curvy drive through the hills, in search of Pralines 'n Cream.

How much better does it get than this—driving on a sunny Saturday morning along Mulholland Drive—the legendary road that Jack Nicholson drove on in *Chinatown*, that James Dean sped on to get to the set of *Rebel Without a Cause*, (and years later, the iconic road of the David Lynch film *Mulholland Drive*)—with a legend sitting in the front passenger seat, pointing Marlon Brando's house to you, and then regaling you with stories of the girls he used to steal from Marlon back in the 50s.

So we got our ice cream, and returned to the house, and to more stories of dating Marilyn Monroe, bailing out of a burning B-24 Liberator bomber, and—well, who can remember them all? We also finally got around to talking about *Treasure Island*, the film we were going to be shooting together in two months. The five minutes he told me I could have with him grew to six hours.

I left Los Angeles thinking he was a warm and generous guy, and would be great to work with later that summer in the U.K. Well, he was—and he wasn't. There were perhaps a number of reasons why the dark, grumpy side of Jack came out on the Isle of Man. He was nearly eighty years old. He did have to do a lot of his acting aboard a rolling pirate ship in the Irish Sea—while balancing on a wooden leg. To do this we had to strap his foot up behind his leg, then fit the wooden leg on to his knee. His other foot wasn't a lot of help, as he had a painful bone spur on it. For days he suffered from jet lag from the nine-hour time difference. He did have to perform with a big beauty of a macaw on his shoulder, who mostly behaved, but occasionally got bored and tried to get some attention by taking a nip out of Jack's ear. He was hounded by the British press, and by holidaying autograph-seekers. But mostly, he suffered from the failure of that old bugbear, memory.

Back in his early days, when he was doing *Shane* and *Panic in the Streets* and the like, he probably had a memory like that of his thirteen-year old Canadian co-star on *Treasure Island*, Kevin Zegers. Zegers, a fabulous kid actor, and splendid today as an adult, simply was perfect. He never once flubbed a line, missed a mark, fell out of character, or dropped the Brit accent he had to adopt as Jim Hawkins. Palance's memory was fading with age. And as the shoot moved on from action sequences on the high seas with minimal dialogue to scenes of heavy drama and long speeches, I began to tear my hair out. It became more and more frustrating for everyone—not least, of course, for Jack.

My wife and two young daughters had come over to visit for a week at the back end of the month-long shoot. I sent them out on a furtive mission to an art store to buy white card and markers, and they, along with Kevin Zegers' siblings, also on summer holidays, had a top secret session, well away from anyone else, writing out all of Long John Silver's lines on the cards. I had them discreetly brought to the set. When the next memory meltdown occurred, I shooed all the British actors away from the set, and quietly produced them.

In England, if you want to cast the part of a working class bloke, you generally find an actor who is…a working class bloke. If the part calls for an upper crusty toff, then the likelihood is you'll get an upper class toff for the part. We had two such toffs playing Dr. Livesey and Squire Trelawney. They were so upper crusty, in fact, that when Lady Diana died on the last week of our shoot, the pair forced me to re-jig the final days of the schedule so they could rush out early, in mourning, to attend her funeral (more likely to watch it on TV, but they claimed to have tickets). They had already expressed their complaints that Palance was making 'way more money than them, staying in a fancier hotel, getting all the attention—*and* that he couldn't remember his lines. I didn't want them now to see him using cue cards.

Jack railed against the cards. He had done *Streetcar Named Desire* on Broadway! He was a method actor—had studied with Michael Chekhov at the Actors Studio. He didn't need any #@$&^%$ cue cards! He railed. I persisted. Finally, I *insisted*. I persuaded him I could place the cards so that no one would know he was using them. At last he relented. Magically, the problem went away. Without the damn issue of memory, his acting improved immensely. So, of course, did the schedule. No more take tens. We were back on track. And no one watching the film can tell the *aides-mémoire* are being used. In the end, though, it wasn't a perfect shoot for Jack. He enjoyed lots of things about it, but he hated the memory embarrassment.

A year later, *Treasure Island* was invited as the opening night film of the WorldFest Flagstaff Film Festival in Arizona. Jack flew in from his ranch in California; I flew down from Halifax, where I was shooting the series *Black Harbour*. The film got a great reception from the audience, and Jack was once again smiling and in fine form. Following the film he bounded down the aisle of the theater with me, answered questions, and entertained the crowd for thirty minutes. Without scripted lines and memory to bog him down, his mercurial mood swung back to the happy side of the meter. As *Treasure Island* was his last released film, I'm glad his final experience with it was that upbeat well-received festival screening in Arizona.

Jack Palance died in 2006, and that same year, I got a chance myself to play the part of another crusty, moody icon of American culture—Hunter S. Thompson. A transatlantic collection of producers had put together a Canadian-American-British coproduction for broadcasters in the three countries for a series they called *Final 24*. The idea was to chronicle the last 24 hours of various dead celebrities such as John Belushi, Robert Kennedy, Marvin Gaye, and…the drug-fuelled alcoholic gonzo American journalist Hunter S. Thompson. Their plan, popular back then, was to use a combination of documentary and dramatic techniques—interviews, stock archival footage, narration, graphics, and also elaborate dramatic re-creations—to tell the story.

I'd just directed a similar series called *On the Run* that used the same techniques—this time to tell stories of notorious con men and white-collar crooks. I had just done the story of Steven Jay Russell, the man who had famously escaped four times from Texan prisons. (After our docudrama, the story was done as the feature *I Love You Phillip Morris* starring Jim Carrey and Ewan McGregor.) At the wrap party for our film, our casting director looked at me with a cocked eye for a few minutes, then commented that he thought I might be a contender to play Hunter S. Thompson in the new series. Would I like to read for the part?

Why not? I read once, then got a callback, and read again for them. There wasn't a formal script to read, but rather some directions that would lead you to improv and riff a scene for them. Before the second audition I quickly re-read Thompson's *Fear and Loathing* books and his *The Rum Diary* to bone up on his style and character, and perhaps more importantly, got a buzz cut to match his near-bald look. I pulled a good audition, and got the part.

It was a very odd shoot for me. On the one hand, it was a ball. As an actor you have a fraction of the problems and concerns you have as a director—and you also have pretty 24-year old girls fussing over your hair and wardrobe, and asking if they can't get you another coffee. On this shoot, I spent much of my time playing with guns, blowing stuff up, snorting cocaine, and drinking whisky (well, snorting icing sugar and drinking apple juice—but almost as good). And playing a legendary character who had last been portrayed by Johnnie Depp (and just as well, if you ask this unbiased observer).

On the other hand, it was a very strange week for me, because on Tuesday, my father, after a long life, and many years first as a kid in England, then as a World War II flyer in the Royal Air Force, then as a very successful journalist and writer, died. On Tuesday night, after leaving the hospital, I spent the evening composing obituaries for the three newspapers, then showed up early the next morning to begin the recreation of another journalist's final 24 hours. My real life collided with recreated drama—very real death blending surrealistically with fake death. Hunter Thompson blew his brains out with a plated revolver rather than waste away because as a kid he had watched his father die in hospital, ignominiously plugged with tubes. Now, I was portraying Thompson and recreating his violent death, only hours after sitting with my father as he passed away, his body injected with tubes just as Thompson's father had been.

It may seem peculiar that I continued with the shoot, but I felt my father, who loved drama and film and theater and writers (television, and Thompson, not so much, but hey…) would have approved of my moving forward with this, as I did. And, because no memorization was required, because it was all about improvisation, the shoot became more like play than like work. For me, and for the actors portraying Thompson's wife, kids, friends, and associates that were part of his life, making the film felt like filmmaking must have felt back in silent movie days—loose, free, fun. When you portray a character in a conventional drama, you don't really inhabit the character so much as inhabit another person's (the writer's) vision of the character. When a recreated docudrama like this gives you the look, the clothes, the props, and the location for a character, then encourages you to improvise with your own interpretation of the words (within reason, of course), it is a creatively liberating form of filmmaking. Of course, the downside as a performer is that this genre of filmmaking is liberating for the editor as well, and the likelihood is that however creative and appropriate your creative riffing may be, 90% will likely be dropped under narration or interview voiceover. That, you'll discover later. On the day, it's amazing how the elimination of the memory issue puts the fun and the creativity back into performing.

Of course memory is also an issue when writing a memoir. So far, I've been doing okay—but I've been mostly telling you recent stories about the 90s and the new millennium. Now I want to go 'way back and tell you about my favorite decade—the 60s. You know what they say—if you can remember the 60s you weren't really there. Well, I *was* really there. And I *do* remember.

Chapter 3
The Sixties Rocked

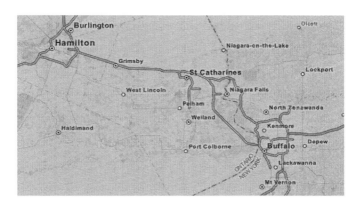

The sixties started out as a terrible decade for filmmaking. The Golden Age of Hollywood was long over, but almost no alternatives to the big bloated Los Angeles-based industrial film model existed. Hollywood was churning out big, boring westerns and comedies starring dinosaurs like John Wayne and Doris Day. Even the masters like Howard Hawks and Alfred Hitchcock were making crummy bloated movies like *Rio Bravo* and *Marnie*. It was time for a change, but change would require a revolution. We baby boomers had one in mind, but it would take a few years.

There was virtually no filmmaking going on in my hometown of Toronto in the early sixties. What little existed was mostly television commercials, or industrials. If I was going to get a start in showbiz, I had to start with live theater. Fortunately I had a mentor from my first days of high school. From 1974 to 1999, Elwy Yost was the ebullient, avuncular, and very well-known host of *Saturday Night at the Movies*—a commercial-free double bill of classic movies mixed with his enthusiastic interviews with actors and directors that was one of the biggest successes of TVO television. But in 1961, his TV career still ahead of him, Elwy Yost was my homeroom teacher at Burnhamthorpe Collegiate. He taught geography, but his passion was producing elaborate school plays. I got my start there, stage managing student versions for him of old Broadway chestnuts like *Death Takes a Holiday* and *The Man Who Came to Dinner*.

I was impatient to move into professional theater. There wasn't even that much of it going on then—seven professional theaters in town in those days. My first job in professional showbiz was for the smallest and funkiest of these - a little eighty-seat joint called The Village Playhouse. Before Yorkville developed as Toronto's answer to Greenwich Village, the Gerrard Street Village had grown up as the city's center of bohemianism. Just before I arrived, the city expropriated all the coffee houses and art galleries, turning the land into parking lots for the big hospitals in the area. The little theater and one funky bistro were the last remnants of the village. The producer, a woman named Elspeth Gaylor, kept her three cats living in the place to keep mice from chewing up the scenery. I suppose it was a plus that the audience didn't have mice running past them, but they'd often be startled to instead see cats strolling across the stage in the middle of a performance. Actually, they probably weren't too startled, as the place had a ripe odor of cat urine during the hot summer of 1962.

Elspeth's preference was for the tough kitchen-sink dramas that were coming out of northern England at the time—hard edge stuff that was a bit of a tough sell as summer theater. I had an hour commute to get to my (unpaid) job as assistant stage manager and lighting guy at the little stage. I'd work every day as a bike courier for a drugstore at forty-five cents an hour to pay for my streetcar fare downtown. I was also supposed to put up little posters for *Look Back in Anger* and our other offerings on telephone poles around town. It was sometimes hard getting much of an audience. The worst night, I remember, we had exactly three people in the audience—for a play that had a cast of eight. Before the curtain rose, a beefy character actor named Len Doncheff, a regular in the company, went out and told the three that there was a theater tradition (and, I believe, an Actors Equity rule—though we were non-union) that the performance can be cancelled if there are more players onstage than customers in the audience. Instead, he told them, the Argonauts were playing that night, he had beer in his fridge, and they were welcome to join him and the rest of the cast to watch the game at his flat. They agreed, we shut the theater down, and all—audience, cast, and crew—traipsed off to his place to watch the football game.

By the next summer I'd moved considerably more upscale. The Lakewood Theater, sitting on a northern lake near Skowhegan, Maine, is one of the oldest, grandest, and best-known summer theaters in America. It is a big, beautiful theater full of velvet and brass, balconies and boxes, fly lofts, and Barrymore-autographed dressing rooms. In its heyday in the thirties, it was considered the number one spot to try out new plays before they hit Broadway. In 1963, it was still going strong (and still is today, though with a different formula). Every summer the theater hired ten apprentices; that year, I was one of them.

The formula then for summer theater was that every spring about twelve travelling companies would come together and rehearse in Manhattan. In late June, they would fan out to a collection of big old summer theaters, of which Lakewood was the jewel. The stages were spread around from Maine through New England to the Catskills, and up to the sole Canadian part of the chain, Vineland Theater near Niagara. Every Saturday night would be the final performance of each of the plays. As it closed, the actors would all pile into cars or buses and head off to the next town. Meanwhile we apprentices would work through Saturday night and Sunday morning, ripping apart the old set, and then putting up the new one. Sunday we'd be painting, setting up the lights, and the new actors would arrive. Sunday night and Monday morning they'd rehearse the play with us on the new set, and we'd open the new play Monday night. As it ran the week, we'd spend our days building the sets for the next week's play. Friday night we'd have a blowout party, and Saturday night, after the play closed, we'd start the process over again.

The shows were mostly headlined by actors coming off a big Broadway hit or a television series. So for instance, one week, on top of my set building duties, I worked as dresser (a weird theater expression, really meaning assistant) to John Forsythe. At the time we apprentices, all full of ourselves with pomposity, considered him a TV has-been, as his big series "Bachelor Father" had been off the air for a year. Little did we know that he would return to television with a vengeance, becoming the highest paid star (per hour) in the world for his pivotal off-screen role in "Charlie's Angels", then doing eight years as the lead patriarch in "Dynasty".

There were many stars who have signed the dressing room walls of Lakewood Theater over the years, most famous of whom today is probably John Travolta, who played there in *Bus Stop*. The wildest star from the year I was there was the legendary Tallulah Bankhead, a woman with a very large and profane appetite for life—and liquor. I once saw her, when the washroom was in use at one of the wild parties that were a feature of the summer, pull her dress up, panties down, and pee in a sink in full view of everyone, all the while continuing to drink her bourbon, smoke from her absurdly long cigarette holder, and continue, in her velvety thick Alabama drawl, to tell the elaborate dirty joke she was entertaining us with. A crazily promiscuous woman, she had the reputation for cracking the cherry of the youngest boy (or girl) in the room. At the time, that was likely me—but we were two ships in the night (more like a giant, listing liner (her) and a little Optimist dinghy (me)). It never happened, I'm sorry to say.

Groucho Marx was supposed to headline one of our last shows, but he fell ill in Los Angeles and so was replaced by a flash-in-the-pan performer named Vaughan Meader. Oddly, at the time Meader meant much more to me than Marx. He was a comic with three best-selling records in which he imitated and did shtick about

56

President Kennedy. As Kennedy would be assassinated within three months, Meader's performance at Lakewood was likely one of his last. The comic's career pretty much ended with the President's, and he is largely forgotten today. Groucho Marx, on the other hand, will likely be remembered forever.

Another old star who brought in the crowds was the old Hollywood actress Spring Byington. Again, she meant little to me at the time but a lot to the grey hairs in the tourist town. One of her claims-to-fame was playing Mickey Rooney's mother in the Andy Hardy films. Little did I suspect that thirty years later I'd be directing the kid she helped turn into one of the biggest, highest-grossing stars in the world.

The sixties were finally getting going, and so the next summer was even wilder. By now I had graduated from apprentice to Assistant Stage Manager at the Straw Hat Players in Ontario's Muskoka cottage country. The personalities were not quite as flamboyant in Port Carling as they were in Skowhegan, but the artistic sensibility was considerably more radical. We put on sophisticated versions of plays by Chekhov and Dylan Thomas, along with more standard fare by young hit-makers of the day like Neil Simon. I was becoming somewhat expert at the most cinematic of the theatrical crafts, stage lighting, so that became my usual role, but I also got a chance from time to time to come out from behind the dimmer board to deliver one or two lines as a bit player in the summer productions.

I also had the opportunity to work with actors that I would cast in shows for the next thirty years. Stephen Markle, the stud young leading man of the company, came from rich showbiz roots. His father was Fletcher Markle, a powerful producer/director/actor who at the time was hosting the long-running CBC celebrity interview show *Telescope*. His voice was a booming, oft-parodied baritone —a clone of Orson Welles's—not surprising, since he'd written *Lady From Shanghai* for Welles, and acted for him through the 1940s.

Stephen's mother was whiskey-voiced Mercedes McCambridge, co-star with Joan Crawford in the lurid cult western *Johnny Guitar*, and the voice of demonically possessed Regan in *The Exorcist*.

Stephen would go on to achieve considerable success in theater and television. I cast him sixteen years later in my series *Vanderberg* and some other films. By the 1990s he had become a fixture in American regional theater, appearing over and over at places like the Guthrie Theater in Minneapolis and the La Jolla Playhouse in San Diego, and guest starring in television series like *House*, *The West Wing* and *The O.C.* In 1964 at the Straw Hat Players, our goal was to have as much fun as possible. He and I organized the first (and only) orgy I've ever been part of. It was mainly memorable because the mother of a teenage girl who was enamored with stud muffin Markle finally broke up the shenanigans at 4 a.m., taking her daughter back to their lakeside cottage in her Pontiac Parisienne convertible, and forcing the rest of us to wander the streets till dawn broke over the quiet resort town.

On the one day of the week our theater was dark, we absconded with the prop truck and hightailed it for Toronto, hoping to see the Beatles in their first performance at Maple Leaf Gardens. Of course, no last-minute tickets were available, so we had to settle for *A Hard Days Night* instead. Seeing the Beatles' films, and the other films coming out of England and France at the time by guys like Richard Lester, Tony Richardson, Lindsay Anderson, Jean Luc Godard, and Francois Truffaut convinced me I really wanted to get out of theater and into film.

Of course, it wasn't easy in those days. My first camera was a Keystone 8mm. Silent, of course (actually not at all silent—very, very noisy). I tried to sync it with a ridiculous portable tape recorder running at 1 7/8 inches per second—decidedly low-fi. Here's how 8mm worked. The film, which was sold on little fifty-foot spools, was actually 16 mm with twice as many perforations on it as regular 16mm. You could get color film, but it was too pricey for me, so I shot black and white. In a black bag or a very dark room you'd load the camera, fiddling to insure that the loops were sized right, or it would jam. After filming for two minutes, it would run out and you'd return to the dark room, flip the film over, re-thread it, and run it through the camera again, exposing the opposite half. Then—making sure you didn't forget and run it through a third time (or else you'd be making arty and probably useless superimpositions)—you would package up the film and send it off to a lab, where they would process and print it, then use some kind of weird machine to slice it down the middle, tape the end of part one to the beginning of part two, and send it back to you. Then you would go out and borrow someone's projector, set up a screen, darken all the windows, and look at it. Hey there, HD/iPhone/GoPro/YouTube/Vimeo Generation! Sounds pretty archaic, doesn't it? Oh, yeah. It was.

My first film was a harbinger of the sort of material I'd continue to shoot for the next forty years. After World War II, large numbers of German immigrants had started pouring into Canada. A few of them introduced the country to the new sport they had developed in the 1930s in Germany of competitive whitewater kayaking. Since it was the hot new thing I decided to go out to the Credit River to make a film about them. Fifty years later, I took up whitewater kayaking myself, and coincidently discovered that one of my instructors was not only a past world champion, but also the daughter of the star kayaker in my first little film.

The next summer I could no longer afford the luxury of low-paying theater and had to make some real money for university. I ended up with a crazy job working for a pair of conmen selling pantyhose door to door. I can still remember the spiel: "Hello ma'am. I'm a student working my way through college. We have an amazing bargain on the newest pantyhose. Only $5.99 for a dozen pair. Wonderful new colours – Tip Toe Taupe, Midnight Lace, Nearly Nude." A bunch of us fanned out across the city selling these things. Unfortunately, our scam-artist bosses stole most of our

59

salaries so that they could buy themselves an MGB, and we ended up with almost nothing.

Our home base for this racket was an empty unit in a mini-mall on Islington Avenue. Beside us was a little operation called William F. White. I didn't know what they did, until I saw a big boat of an old Cadillac parked out front, with the top chopped, the rear seat removed, and crane welded into it, turning it into a primitive camera car. At the time William F. White was probably no bigger an operation than our little door-to-door pantyhose sales company. Little did I suspect it would turn into one of the largest movie equipment companies in the world, with branches all across Canada, and a European base in Hungary—supplying gear to some of the biggest movies made. Its headquarters are still on Islington Avenue—just down the street from the old place, but now housed in a 338,000 square foot building.

The film business was starting to get going. As White was starting his equipment house, cameraman Bob Crone was starting his lab, at that time called Film House. Again, it started as a basement operation with one processing machine, and moved on to become eventually Deluxe Toronto, one of the biggest labs in the world, at one point producing over 80% of the prints shown in all North American theaters. But back when they were just Film House, they called in the Toronto Police Morality Squad to try to confiscate the rushes of the next film I was involved in. Stay tuned for that tale.

There were very few film schools in the world in the sixties, most notably UCLA, USC, NYU, and the Lodz National Film School in Poland, whose most famous graduate was Roman Polanski. It wasn't in the cards that I was going to attend any of those, so instead I went to McMaster University in Hamilton, which in two years we managed to turn (largely against its will) into a productive, though highly controversial crucible for underground filmmaking. I began by becoming a reporter and the film critic for the student newspaper, The Silhouette. Instead of wasting much time in classes studying

Chaucer or Charlemagne, I spent most of it either covering Viet Nam protest marches or writing reviews of films like *Blow Up* and *Wild in the Streets*. Through the Silhouette I became involved with a group of people organizing screenings of new alternative cinema that that had to begun to emerge in the mid 60s.

There were four Canadian filmmakers who inspired the rest of us and got us emulating their nascent attempts to create an English Canadian cinema. Larry Kent was a South African guy who ended up at the University of British Columbia, and caused a great ruckus with his first two underground features, *The Bitter Ash* and Sweet *Substitute*. Don Owen was a young filmmaker who got a commission from the National Film Board to make what was supposed to be a sober-sided twenty-five minute film about teen pregnancy. Instead he secretly used the money, gear, and crew to make a gritty feature film (still with the provocative theme) called *Nobody Waved Goodbye*. Meanwhile David Secter—probably the first student filmmaker in Canada, made a somewhat similar film called *Winter Kept Us Warm*. Again, more commentary on the sexual revolution, but this time with a gay theme (though so subtly and obliquely understated as to be almost unrecognizable). Although its domestic release was limited to college campuses, the film does have the honor of being the first Canadian film ever shown at the Cannes Film Festival. Finally Arthur Lipsett made a series of remarkably cool and eccentric films out of found-footage culled from the dustbins of the National Film Board. I was not the only person blown away by his wild editing techniques. His short film *Very Nice, Very Nice* was nominated for an Oscar. George Lucas credits Lipsett with many influences on his Star Wars film, including the concept of "The Force". Stanley Kubrick was so impressed by Lipsett's work that he offered the reclusive Montreal filmmaker the opportunity to create the trailer for Dr. Strangelove. (Lipsett foolishly turned down the opportunity).

The four got little support from the hidebound local establishment and press. Kent's self-financed films got huge audiences at UBC, but were slammed as "filth" and "stag-movies" by the Vancouver press. Owen had difficulties getting his film shown, with the most prominent exhibitor of the day stupidly calling it "night out in amateur-ville". Secter had it even worse, as, unbelievably, IATSE, the cinematographers' and projectionists' union, refused to allow his films to be shown, as he did not shoot them with a union crew. As for Lipsett, his films were so off the wall that they were shown only in underground venues and at university campuses like McMaster, where young wannabe filmmakers like me reveled in their kaleidoscopic imagery.

Oddly, none of these four were able to parlay their early pioneering success into a continuing career. Although they each made a few more films, Kent, Owen, and Secter all soon drifted away from filmmaking. Lipsett had the worst luck of all. Too weird and crazy for the National Film Board that had supported his early films, he was let go, and ended up homeless on the streets of Montreal. He committed suicide in 1986.

"Never be a pioneer," Ivan Reitman once advised me. It seems to be good advice. While these early pioneers struggled with very limited success, the gang of us who were influenced by them, and followed directly in their wake—Reitman, his producing partner (and ex-U of T professor) Joe Medjuck, David Cronenberg, Don Shebib, and Michael Hirsh (co-founder of Nelvana)—are all still making films today.

Novels influenced us just much as movies and music in the 1960s, and none more so than Salinger's *The Catcher in the Rye* and Kerouac's *On the Road*. In 1966, my pal David Martin and I both had dead end summer jobs. I was distributing newspapers along the Wasaga Beach strip. He was working in one of Hamilton's steel mills. We both had an itch for adventure, an itch to ditch our jobs and head out, like the characters in Kerouac's novel, to discover America. In early July, we did. I bought my first car for $125—a ten-year old MG Magnette (built by MG, but a small four door sedan, not a sports car). I picked up David at his parent's home in Hamilton. His parents so disapproved of the wild venture they wouldn't even say farewell to him. He told me the scene inside was frosty and I would be best not to come in, so as I sat in the car, I watched him on the front porch, shouting his final goodbyes into the house. With no reply from them after three tries, he closed the door and climbed in my car.

We headed out on to the highway—but as we approached the entrance to it we were still unsure we way we should head. Should we go out west to California, and see what was happening in the movie business? Should we head east for New York, where the village folk music scene was exploding with Dylan, Baez, Phil Ochs and The Blues Project, Simon and Garfunkel, and all the rest of them? Or, as Peter Fonda and Dennis Hopper would do in the famous road movie *Easy Rider* three years later, should we head south to the Big Easy—New Orleans? At the last minute we made a decision, and I veered onto the highway. We had decided for none of the above, and instead headed for the cool midwestern college town of Madison, Wisconsin, where one of David's many girlfriends lived.

After a week enmeshed in the radical anti-Vietnam politics of Madison, we headed for the Deep South. I suppose, if we were looking for adventure, we were now headed in the right direction. The battle of the Civil Rights movement had been boiling over in Mississippi, Georgia, and Alabama for the past two years. We started getting the sense we were entering a different world when, in Memphis, Tennessee, we asked directions how to get to Highway 61.

"You jes' head down there, you'll see a li'l nigger gas station," said the old boy. "Jes' turn there and yer on yer way to Mississippi."

Late at night, just outside the town of McComb, Mississippi, our car came to a shuddering halt. It had chosen an auspicious little town to break down beside, for McComb was one of the most notorious battlegrounds of the civil rights movement. A hotbed of the Ku Klux Klan, it had a mayor who was Chairman of the White

Citizens Council and a police chief who headed the local chapter of the virulently racist "Americans for the Preservation of the White Race"(APWR). It had recently seen violent disruptions by the Klan of black voter registration drives, and also the murder of NAACP worker Herbert Lee by local State Representative E. H. Hurst. Jane Fonda's husband Tom Hayden was beaten up on the streets of McComb for supporting the local black demonstrators.

Perhaps fortunately, none of the details of this were known to us at the time. In the heat of the dark, Southern night, we somehow found a tow truck operator. We were ignominiously towed into town, and the next day, searched for a place to stay. It wasn't easy finding a place that would take in two boys from the north. The assumption was we must be civil rights agitators.

"Yer from Kenada?? Izzat somewhere near London, England?" asked the lady. But she did give us rooms in her mildewed old antebellum house. If you remember the boarding house where the young Forrest Gump met Elvis Presley, that's where we were. But Elvis had left the building, ten years previous.

As for the car, it was even more shunned than we were.

"What the hell kind of a communist car izzat?" said the Dixie Auto mechanic. "We just deal with Chevy here." But he finally looked at it, discovered it had a cracked cylinder head, which is a pretty serious repair, and he called around, and found the nearest parts distributor was in New York City. The price of buying it and getting the big part down to McComb was way out of our financial ballpark. We dithered for while, wondering what to do.

One night we went to slightly upscale restaurant (by 1966 McComb standards). In those days, there was a white side of town – and a black side of town. This was definitely in the white side of town. As we entered, the restaurant fell to a hush, with everyone looking at us. We took a seat, and sat for a while. After a huddled

64

conversation with staff, the manager came over and told us he couldn't serve us.

"This is a private club. You boys understand. I know you boys are okay, but we gotta be careful against them FBI comin' in and making trouble." It wasn't a private club. It was a normal restaurant. But blacks were forbidden entrance, and only by being careful could they keep it that way. Whatever he said, he did suspect we might be FBI agents.

The South then was such a strange mix of racial hatred and Southern hospitality. The manager couldn't stop himself. As he kicked us out of his restaurant and closed the front door on us, he smiled and recited his standard goodbye: "Y'all come back now, y'heah?"

While kicking around McComb wondering how to proceed, we ran into a good ol' boy—actually a good ol' boy in training, as he was about our age, named Johnny Lee Harper. He was a construction worker, and a son of Dixie, like everyone else there, but unlike the rest he took a shine to these two strange Yankees with their funny accents and their communist car. He was intrigued by our adventure, and offered to help out by giving us seventy-five dollars for my car and my guitar. We took it, he drove us to the edge of town in his pickup truck (Chevy, natch), and we began hitchhiking, heading south for New Orleans.

Forty-two years later, I passed through McComb again. George Kourounis and I had driven south from Toronto in his Honda CRV (the "Storm-mobile"—hail-pocked, but considerably more reliable than the '56 MG) to intercept and film Hurricane Gustav for *Angry Planet*. Once again, it was three in the morning. We were almost the only vehicle heading south, against a steady stream of headlights streaming away from New Orleans, heading north. Gustav was a serious Category Four hurricane at that point, aimed directly for the same bull's-eye that had been hit by Katrina only three years earlier. A torrent of dire pronouncements from the Governor's office issued from the radio. There was a mandatory evacuation, which would become the largest evacuation in American history. We were heading into it—but as we still had twenty hours before the big storm would make landfall, I convinced my star (and driver) to take a quick detour off Interstate 55 so I could see McComb again.

Things had changed, of course. The old hand-painted signs on the sides of barns and buildings advertising Mail Pouch chewing tobacco ("Treat Yourself to the Best") had been replaced with McDonald's golden arches and fluorescent Walmart signs. The biggest shift, though, was invisible. Of the changes that have happened in my lifetime, the most profound are the changes in attitudes in the American South. Things may not be perfect today, but in the mid-sixties it was impossible to imagine the level of tolerance that has evolved since then.

In the hot summer of 1966, when we arrived in New Orleans, we were entering not a hurricane but rather a firestorm over swimming pools. Among the last holdouts against integration were the public municipal swimming pools of the Big Easy (not so easy, that summer). We were thrown into that debacle for a while, then eventually decided it was time to hit the road again to put some serious miles under us. The Newport Folk Festival was in three weeks time. We thought we'd try to make it there.

It was not at all easy for two lanky 6'3" guys carrying packs to get rides from passing motorists. It was possible back then (I would think it would be almost impossible today), but it wasn't easy. One problem was that when you finally did get a ride, it would be down the freeway thirty or forty miles to the next city, where you would be dropped off usually at the first big exit off the highway. People leaving that town to head north would be entering the freeway on the last exit out of town, so we would be stuck in this no-man's land, often waiting for hours for the next ride.

66

As we baked in the afternoon sun, cars and trucks roaring past us, we had a fantasy that a pair of girls in a Mustang convertible—top down, of course (the car, and maybe the girls, too)—were going to pull up and offer to drive us all the way to Newport. Never happened, of course. Instead, we were grateful to get whatever combination of crappy old car and weird driver would stop for us. One drizzly morning we waited for hours for a lift. People slowed down, and stared, but no one stopped. When we were finally picked up, we learned why the wait had been so long. The radio was running bulletins about a local prison break, and warning people to lock their doors, and to not pick up hitchhikers. Turned out the only reason our driver had picked us up was that he thought he might get a reward, returning two cons to the pen. He was only dissuaded from this endeavor after stopping at a 7-Eleven to buy a local paper, which had pictures in it of the escapees. Disappointed, he drove us on to the next town, Gadsden, Alabama, and dropped us off, as usual, at the first entrance into town.

We stood beside the highway near Gadsden for fifteen hours. Cars and eighteen-wheelers roared past us. It was a terrible spot. Even if they wanted to stop for us (which they mostly didn't), it was a difficult and dangerous place to try to pull over, so they blasted past. It is remarkable how much air a big transport pushes out of the way. Standing by the shoulder as one passes, you are almost blown over. Once the sun went down, it was even less likely we'd get a ride. By three in the morning there were so few vehicles still out that it seemed pointless. I wanted to lie down on the scrubby shoulder and sleep— but I then discovered that thousands of black caterpillars were now crawling over the dirt. That didn't seem like much fun. Better to stay standing on the asphalt, which they didn't seem to like. Sleep standing, like a giraffe.

At five the sun began to rise. A grey, ugly dawn. The caterpillars went home, wherever that was. At seven, a miracle. A car slowed, lurched over, and stopped. David and I looked at each other in disbelief. Was it a mirage? No, it was real. We grabbed our bags and ran to the car. There were already four people in the big muscle car. We piled in with them, and they took off. They picked our brains for a while, finding out who we were, and then slowly, we learned their story. The driver was a moonshiner. The trunk was full of cases of white lightning—illegally made, over-proof liquor. The car had a huge engine in it—the biggest Dodge made—to outrun The Man on the highways and back roads of Georgia and Alabama.

Riding shotgun beside the driver was his partner—a tough as nails French Canadian cat from New Brunswick. In the back seat, now jammed in with us, was the driver's father—aging patriarch of the bootlegging family, and the driver's young son—learning the ropes so he could one day take over the family business. They were heading for Chattanooga, Tennessee. Tennessee? After all the long waits we'd had for ten-mile rides, they were going to drive us all the way there? These guys really were our saviors.

There were still dry counties sprinkled through the Deep South and Midwest in the 1960s—and Chattanooga was in one of them. Since people couldn't buy legit liquor in Chattanooga, there was a high demand for our new best friends' illegal moonshine. Of course, the revenue agents were on the lookout for them. If they were caught, there could be jail time—and they'd certainly have their hot wheels confiscated. Didn't seem to bother them much. By mid-day they had already made a few big sales up on the appropriately named Lookout Mountain, and then they dropped down into town, and dropped us off at an entrance to Interstate 75.

We headed north. By late July we were in Newport, for the folk festival. Of course, we didn't have tickets, nor any money to buy them with. Part of the ethos of the sixties revolution was "The Music Should be Free!" We joined the hordes of other ticketless music lovers, storming the barricades and fighting the police to break in to see the headliner Jim Kweskin and his Jug Band. *Jim Who?* you ask. People would battle the police to see *Jim Kweskin and his Jug Band?* Seems hard to believe, I know, but that's the way it was. The group played a unique blend of blues, ragtime, and rockabilly on instruments that included mandolin, washboard, fiddle, kazoo, guitar, tambourine, and, of course, jug. Now, Kweskin did have Maria Muldaur singing with him, and she did have a hell of a sweet voice (best remembered for her 1974 hit *Midnight at the Oasis*)—and her husband, Geoff Muldaur, played in the band—and Geoff was a fabulous guitar player. But still...

We bummed around New England for a while, taking jobs weaving fiberglass on giant looms in a factory in Providence, Rhode Island (skin's still itching from it!), then as handymen and gardeners (though all thumbs and none of them green) for a semi-famous abstract artist in Provincetown, Massachusetts.

We thought we wanted to meet Leonard Cohen, so we headed north for Montreal. Cohen was already well known in Canada as a poet and a novelist—though his days as an internationally known troubadour were still ahead of him. We vaguely searched around for him in Notre-Dame-de-Grâce and the Plateau, but never connected. We did meet one of his girlfriends (neither Suzanne nor Marianne, but rather, Rose, who was probably more fun, anyway). We had no place to stay, so we hung out in Bens, the famous twenty-four hour deli on De Maisonneuve. I would pass the long nights in Bens by studying their massive "Wall of Fame", a long wall covered with hundreds of framed eight by tens of Quebec and American showbiz personalities who had eaten there. Remembering those penurious nights, I was totally stoked when thirty years later, while shooting a feature called *The Best Bad Thing* in Montreal, Bens mounted a picture of me alongside one of George Takei (yes, Sulu from *Star Trek*), the star of the film, up on their wall.

It was time to head back to Ontario, so we stuck out our thumbs and headed back down the 401 to a wild year at McMaster University. I returned to being a student film critic, David to directing risqué theater. We were both part of a crowd of black-sweater hipsters who took our cues from New York City. The biggest influence on us was Andy Warhol. That year, the famed New York painter and filmmaker had teamed up with the alt-rock group The Velvet Underground to create a quintessential piece of sixties craziness called The Exploding Plastic Inevitable. On our quest to turn McMaster from the Baptist bible college it had started as into the hippest campus in the country, we were determined to bring Warhol's psychedelic happening to Hamilton. Was the Hammer ready for it? Probably not. The quintet that made up the Velvet Underground were extreme by Manhattan's standards—let alone those of our little working class steel town at the end of the lake. The University administration, and the more conservative elements of the student council fought our plans, but in the end we prevailed. In the late fall of 1966, we managed to book Warhol and the band to perform at the campus.

I got involved in my first year at university, with a sleek young coed named Michaele-Sue Goldblatt, daughter of a rich Hamilton steel baron. One of the cool things about her, though by no means the coolest, was that she had easy access to her mother's Pontiac Parisienne convertible. (The observant reader will note that this is the second reference to mothers driving topless versions of this fine— now defunct—premium brand from General Motors. This was the sixties. Even soccer moms wanted to be cool back then. Minivans were not yet even a gleam in Lee Iacocca's eyes. In 1966, convertibles were an application for approval by the Pepsi Generation.) Since Michaele-Sue was the only one of our group to have access to wheels, she and I were assigned the task of driving to Buffalo airport to collect some of the band and bring them across the border into Canada. When we arrived at the airport, we discovered that four members of the group, Lou Reed, John Cale, Sterling Morrison, and Maureen Tucker, had all at the last moment flown instead to Toronto. However, the woman who was by far, in my wide eyes, the most interesting member of the band, their "chanteuse", Nico, was standing before us, with her flowing scarves, blonde hair, rock and roll baggage, and long-haired five year old son, ready to be driven to the gig.

70

Nico was an intensely exotic German-born model, actor, composer, and singer whose first big break had been playing in Federico Fellini's *La Dolce Vita*. Her career as a singer began in London and Paris with Rolling Stone Brian Jones and with Bob Dylan, and after giving birth to her son sired by French star Alain Delon, she moved to New York, starred in Warhol's *Chelsea Girls*, and linked up with the Velvet Underground.

Her plane arrived late in the evening. By midnight, the four of us were at the Peace Bridge, trying to cross the Niagara River into Canada. Canadian Immigration was very suspicious of rock and rollers in those days. (Within a few years they would have busted a long list of musicians trying to get into the country, a list led by Jimi Hendrix and Keith Richards.) Neither Nico's (nor Michaele-Sue's) gorgeous looks seemed to help, nor did the rock star's long confusing list of Eurotrash home addresses, mixed nationalities, missing work visas, and questionable, unverifiable connection to the sleepy long haired hippie child she was travelling with. All sounds pretty suspicious. Application for entry into the Great White North— denied. Turned back into Buffalo, we reassured the rattled rock queen that we weren't done yet. There were two other crossings into Canada.

We headed north for the Rainbow Bridge in Niagara Falls. I don't know if Nico was wired on heroin at that time, but the drug was the name of the Velvet Underground's most famous song—and she was an addict for fifteen years later in the 70s and 80s. From the driver's seat, I suggested she get rid of anything she thought might be a problem. She rolled down the window and dumped a bag of pills onto the I-95. Good thing, as we were hassled again in Niagara, and again were refused entry.

We had one last entry point to try, the Lewiston-Queenston Bridge just south of Lake Ontario. It was now four in the morning. If we were unsuccessful this time, our big light show/rock concert/underground movie presentation would have to be cancelled. Michaele-Sue came up with a new plan. She suggested that Nico feign sleep in the backseat with her child, and speak only in French if woken by the border guards. It isn't much of a stretch asking a smack user to nod off, especially at that hour of the night. Nico played her part well, and we made it across, and on to Hamilton. The rest of the band arrived, and they got their musical extravaganza underway. Nico, Lou Reed, and the other partners in crime wailed, Warhol's wacky movies unspooled above them, oily iridescent colours superimposed over everything, and smoke swirled through the rapt audience.

It was my last experience as a human smuggler, though not Michaele-Sue's. Over the next two years she and her group were involved in bringing over 2,000 draft dodgers and deserters from the Vietnam War across the Niagara River into Canada. It was an incredibly brave thing to do, in a dangerous time. She could have been arrested on a number of counts, and thrown into an American prison. She knew that she and her associates were being watched by the FBI, but they continued to bring the young men into Canada, most of whom stayed in the country for the rest of their lives. They did it even though facing disapproval by all but our generation. They knew, like all of us did, that our generation was right—and our generation was really the only one that mattered to us.

Within six months, I would turn elements of the experience into my first film, *Buffalo Airport Visions*. Later, after my involvement with Michaele-Sue had cooled off, I went down to try and connect with Nico at Warhol's "Factory" in New York. I never found her there, though I met Warhol a couple of times—a guy just as glacially icy as she was. I didn't have a snowball's chance in hell with her, anyway. Seriously competing for her affections were Leonard Cohen, Jackson Browne, Iggy Pop, Jimi Hendrix, and Jim Morrison. And at least three of them were writing love songs to her.

Back in Hamilton, our gang became inspired. We wanted to move up from working as drivers and impresarios for Andy Warhol's troupe to making films ourselves. While the idea of student and independent underground filmmaking was starting to take hold in 1966, the practice of it was limited and sketchy. We only made it happen by dint of ramming forward until someone told us to stop. That winter, we arbitrarily created what we called the McMaster Film Board, and somehow convinced the Student Council to allow us to purchase a movie camera and some 16mm film. Our efforts that winter were uninspiring, but we did assemble an interesting group of people—the hippest of the hip. Four of us were the ringleaders of the crowd. I of course was the film guy, with my weekly columns of film reviews, and my de facto role as cameraman on any ventures with the shiny new Bolex. My pal David Martin ran the Theater Society, and regularly upset the university establishment with his choice of wild off-Broadway fare, just as we soon would with our films. Patricia Murphy was a drop-dead gorgeous beatnik chick who scandalized the university by conducting simultaneous affairs with the Head of the Mathematics Department and a bohemian poet in the English Graduate School. She served as organizer and social convener for our activities. Within ten years, she would become an onscreen fixture on Moses Znaimer's radical new television station, CITY TV, and she and I would be living together.

The fourth musketeer was Dennis Murphy, who started the rock band The Gass Company that provided the soundtrack for our misspent university years. He went on to become a major record producer for Electra Records in Los Angeles, then ran the National Film Board's Ontario operation for a while. In 2004 I directed a series he produced for Discovery Channel and Court TV. In the middle of shooting, to the bewilderment of the crew, cast, and me, he was fired by the network. He left television, and took up his lifelong ambition, which was to write crime thrillers. One day in 2006 he had two meetings. At the first, his agent told him that Harper Collins had just approved his novel for publication. At the second, his doctor told him he only had three months to live.

There was no structure at the school for filmmaking, but there was a wild character hanging around the school named John Hofsess whose motto, years before Nike adopted it, was "Just Do It". Nobody authorized us to set up a McMaster Film Board, to go out and buy a camera and editing system, to buy film from Kodak and send it all off to Film House for processing and printing—and to send all the bills to the student council. John just convinced us it was much easier to ask forgiveness than to ask permission. As John was not even an officially registered student at the school, he needed a proxy to help him develop his grandiose plans. I was appointed first President of the new Film Board, allowing him to spend his time coming up with ambitious and provocative scenarios to shoot, while I would be officially responsible for trying to convince the student council and administration to allow us to bring underground filmmaking to Hamilton.

Our big production was originally titled *Black Zero* but for reasons now forgotten was re-named *Palace of Pleasure*. Writer and Film Professor Stephen Broomer, who has chronicled the full story of our McMaster Film Board adventures in his book *Hamilton Babylon*, has recently organized the re-discovery, restoration and exhibition of the underground classic. I always remembered the stories and the scandal connected to the film as being more amusing than the film itself, but Stephen claims that a new generation of students today are responding as enthusiastically to the film as people did back in 1966.

John directed the film. I photographed it—and I cast it, with my girlfriend Michaele-Sue Goldblatt, and my hitchhiking-around-America pal David Martin. It was a nutty shoot, with no real script, but instead mostly late night improvisation consisting of moody shots of Michaele-Sue and David smoking cigarettes. John did convince the two of them—and another student actor named David Hollings—to climb into a bed together. Sexual adventure was de rigueur for 60s underground filmmaking—but John found the results a little tame, and determined to add some bare skin (specifically, of course, bare breasts) to the scene.

74

By then we were linked to other student filmmakers, mostly in Toronto, and so John convinced our pal at York University, Michael Hirsh, to film our pal at University of Toronto, David Cronenberg, in bed with a York coed willing to bare all for our McMasterpiece production. Matching of the faces or other body parts didn't really matter, as both shoots were done with deep green and magenta gels on the lights, and in any case the whole film was going to be run through a mirrored kaleidoscope contraption before release, so it would become quite abstract.

Before we ever got there, though, the proverbial fan was covered in you-know-what. Someone at the lab we were using, Film House, saw the footage and decided to call in the Toronto Police Morality Squad to review it. Although in the end the cops didn't seize the film, they threatened to. When word got back to Hamilton that "Mac coeds" were being filmed in *ménages* à *trois* for a university-sponsored film, the student council, the administration, and self-righteously pontificating scribes in the student newspaper all went on the warpath. One columnist, Mary Lou Smitheram, claimed that the school's Baptist forefathers would be "spinning in their graves" as the image of the school became one of "dirty movies, and pot-smoking, acid-dropping, bearded protestors".

The story spread from the McMaster campus to the Hamilton Spectator, then on to Canada's newspaper of record, The Globe and Mail, where their humorist George Bain filled his column with a collection of limericks that he claimed had been penned by his alter-ego, Saskatchewan yokel "Clem Watkins Jr.". Here's one:

> Said the film-man, "How gay, having three
>
> Two-to-one is quite best, you'd agree?"
>
> Said the girl, 'This lark here would play hell with an arc
>
> But by George, it's just dandy by me."

Just as the story was going national, Hofsess complicated the issue by getting himself arrested over the film. In those days—and for the next ten years or so, most film cameras, lights and other equipment in Toronto were rented out of a shacky house opposite Maple Leaf Gardens by a wildly colorful old broad named Janet Good. Janet was an hilariously profane Scottish woman of considerable girth, who presided over her notoriously unreliable cameras, and her harem of young filmmakers and cameramen who came in to rent them, usually decked out in a flowing muumuu, giant diamond rings on her fingers, a Kool cigarette with a precariously long ash on it in one hand, and a glass of Scotland's finest in the other.

"John focking Hofsess!" she would tell you, if she were still around (she passed on to the big rental house in the sky at the turn of the century), "Focking bugger rented two of me best focking projectors, went down focking Church Street and pawned them in focking McTamney's!"

Since the student council was no longer accepting bills on behalf of the Film Board, John needed some cash to get our rushes out of the lab. Unfortunately, his solution resulted in his getting charged with theft over $50. Not only had Janet's projectors been pawned, but their original rental was again charged to...the McMaster Student Council. It was getting harder and harder for me, as President of the MFB, to defend his activities to the student authorities. Rumors swirled around the school that I was going to be fired.

At this point CBC National News picked up the story. In those days Peter Mansbridge's only connection with a microphone was as a baggage handler (and announcement maker) in Churchill airport. Instead, in 1966 the nightly news was read by the stern voice of Earl Cameron, and so his stentorian tones informed the nation of the filmmaking shenanigans at McMaster. (Ironically, another graduate of the McMaster Film Board, Eugene Levy, would later parody Cameron as newscaster "Earl Camembert" during his stint at

Canada's best-ever TV show, *SCTV*, performing in the show with Joe Flaherty's character, co-anchor "Floyd Robertson", modeled on long-time CTV anchor Lloyd Robertson.)

Cameron's brief piece on the national news inspired Daryl Duke, the producer of the muckraking newsmagazine show *Sunday*, to send his star reporter Larry Zolf and a crew down the QEW to investigate what was going on in usually news-bereft town of Hamilton. Zolf was one of the few survivors of the bloodletting the previous year when *Sunday*'s predecessor, the fabled *This Hour Has Seven Days* had been axed into bloody defeat. His favorite beat was Ottawa, his favorite style blowing the lid on scandals. For months, he had been covering the story of Gerda Munsinger—the East German prostitute and alleged spy who had conducted affairs with at least two members of John Diefenbaker's Conservative cabinet. If anyone personified the cliché of a journalist with "a nose for news", it was Zolf. He had a schnoz—and an ebullient personality—bigger than Jimmy Durante's. And now he was on McMaster's campus, doing streeters with students and faculty, asking them what they thought about the fact that, as he put it, "Hamilton has replaced Ottawa as the sex capital of the country".

It all became way too much for the administration—and the student council. On January 13 of the new, bright centennial year of 1967, the Student Executive Council held a six hour (!) meeting about *Black Zero*, the McMaster Film Board, and me. On January 20, The Silhouette blared a headline that I was out as MFB President. Inside, the editorial page cartoon showed me, hands tied behind my back, my head on a chopping block, surrounded by the paraphernalia of a movie set, a guy with a giant cleaver about to chop my head off. An excited director, personifying the student council, gesticulates from his chair bellowing, "Cut!"

In truth, I was not unhappy losing the mantle of MFB President. I didn't really want to be a student film administrator—I wanted to make films. I had supporters who felt I had been

77

railroaded, and as I left they managed to get my pal David Martin in as the new President. (Incestuous bunch, weren't we?) One of his first moves was to approve the new film I wanted to make inspired by my activities the previous year with Nico and the Velvet Underground. If you're handed a lemon, make lemonade. I also parlayed my new connections with Larry Zolf and his producer Steven Patrick into a summer job in the editing department at CBC.

The film scene was suddenly exploding, and there seemed to be a sea of possibilities. IMAX had just been invented (partly at McMaster), and the world's first IMAX theater was being built on the Toronto waterfront. Chris Chapman's shape-shifting multi-screen ode to Ontario, *A Place to Stand* was the hit of Expo 67 and would go on to win an Academy Award. Our *Black Zero*, though still under clouds of financial malfeasance, somehow got finished and became one of the hits of the summer's big film event, the twenty-four hour long Cinethon. Twenty-four hours of trippy underground films? Yes—and for me, on acid, to boot. Meanwhile, in Montreal the National Film Board was turning out all kinds of interesting new *cinéma vérité* films, documenting rising stars like Paul Anka and Leonard Cohen. As for me, with a camera in hand, a film to make, and a job at the biggest TV network in the country, I was stoked to dive in to the scene myself.

The summer of 1967 was also of course the Summer of Love. Haight Ashbury, the Sunset Strip, the East Village, and, in our neck of the woods, Yorkville, were all exploding with music, dope, action, and change. In order to participate, we created a hippie crash pad for ourselves. If the expression suggests undisciplined squalor to you, I have used the wrong turn of phrase. The house we rented for the summer is gone, but if it were standing today, it would be worth well over two million dollars. A large Victorian home at the corner of Huron and Sussex Streets, it was then owned by the University of Toronto. Wanting to bust the block up so they could tear the houses down and built a massive new library, they rented it to us for a hundred dollars a month.

My high school girlfriend Maryke McEwan and I took the lead on the rental of the house, and then found six other kindred free spirits to share the rent. The eight of us each had our own room, and each paid…twelve dollars a month rent. The house quickly became known on the hippie trail, and it would not be uncommon for us to have couples arriving on the doorstep with their backpacks, telling us they'd been told of our place at the beginning of their journey, in San Francisco. We let people like that crash in the basement. Time Magazine mentioned us on their cover story on the Summer of Love. The fabled Rochdale College, an alternative cooperative residence and educational institution, soon to become known for its drug-fuelled counterculture, was conceived in our kitchen, and built just a block up the street.

We were hippies by night, working stiffs by day. After swearing an oath to the Queen (which all employees had to do in those days), I punched in to a time clock every day at the Corporation. Maryke worked as a bank teller—though within a few years she would go on to become a television producer herself. One of her claims to fame is that, after screening nearly a thousand other possibilities for her film *The Diary of Evelyn Lau*, she discovered and gave Sandra Oh her first screen role.

We painted the entire first floor of the house, and everything in it, silver—then inscribed "Love or What?", the title of the new feature script I was writing, in giant psychedelic lettering, across it. The freezer in our battered fridge was filled with thousands of tabs of Owsley acid, which our in-house dealer living on the third floor dealt on the streets of the Yorkville Village. 1967 was the summer of Sgt. Pepper, Jefferson Airplane, and Buffalo Springfield. The tunes were always cranked to eleven. Fortunately another recent graduate from The McMaster Silhouette was now working on the police beat at the (soon to be defunct) Toronto Telegram, and he would warn us whenever he heard on the police scanner that the cops would likely be trying to bust us for a noise complaint. Convenient, since a noise complaint could have led to something much more serious.

I filmed the love-ins and happenings of the groovy summer, and used our spacious house to stage scenes for my film. To play a young director in a trippy filmmaking sequence, I brought the ever-willing David Cronenberg back for another performance. For another scene, we got local biker gang the Satan's Choice to roar around on their Harleys. By September, though, the Summer of Love was over. Our lease ended, and as we vacated the wrecking ball was already hanging over our psychedelic pad. My summer job at the CBC had come to an end. I finished shooting my film—and got a call from Hamilton telling me I had to get the camera back to McMaster right away. There was a new first-time filmmaker named Ivan Reitman who wanted to use it to make a short comedy about a freshman's first week of school. His McMaster film, *Orientation* was a modest but successful model for him for the camp and campus comedies *Meatballs* and *Animal House* that he would soon make his name with.

As I'd been burning the candle at both ends for several years, I decided it was time to return to the quiet and good cooking of my parents' suburban home. I also needed a clean retreat in which to cut the negative of my film. For years I've been known as someone who wants to do just about everything in the field of filmmaking (a profile on me in Canadian Cinematographer magazine was titled "A Master of All Trades: Writer-Director-Producer-Cinematographer"). In my long career, however, this is the only time I ever cut the negative for one of my films. Neg cutting is a fussy task best left to anally precise women of Germanic or Scottish descent, but I wanted to learn every craft in the filmmaking quiver, so I donned a pair of little white cotton gloves, messed with glue and a hot splicer, squinted at edge code numbers, and neg-cut my little film.

But with that and the network job both finished, prospects for professional film work looked bleak. In those days, there was only a tiny fraction of the film and television business there is today. I was so desperate I actually went out and took a real job. A neighbor worked at Canada Packers, the huge meat packing plant in the north end of the city. He told me he could get me a job there. I lasted one day. As this good fellow drove me to work that day, earnestly telling me about retirement plans and dental benefits, I got the distinct sense from him that he thought he was driving me to a career at the meat packer that would last me until I was sixty five. I pushed an internal mail cart around the massive building for the day, and told him that evening I wouldn't be returning. I am happy to report that was the one and only day of a "real job" I've ever had to endure.

If I wasn't going to work nine to five at the meat plant, I'd have to be on my toes for an alternate way of earning a living. Fortunately, I was at the right place, at the right time. *Cinéma vérité* had developed quickly in the mid sixties as a new way of shooting film and telling raw, unvarnished stories. Technical innovation was at the heart of this revolutionary way to make films. A Polish inventor named Stefan Kudelski created the portable Nagra tape recorder and the crystal that could sync it to a camera. At the same time New York filmmakers Donn Pennebaker and Richard Leacock chopped down the old-school Mitchell cameras, turning them into relatively lightweight, reflex cameras that could be thrown on to a shoulder and taken virtually anywhere.

A radical new way of filmmaking was born—and two of its most accomplished advocates were just down the street from me. Director Allan King and his cameraman partner Richard Leiterman had started filmmaking in Vancouver, and spent much of the late fifties and early sixties in London, England, and Ibiza, Spain, honing their craft and creating a sort of co-operative/film company called Allan King Associates. In 1967 they returned to Canada, and set up shop in Toronto. Within a few months of their arrival, I was hired as an assistant editor/assistant cameraman at the exciting outfit. It is hard to overestimate the role our ever-expanding company had in the city in the period. Allan's film *Warrendale*, a fly-on-the-wall look at emotionally disturbed kids, was banned by the CBC—the network that had commissioned it—but the controversy over the banning made King's career. It was invited to the Cannes Film Festival, and won the Prix d'art et d'essai there, and in my first year at the company it was playing theatrically in town, while I and a gang of others worked furiously turning out a series of short sequel films to the notoriously foul-mouthed doc.

Meanwhile we were turning out all kinds of other films for TV networks and others. The buzz on the company was so hot that, almost unbelievably, we shot the campaign films for all three political parties in the 1968 federal campaign. I worked on all three films. I was just an assistant editor on a film for the Liberals, but it was perhaps the most fun, as it was Pierre Trudeau's first campaign for PM, with mini-skirted screaming Trudeaumania following him on every campaign stop. On an even grander film we did for the Conservatives, I was a Production- and Post-Production-Coordinator. And with everyone else working away on films for the big boys, I was the Director (!) of the film we did for the NDP.

No sooner was that campaign over than I jumped on a plane with Richard Leiterman to fly to California to make a film about the Los Angeles Police Department. It proved to be one of the nuttier adventures in filmmaking I've been involved in. We were working with another big name in the history of *cinéma vérité*, Fred Wiseman. Wiseman made his name with *Titicut Follies,* a documentary about the patient-inmates of a hospital for the criminally insane in Massachusetts, and followed it with a long string of provocative films with bland titles like *Public Housing, Welfare, High School*, and *Zoo*. Ours, of course, was going to be called *Police*.

The idea was that we were going to drive around Watts and South Central L.A. with Richard filming, Fred recording sound and directing, and me assisting. Basically *Cops*-style, but twenty-five years before *Cops*. The cops we were dealing with didn't know what to make of us. The filmmaking model they were used to was Jack Webb and *Dragnet*, a realistic drama, which featured the terse but earnest Sgt. Joe Friday. Our trio of two long-haired Canadians and a pudgy eastern liberal academic with a tape recorder and microphone 'round his neck—well, it didn't seem to work for the cowboy cops of South Central. We all tried to make a go of it for a week or so. We'd show up for the night shift, and head out with different units in the mean streets—Richard and Fred in the back seat of the patrol car, me following in our rental station wagon, the back filled with Sungun lights and extra magazines and rolls of film and tape. When they got a call, they would take off, sometimes with lights on and sirens wailing, sometimes just at high speed. I was expected to keep up, with no knowledge of the area, no training in high speed driving, and no siren or flashing lights. When and if I managed to follow them to the crime scene, everyone would pile out and we'd follow the cops around, filming them making high risk takedowns in one of the most dangerous neighborhoods in America. The disconnect between the L.A. cops and the eastern filmmakers eventually resulted in the whole shoot imploding after a couple of weeks, and we returned home, to move on to other, less difficult projects.

The federal government had just set up the institution that would become Canada's feature film production studio/bank— Telefilm Canada. It was then known as the Canadian Film Development Corporation. It seems hard to believe today, but when the CFDC went to find themselves a first director for the Toronto office of the crown corporation, they choose a twenty-one year old kid still in law school at the time named Chalmers Adams. (He did have prematurely grey hair, so perhaps that helped.) For one of his first advisors on the new organization, Chalmers chose another twenty-one year old named...Peter Rowe. One wintery day he showed up at our film office to take me to lunch to pick my brain about how the new operation ought to work. It gives you an idea of the fixation on youth in that era—one reason I call the Baby Boom Generation the Lucky Generation. I suppose it had happened before. For instance, film producers Louis B. Mayer (who grew up in Canada) and Canadian-born Jack Warner began the studios that would become MGM and Warner Brothers while they were in their twenties. But I don't think it would happen today.

I decided if I was going to become a film director I would have to figuratively hang up a shingle that said "Film Director" and stand firm that that is what I had become. You can't expect others to take a chance on you, unless you are prepared to take a chance on you. With that shingle up, there may only be one person in the world who believes it, but that is one more than there is if you're drifting without it. Eventually there'll be a second, then a third, and a fourth person that agrees with you. I had the idea that I wanted to make a film comparing the culture of the 1950s with those of the 1960s. I wrote an outline for the film, and took it to the boss, Allan King. He liked it, and wanted to produce it. He wanted the bring in his old pal from Vancouver, a guy named Gene Lawrence, to direct it, and he wanted to try to get that hottest of hot sixties writers, Tom Wolfe, to write it. It was a major crisis for me. I wanted to help Allan's company, which I loved, but not by handing what I thought of as my baby to Gene Lawrence and Tom Wolfe, however skilled and famous they might be.

After a good deal of soul-searching, I returned to Allan to tell him I didn't want to do it that way. Nothing against that plan, or those guys, but I wanted to write it, I wanted to direct it. I thought I was going to be fired, but to my surprise, and I think to his credit, he accepted my plan. I could do it my way, using his organization as a base. Only thing is, if I wanted to write and direct it, I'd have to find the money and basically produce it as well. Fortunately, I had some connections that allowed me to do it. Through my friendship with Chalmers Adams I learned of a special opportunity to get some money from the CFDC. I put together a wild looking presentation featuring a photo of me decked out as a fifties greaseball hood. Apparently my unorthodox pitch divided the jury, but the chair of it, Quebecois director Claude Jutra, argued in my favour, and I got the dough. The other two recipients of that one time CFDC experiment in film financing were Don Shebib, for his film *Goin' Down the Road*, and feminist filmmaker Sylvia Spring from Vancouver, who became known for *Madeleine Is...*(1970), the first Canadian feature film directed by a woman since the post-WWI days of Nell Shipman.

While working at Allan King Associates I'd also been involved with John Hofsess, David Cronenberg, Michael Hirsh, and some others, in setting up an outfit we called the Toronto Filmmaker's Co-op. (It later morphed into an organization called the Canadian Filmmakers Distribution Center, which is still in operation today). One of our first members was a guy named Lorne Michael Lipowitz, who later changed his named to Lorne Michaels, moved to New York, and created a new TV show called *Saturday Night Live*. Through the Film Co-op I connected with a burgeoning new distribution company called Film Canada, which also got involved in the micro-financing of my film, now titled *Neon Palace*.

Shebib and I both shot our films out of Allan King Associates in the summer of 1969, both using the same camera. One day he would be out with Richard Leiterman shooting his gritty drama with King's trusty Éclair NPR on the streets of Cabbagetown; the next my filming partners Jim Lewis and Tony Hall and I would be using the same camera to film our wacky and elaborate underground docudrama.

Everything was communally shared back then (even, one has to confess, girlfriends). Once I got the film finished my distributor, Willem Poolman, rented a Moviola for two of us to use to edit our films. Cronenberg had just shot his first feature—an art film called *Stereo*. I had more money for my film than David did for his (last time that's happened) so I got to use the cutting room in the daytime, and David took it over every night.

The film won me a Canadian Film Award (later called "Etrogs", then, for thirty years, "Genies", now, "Canadian Screen Awards". It's the Circle of Life.) We released the film a year later in Poolman's Yonge Street theater. We had some pretty good luck with the critics. We got a great review in *Variety*, some good spreads in the Toronto dailies, and what was going to be a rave in *Rolling Stone*. I was ecstatic when I saw a preview of the magazine critic's review, but he was fired the week before it was to run. He later sold the review to *CREEM* magazine, which ran it, but it was hardly the same.

My two partners and I came up with some novel promotions to try to get people into the theater. Our trailer for *Neon Palace* had run for three months with the Stones' film *Gimme Shelter*, so a lot of people knew of the movie—but we wanted to maximize the turnout. As part of the film I had shot an interview with an old-fashioned straight French Canadian businessman in Montreal who was making a fortune importing Zig-Zag cigarette papers and selling them to dope smokers and head shops all over North America. We now got him to send us about 5,000 of the packets of papers, pasted a little neon colored label on the back of them that read "Light up—before entering The Neon Palace" and gave them away all over the streets of Toronto.

We then took the film to New York, and tried to get an American distribution deal for it. We showed it to Paramount, Warner Bros., and the rest. A lot of hot young (and not so young) film executives and producers came and saw the film, but in the end nobody bit and I never got a distribution deal. I did, though, later wonder about the influence of those screenings. At the time we showed it to them there was no nostalgia for the 50s, no looking backward to the past. Within two years, there was all kinds of 50s nostalgia coming out of Hollywood—*American Graffiti*, *The Last Picture Show*, rock and roll revivals, *Sha Na Na*, *Happy Days*, and *Last Summer*. Maybe *Neon Palace* got those executives thinking. Or maybe it was just in the zeitgeist. I was certainly one of the first to tap into fifties nostalgia—if not the most successful. My goofy feature did become a fixture as a Friday night midnight show at various rep houses, then ran numerous times on Moses Znaimer's CITY TV, then once home video was introduced ten years later, got released by Garth Drabinsky's Cineplex Video label.

Film was a big deal in the late sixties, but music was an even bigger deal. We had orchestrated and filmed an elaborate reconstruction of a fifties rock and roll movie as part of *Neon Palace*. Through that, I got more and more into filming music. I believe the first band I filmed was the Mothers of Invention. While I was setting up to film him, my girlfriend of the moment went backstage and threw herself at Frank Zappa. How fair is that? Many musicians in those days of course believed they ought to play stoned. We in the camera fraternity thought we should emulate our onstage brethren. Really bad idea. I don't know how you can play a guitar stoned—and I certainly learned you can't operate a camera after smoking up. One weedy concert of the Jefferson Airplane, I was on a scaffolding, filming Grace Slick and Marty Balin when the lens fell right out of the camera. It landed on some blissed-out cat below, who picked it up and handed it back up to me. Without even turning the camera off I re-inserted it and kept shooting. They probably used the footage as is. Wow, man. Psychedelic.

In the spring of 1969 John Lennon and Yoko Ono flew from the Bahamas into Toronto and on to Montreal to stage their famous Bed-in for Peace. We combined forces with Allan King's sister company in London to film their pajama party. It was a bit like *The Bill Maher Show*, except in a big bed, and not as funny, with visiting celebrities, some sympathetic, others antagonistic, talking with John and Yoko about big issues. Timothy Leary showed up, as did Al Capp (whose abrasive personality endeared him to no one), Dick Gregory, Murray the K (who styled himself as the Fifth Beatle), Norman Mailer, and Tommy Smothers. At one point they all got together and recorded "Give Peace a Chance". In the midst of it a young political science student named Allan Rock (who much later would become a Minister of Justice and Attorney General of Canada), drove John and Yoko in his Volkswagen up to Ottawa to meet Pierre Trudeau. My own minor bit part in the production was to take the reams of footage coming out of Montreal, sync it up through the night and get it back the next day to John's press officer Derek Taylor, so that some of it could be screened for the two bed-bound stars/producers in their down-time between celebrity visits.

Sounds simple, doesn't it? "Sync it up." These days you can do it with one mouse click. Back then, given the exigencies of catch-as-catch-can *cinéma vérité* shooting, it was frequently a nightmarish, pull-your-hair-out task. Filmmakers today talk wistfully of the old days of 16mm film, flatbed editing benches, double-system shooting, Arriflexes, and Moviolas. I don't have an ounce of nostalgia for any of it. Thank God, I say, for Japanese cameras, digital chips, and Final Cut Pro.

There are other things I don't miss about the late sixties. Witchcraft, for one. Very big back then. I decided I wanted to go to the famous Woodstock Festival—and I had a motorcycle to get me there. I took off across upstate New York, but somewhere along the line got massively off in the wrong direction. Navigation can be difficult on a motorcycle. I was so far off course that I decided the hell with it—I would go back to Provincetown, instead. It's a great town, and no one really knew if Woodstock was really going to happen before it did, anyway.

Later that summer my motorcycle died a fiery death. I was sharing a house split into two apartments with Moses Znaimer. He was at the time an afternoon television host—three or four years away from his revolutionary move to create CITY TV (and its spawn of MuchMusic, Bravo!, Fashion Television, etc). One night he banged on my door to alert me to the fact that my motorcycle, parked in the driveway beside the broad lawn, was now ablaze in a ball of flames. I had just ditched a rather strange girl who had a sick passion for witchcraft, but I never really found out for certain whether she was the one who lit it on fire. The sixties were starting to get weird.

In the late summer of '69 Lennon would return to Toronto, for his first public performance after the breakup of the Beatles. We were there again to film that. A couple of promoters, Ken Walker and Thor Eaton, decided to stage what they called the Toronto Rock and Roll Revival in Varsity Stadium, with the likes of Jerry Lee Lewis, Bo Diddley, Chuck Berry, Gene Vincent, Chicago, and Alice Cooper on the bill. New York based Donn Pennebaker, who had just had a big hit with his Bob Dylan profile *Don't Look Back*, decided to come up to film the concert. He came, naturally, to Allan King Associates, to find his crew. I had the best job of the day. Richard Leiterman was assigned the position of onstage cameraman. I assisted him—sitting immediately in front of the stage, my arms in a black bag, loading dozens and dozens of rolls of film into magazines. It was a twelve-hour concert, so occasionally Richard would have to take a break, and I'd shoot, but mostly he shot, and I got to sit in my front row seat, digging all these amazing musicians while performing an easy task I could do in my sleep.

What none of us knew was that the night before John Lennon had decided he wanted to join the party. According to Albert Goldman's salacious and highly controversial biography of Lennon, he had arranged to meet Eric Clapton, Klaus Voorman, and Yoko at Heathrow Airport to fly to Toronto for the festival. When the heroin-addicted Lennon couldn't climb from bed Saturday morning, he received a call from Clapton (also wired on heroin at the time) at Heathrow. Goldman quotes Clapton shouting to the famous ex-Beatle, "Listen, motherfucker—I'm not at the fuckin' airport for a joke! You guys get your asses out here—or don't ask me for any more favors, ever!"

Lennon and Ono roused themselves and made it to the airport to catch an afternoon flight to Toronto. Apparently it was a grim flight, with the rockers desperately trying to rehearse and remember the lyrics to old hits, while suffering cold turkey from their forced withdrawal from their smack habits. When they arrived at the Toronto airport, they were accompanied into town by a large phalanx of Vagabonds motorcycle gang members on their Harleys, and they went onstage at about 10 that night. It was the first performance anywhere of Lennon, after the break-up of the Beatles, and so the mood was electric. I found it a bit ridiculous—the rock gods Clapton and Lennon performing in front of me reduced to guitar sidemen for an absurd performance of yodeling and howling inside a bag by Yoko Ono, the woman who had recently broken up the greatest songwriting team in history (according to Goldman, by alerting her connections in Japan so that Paul McCartney would be caught in a marijuana bust as he entered the country.).

The concert, which we immortalized in a film Pennebaker released as *Sweet Toronto*, also saw two other famous moments in rock history. Alice Cooper got involved in a crazy scene involving biting the head of a live chicken off and flinging the bird into the audience. (He now denies it, and although I was certainly there for it, hey, it was the 60s—who now can remember who exactly bit what?) It was also the first instance of the ritual of the audience waving lighters and matches to the music. Master of Ceremonies Kim Fowley persuaded the audience to pull out their lighters—of course nearly everyone had one in those days—to light them up "to welcome John and Yoko to Toronto"—and it became a rock concert tradition that continues to this day (though now done digitally, with waving cell-phones).

Unbelievably, John Lennon was not the headliner of the show. After he and his Plastic Ono Band left the stage, we learned that there would be one more group that would perform that night—the chart topping Jim Morrison and The Doors. Morrison was on good behavior (no flashing) after his recent concert arrest in Miami, the band gave a great performance, and Morrison graciously introduced the last song of the night, "The End", by saying he was honored to be on the same stage as all the "illustrious musical geniuses" that had been on it before him that day.

After their success at Varsity Stadium, the next summer the same two promoters had bigger plans that, once again, I got involved in. Their idea was to invite a large group of performers on a "Festival Express" train that would tour Canada from Montreal to Vancouver. There were battles from the start, with the mayors of both Montreal and Vancouver cancelling concerts in their cities due to concerns about security and possible violence. Instead, it became a train tour that started in Toronto, and ended in Calgary. Maybe the mayors were right. The Toronto concerts began with more battles and riots around the issue of how "the music should be free", and "The Man is ripping us off". In the end, Jerry Garcia arranged a free "rehearsal concert" in a park in order to cool down the ridiculous riot. The free concert, which lasted from 7p.m. to 4 a.m. included performances by The Grateful Dead, Ian & Sylvia and the Great Speckled Bird, and James and the Good Brothers, among others. The "rip off" ticket price fans were screaming about? Ten dollars. (Nine dollars advance.)

Following the contentious Toronto concerts, the Dead, Janis Joplin and her Full Tilt Boogie Band, Buddy Guy, Delaney and Bonnie and The Band, and a team of cameramen and sound guys to record their every drunken move, jumped on a fourteen-car CNR train heading across northern Ontario for more gigs in Winnipeg and Calgary. I was right in the middle of completing my *Neon Palace*, so I was not able to get very involved with the tour. However I was a player in a sidebar story to it, without which the film would never have been made.

These rock films were all thrown together very much at the last moment, often with the financing and artist releases all still pending as the cameras began to roll. Today, if you suddenly decided you needed to film a rock festival, you could just format all the memory cards on your camera and go out and shoot it. Back then you needed film. Lots of it. It wasn't cheap, and it was only made by one company (Eastman Kodak) and they didn't give it to you on credit.

Willem Poolman, the producer of the film that would eventually be called *Festival Express*, and the distributor of my *Neon Palace*, called me in a panic asking for assistance. It was the afternoon of June 29, the Friday leading into the Canada Day holiday long weekend. In a few hours, the train full of rock stars and cameramen would be leaving the station on its cross-country journey. They had everything they needed except...film stock to shoot it with. Hey,

91

that's a bummer, man. The Eastman Kodak plant that had the film stock was way out in Brampton—twenty miles from our downtown headquarters. There were several cases of it being held for us, which they would be glad to release to us if we got there before five, and if we paid them for it—cash on the barrelhead. Few people had credit cards in those days. Visa (then called Chargex) had just been introduced, and I'm sure Kodak didn't accept it. They wanted dollar bills, and lots of them—just like those Congolese shakedown artists in Chapter 1.

We had to get to Poolman's bank—and it would be closed at four o'clock for the holiday weekend. If we missed either the bank or Kodak, the film would be down the drain. By the time they both re-opened on Tuesday morning, the train would be steaming across Saskatchewan. We tore over to his bank, where he went into a long meeting trying to persuade his manager to approve the extension on the company line of credit. I watched the minutes ticking away on the bank's clock, knowing the shipping guys at Kodak were likely doing the same, wondering if they could close up shop a little earlier. Who would be wanting film stock on the Friday afternoon of a holiday weekend anyway?

Poolman got a giant envelope of cash (we didn't want to risk a certified cheque in case we got the dollar amount wrong—the cameramen were still trying to figure out how much film stock they would need). We charged off to Brampton. Of course, everyone else was charging off too. It was the biggest Friday traffic jam of the year, with half the city heading out to the lakes and beaches north of the city. Traffic gridlock. Finally, at 4:45, we sprinted into Kodak, laid the cash on them, and picked up enough film stock to fill the trunk and back seat of the car. Now, how would we get it to the shooters?

We found a pay phone, and Poolman called to find out that the notoriously tardy Grateful Dead had all been rounded up and rolled on to the train. It was leaving the station. We had missed it. He quickly came up with a back-up plan. Was it going to stop anywhere?

No—but CN agreed they would have the train crawl through Barrie station, so we could toss the film cartons onboard. That is, if we could get to Barrie in seventy-five minutes. We took off, roaring along the 401 and up the 400 the sixty miles to Barrie. Actually, wrong verb. We were stuck in traffic gridlock on the 400 with all the weekend cottagers, tearing our hair out as we inched our way to our destination.

Somehow, we made it. As the train rolled slowly through town, we ran alongside, tossing our cartons up to the waiting assistant cameramen. Did we get any gratitude? No, all we got were questions from the rock bands, asking if we had any booze for them. Seems they'd almost already emptied the bar car. No, we told them, they'd have to handle that problem themselves. And they did. Apparently Rick Danko and Robbie Robertson of The Band got the train to stop in the northern hamlet of Chapleau, completely bought out the town liquor store, and loaded it on the train.

That's a story you don't hear in Cat Stevens' famous song *Peace Train*.

A week later, I was on a plane heading for London, where I would spend the summer at Technicolor overseeing the blow up of my *Neon Palace* to 35mm. While there, I learned of the plans for the Isle of Wight Rock Festival, and determined to get to the big gathering. Originally I went simply as a spectator, with my girlfriend of the period—but that changed once I got there.

Canadian music didn't really take off until 1971, when the federal government mandated that radio and television broadcasters must air a certain percentage of Canadian content. The Guess Who, Gordon Lightfoot, Anne Murray, Bryan Adams, and all those who followed them—Celine Dion, Shania Twain, Nickelback, Jann Arden, Corey Hart, Dan Hill, k.d. Lang, and all the others—owe a fair amount of their early success to the programming regulations that got them on the air. Before CanCon, the only real way to become a rock star was to move to New York, Nashville, or L.A. and try your hand there. That's what Zal Yanovsky had done, and it did work for him. When I met him in 1968 he was probably the most successful Canadian rock performer there was—co-founder and lead guitarist for The Lovin' Spoonful. He and his girlfriend Jackie Burroughs were both connected with a quirky and successful little film I partially shot and fully edited called *At Home*.

By 1970 the Spoonful had broken up, and Zal was playing back-up guitar for Kris Kristofferson, who happened to be onstage when I arrived on the first night of the Isle of Wight Festival. How he saw me out in the huge audience I'll never know. The 1970 Isle of Wight Festival, with an estimated attendance of 600,000 to 700,000 people, is believed to have been at the time not just the biggest rock festival ever, but the second largest assembly of people in one place ever on the planet. (It is claimed only the siege of Stalingrad had more.) The Isle of Wight was nearly twice as big as Woodstock. It was just a giant sea of people that stretched as far as the eye could see. There are some massive religious gatherings in India—I filmed a huge (and crazy) one in 2009, but even it didn't compare with the numbers at the Isle of Wight.

For some reason musicians used to take forever to tune their guitars back then. As Kristofferson interminably tweaked the tuning on his electrified acoustic, I squirmed and inched my way closer and closer to the stage. As I got close enough, an impatient-looking Yanovsky, scanning the crowd, caught sight of me. With a quizzical look in his eye, he moved to Kristofferson's mike, and shouted out, "Peter! What the hell are you doing here?" Whatever my answer was, he couldn't hear it. Kristofferson seemed a little taken aback that his session player had taken the spotlight, so he determined that the tuning on his low E string was finally satisfactory, and moved in to take the mike back. Zal shouted at me to come backstage after the set, and Kristofferson launched into his tale of being busted flat in Baton Rouge, waitin' for the train, feelin' nearly faded as his jeans.

Following the Kristofferson set, I made my way backstage, and found the ever-effervescent Yanovsky. He told me that a mutual friend of ours, Toni Myers, was also backstage somewhere, preparing to produce a big film on the festival. Toni has gone on to become (I believe) the most financially successful documentary filmmaker in the world. Her films, all made in IMAX, made with Graham Ferguson and often about the NASA Space program, have grossed close to half a billion dollars. Back then she was fixated, like the rest of us, on music. She had been given the gig of producing a feature film about the British festival, a film thrown together in the usual slapdash manner. When I showed up, I was hired on the spot. The British crew wasn't responding well to their American director—another east-coast academic type named Murray Lerner—and they thought with my North American background I might relate better to him than the Brits did. I was handed an Arriflex BL camera, introduced to Murray, and thrown into a musical maelstrom that last four days and nights.

The festival began every day at about noon, with local Isle of Wight bands. By mid-afternoon other British bands would hit the stage, and by evening the stars would start playing. The headliners would sometimes not appear until long after midnight. At 4 a.m. they shut things down, but by noon the next day the massive P.A. system would be back on again with the volume cranked well past eleven. The line-up included Jimi Hendrix, Miles Davis, Joan Baez, Tiny Tim, Leonard Cohen, The Doors, Emerson, Lake and Palmer, The Moody Blues, Ten Years After, Donovan, Joni Mitchell, Richie Havens, Chicago, Jethro Tull, and The Who.

The festival was an utter organizational shambles. Once again we had the "This festival should be free" crowd attempting to tear down the gates and get in without paying. The area was so huge—hundreds of acres in size—that it was impossible to patrol, and eventually breaches in the temporary fencing were made and the freeloaders stormed in. I filmed the furious promoters—British pirate station disc jockeys—claiming that the interlopers were not British—

they were all outsiders—Algerians. Who knew there were so many rabid Algerian fans of Tiny Tim and Jethro Tull?

Before the third day, when the promoters gave up and threw all the gates open, declaring that the festival was free, I filmed inside an army Bell tent with them. I was cross-legged on the ground, as were they, and a parade of the managers of Hendrix, The Who, Cohen *et al*—mustachioed and buckskin clad dudes with joints behind their ears, came in and sat across from them, angrily negotiating the terms of their stars' performance. From time to time gate managers would open the fly of the tent and unceremoniously dump huge plastic tubs of one and five pound notes on to the ground between us. Once the negotiations were completed, the festival organizers would start picking fistfuls of notes up off the ground, count off five hundred pounds, or whatever the agreed artist fee was, and hand it to the managers.

Backstage was rock 'n' roll pandemonium. At one point a girl suddenly pulled all her clothes off and threw herself on Pete Townsend, just as The Who were about to go onstage. A roadie grabbed the naked girl off the startled rock star, and threw her aside like a used tissue. Murray and I were filming right on the stage, only a few feet from the performers. While Joni Mitchell was crooning her gentle song about getting back to the garden, some mental anarchist ran on stage, grabbed her mike, and began a diatribe about capitalism and freedom and not getting ripped off by The Man. No-one stopped him. Mitchell just stood back as everyone let him have his say, until finally one of DJs grabbed him and booted him off. Joni returned, somewhat shaken, to finish her set.

The temporary stage had a grid of Fresnel lights above it, surrounded by some wide strips of black bunting. During Leonard Cohen's late-night set, the breeze blew some of the cloth on to the back of one of the hot lamps, and it began to smolder. Smoke began drifting up off the roof of the stage. In the middle of "So Long, Marianne", one of the organizers ran on to the stage, pulled the mike away from Cohen, and began shouting at the audience, in his thick cockney accent.

"Look, we got a problem 'ere, aright? Is there a fireman in the 'ouse? Oy said, is there a bloody fireman in the 'ouse?"

Apparently there was. Several louts—looked more like bikers than firemen to me—volunteered. Because the crowd was now so tightly packed together, they had to be lifted into the air, and pushed over the heads of others towards the stage. Eventually, they made it, and enthusiastically clambered on to the stage (big dopey two-fisted waves to their friends) and up the scaffolding toward the smoldering cloth. Cohen waited (probably tuned his guitar—as mentioned, a popular way of killing time). We filmed the volunteer firemen doing their thing. Then came the craziest moment. They put out the little burnt piece of cloth—then, apparently to indicate to all of us that all was now safe, they lit a railroad flare. The crowd gasped. Even the unflappable Leonard stopped tuning and looked up. Then they began waving the flare around, as if to say, "It's all okay", and began to climb down. Cohen returned to his set list.

After my sixteen-hour days of shooting, I would trek through the vast hordes of people searching for my girlfriend, her friend, and our little campsite on one of the hills far above the concert stage. Like almost everyone else there, we had nothing more than heavy paper one-time use sleeping bags we had purchased with our tickets. Fortunately, unlike Woodstock (and surprisingly, since it was England), it never rained. I'd crash from perhaps 5 a.m. until 11, then make the long one-hour trek back through the waking crowd to the stage, for another day of filming rock 'n' roll.

Highlights of the event for me were Miles Davis (insanely great, if you could handle that kind of music) and Jimi Hendrix. As we were filming Hendrix from the side of the stage, I saw the most excessive rock 'n' roll move ever. Hendrix used those tall Marshall speakers popular in the 70s, on either side of the stage. During Mitch

97

Mitchell's lengthy drum solo in the middle of "Foxy Lady", Hendrix moved to the side of the stage, slammed his bare arm against the edge of the Marshall stack, (and out of the spotlight), and a roadie pulled out a needle and shot him up. Hendrix moved back into the spotlight and returned to his wicked guitar playing. Maybe it was just Vitamin B-12 in the syringe.

The festival wound down. The sleep-deprived, eardrum-busted hordes made their way off the island. (Yes, I now have tinnitus. Blame it on all those days and nights filming in front of those Marshall stacks. I'm not alone—Beethoven, Bono, Phil Collins, Pete Townsend, Neil Young, Barbra Streisand, Paul Simon, Eric Clapton—the list of people who should have worn earplugs in their youth is quite long.)

As for the films of the Festival Express and the Isle of Wight, the extraordinary and exclusive footage sat in a mess of litigation, unpaid bills, and unfinished editing for nearly thirty years. I forgot about both of them until 2001. I had just finished my filmed biography of Joshua Slocum, the first man to sail alone around the world. After his epic sail, Slocum moved from Nova Scotia and Boston to live in Martha's Vineyard, where he gave magic lantern presentations about his epic voyage in a town hall. Now, the people who ran the same town hall asked me to come, one hundred years later, to show my new film about Slocum.

During my time there, they mentioned they had a filmmaker living on the island—Murray Lerner. They connected me with him, he came to my screening, and he gave me a DVD of the Isle of Wight film titled *Message to Love*. All those years later, he had finally released it in 1997. A few years later, I got a call from Willem Poolman. He and his son Gavin Poolman and Bob Smeaton had pulled together the footage and added interviews with the Festival Express survivors to make the rockumentary feature film *Festival Express*. He invited me to the premiere. The film became a million dollar box office and DVD success, proving again that as the song from the era had it, people out there are (still) turning music into gold.

Back in England, the reaction to the big festival was negative. The House of Commons passed a new "Isle of Wight Act", banning gatherings of more than 5,000 people on the island without a special licence. The next festival would not be held there until 2002.

Within two weeks, Jimi Hendrix was found dead in his London hotel room. His was the second of four major rock star deaths within a year—the others Brian Jones, Janis Joplin and Jim Morrison, each one of them 27 years old.

It was time to get out of Dodge, to find a new specialty. My girlfriend and I left England for an adventure in Ibiza. On the way to the ferry to Bilbao, I stopped at a bookstore and stumbled upon a reprint of Joshua Slocum's 1901 book, *Sailing Alone Around the World*. I had found a new passion. Music was history. The marine world was to be the new theme.

Filming the Storm Plates for *Lost!* – Lunenburg, Nova Scotia 1983   Tony Hall

Snow Goggles – Pangnirtung, Nunavut 2008   George Kourounis

100

Peter Rowe at the Cannes Film Festival –
both born in 1947

With Maasai tribesmen – Maasai Mara, Kenya 2009
George Kourounis

Fired as President of the McMaster Film Board
Cartoon by Jelte Kuipers, McMaster Silhouette 1967

"Let's just make an edit here, and there..."

The CBC re-edits *Beyond the Red Wall* to appease the Chinese Government 2007
Stephen Taylor

Marooned in the Land God Gave to Cain 1979
With Céline Lomez and Jean-Jacques Blanchet   Rosebud Films

Chasing Waterspouts for *Angry Planet* - Sugarloaf Key, Florida 2008
George Kourounis

Filming *The Spirit of the River to China* 1979   Rosebud Films

Naica Crystal Cave, Chihuahua, Mexico 2009   Speleoresearch & Films

Filming *African Skies* – Krugersdorp, South Africa 1993   Atlantis Films

With Cheetah, West Rand, South Africa 1994   Sean Ryerson

The *Rub'al Khali* (Empty Quarter), Arabian Desert 2010　　Peter Rowe

Jackson Hole, Wyoming 2012　　Frank O'Connor

106

Filming *Alien Invaders* – Eleuthera, Bahamas 2011   Brianna Rowe

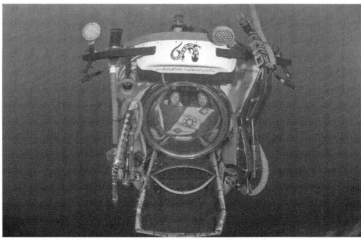

Filming in the Curasub – Curaçao, Dutch Antilles 2012   Barry B. Brown

As Captain Flint in *Treasure Island* 1997   Jake Fry

As Hunter S. Thompson in *Final 24* 2006   Cineflix Media

108

With Boa Constrictor – Monteverde, Costa Rica

Right Hook – A Tall Tail – Cataract, Ontario 2003   Allan Levine

109

With Mickey Rooney on *The Adventures of Black Stallion* 1992
Alliance Entertainment

Angry Planet - HQ Antarctica 2009   Pinewood Films

110

Chapter 4
On the Water

While we were rocking and rolling on makeshift musical stages in the late sixties, a group of sailors were rocking and rolling on the high seas. They were doing something that had never been done before—racing each other singlehandedly in a non-stop race around the world. The *Sunday Times* Golden Globe Race was a strange, memorable sporting event in many ways. The leader of the race, Bernard Moitessier, had a mystical experience after sailing most of the way round the world, and so instead of returning to the finish line, carried on and sailed almost two-thirds of the way around a second time. The man considered to be the least likely entrant in the slowest boat, ended up not just winning the race but would go on to be the most celebrated British sailor of the era, knighted as Sir Robin

Knox-Johnson. But by far the most intriguing entrant in the race was another Brit, Donald Crowhurst, who mortgaged both his house and his business to put a slapdash entry together, then, when he got down in the South Atlantic getting ready to round Cape Horn, realized he would never be able to do the race legitimately, so instead began sending back faked positions, while sailing in circles. His deception worked, but the guilt drove him into madness and eventually suicide. His empty boat was found adrift without him ten days after his last logbook entry.

Great story, and I determined I wanted to dramatize it. The celebrated theatrical director John Hirsch was now running the drama department at CBC, and was taking chances on people like me, so I lucked into a bit of money from them. Putting it together with some other funding I cobbled together, we were off and running. I wrote a script, and was able to get the legendary Gordon Pinsent to play the lead in what was almost a one-man story. Gordon and I were able to plumb some fairly wild psychological depths with our portrayal of this poor misguided character driving himself crazy thousands of miles away from the nearest other human being. I called the film *Horse Latitudes*, after the windless doldrums of the Atlantic that Crowhurst ended up in, where becalmed ship captains, out of food and water, supposedly once jettisoned their cargos of horses into the ocean.

It was not an easy shoot for Gordon, as he was performing nightly at the Stratford Festival. We chartered a large trimaran to shoot the film on, and shot far out on Lake Ontario. At the end of every shooting day, we'd put him into a waiting speedboat, rush him back to a waiting car on the docks, and drive him the ninety minutes to the theater so that he could make the 8:00 p.m. curtain call. It was also tough for him because, paradoxically, as a Newfoundlander, he never learned to swim (water's too cold there to bother), so he never felt very comfortable on board the boat, and he certainly wasn't going to do the final shot in the film, where the character jumps off the stern of the moving boat. (We got the boat's captain to double for him.) But for the important stuff—creating a fascinating, flawed character, he nailed it. At least, I thought he did, and so did the Yorkton Film Festival—a big one back in those days—which gave us three awards—one for his acting, one for my directing, and one for the film itself. In France, the Toulon Festival gave the film another award.

Before it got to those festivals, it had to get on TV. There was a weird controversy about the film, over, of all things, its length. Hirsch had originally commissioned it for a half hour non-commercial slot. The story was always too big for half an hour, and the cut of the film came in at the peculiar length of 47 minutes. Hirsch wanted me to cut the film almost in half, which would have destroyed it. I resisted, and suddenly he had another to add to his many battles going with his CBC producers and directors. To be blunt many of us thought of him as a kind of high-minded theater guy who didn't really get television. To help him resolve the issues he was having with all of us, the network brought in two Hollywood television guys to assist him. One of them, Stan Colbert, had been a producer of the old *Flipper* TV series. The other, Jerry Mayer, was Hollywood royalty—a descendent of Louis B. Mayer, who still owned a tiny share of MGM. He was a producer who thought he could do everyone else's job better than they could. A year later I directed another film for him. He used to look over my shoulder and second guess every shot I set up, claiming to think that I was going to be crossing the axis. Finally my cameraman, an old guy close to retirement, just told him to fuck off and leave me alone. CBC crew could do that in those days—they were well protected by their union. In that instance, though not all others, it worked out well for me—he went back to his office and I never did cross the axis on any of the shots in the film.

In the case of *Horse Latitudes,* I figured these two new hired guns were going to side with Hirsch. I was wrong—Colbert brought me into his new office, told me he'd screened the film, and he decided it ought not to be cut down, but rather expanded into a feature. Pinsent was brought in to the discussion, and he too, as he describes in his memoir *Next,* thought it worthy of being transformed into a feature. Of course, I didn't object—but I wanted to know where the money was going to come from for this grand plan. When no one seemed to have an answer for that, I (the eternal skeptic) began to suspect this might be a ploy to bury this little programming problem child of a film. In the end, the network acquiesced, and broadcast the film at the length I cut it to. The sky didn't fall, and we got some nice notices for the picture.

One day while we were shooting the film, a catamaran with a multi-hued sail went zipping past us at about twice the speed we were moving at. Intrigued, I asked our captain what it was, and he told me it was a new design of boat, only about a year old, called a Hobie Cat. I determined that I wanted to try out these revolutionary speedsters, with their fast, asymmetrical hulls. Shooting *Horse Latitudes* I realized I didn't really know enough about sailing and seamanship to be a master marine filmmaker, and I thought sailing these athletic little boats would be a good way to learn. The next summer I found a group of people racing Hobie 16's, and soon began crewing for the best of them, an amazing Austrian sailor named Herb Ponta. Within a few months we were cleaning up on races around Ontario. He and I didn't have a lot in common other than our shared passion for sailing. I used to call him my Nazi skipper, as he would, in the heat of the moment, call every one of our competitors (regardless of their race) "focking niggers". But I loved sailing with him, as he was a brilliantly skilled racer. How good was he? In one race in the Canadian Championships (which we won—two years in a row), we crossed the start line early (we were very aggressive starters), and had to circle around the entire rest of the fleet, return, and start behind them all. Even after starting maybe four or five minutes behind everyone else, we beat *every one of them* to the first mark—and then continued to stretch out our lead for the rest of the race. He was remarkably skilled. I was no slouch on the trapeze—but he was the real brains behind our success.

He was so good that we considered moving from the Hobie 16 to the Olympic-class Tornado, and then trying to see if we could compete for a slot in the 1980 Moscow Olympics. I thought we had a shot at it, but in the end I decided filmmaking meant more to me than sailing did, and I wasn't going to sacrifice my career for a shot at the Olympics. It was a good decision because in the end, of course, the West boycotted the Moscow Olympics over the Russian invasion of Afghanistan. I was one of the relatively few Westerners to see those Olympics, as in the summer of 1980 I was in (the former) Yugoslavia, shooting a film in Lipica, home of the famous white Lippizan stallions. In the evenings I would sometimes see coverage of the games from the USSR, showing on the small black and white TV sets in the lobby of our hotel, and muse that had things worked out differently I might have been there myself.

I was looking around for more marine stories to turn in to films, but couldn't at first get anything going, so returned to my old stomping grounds of music. When I was fourteen I was obsessed with American Top 40 AM radio, and used to spend evenings trying to bring in the big 50,000 watt stations like WOWO in Fort Wayne, Indiana, WBZ in Boston, and the top jocks like Dick Biondi, Wolfman Jack, and Murray the K. By far the best of them, I thought, was Bruce Morrow—"Cousin Brucie" at WABC, New York. Sixteen years later, I got a chance to film a profile of him and so spent an entertaining week with a film crew tracking him (and his pal Dick Clark) around his Manhattan haunts. I also made a profile of the soul group The Chambers Brothers. You may not remember them, but you've likely heard their biggest hit, *Time Has Come Today*, which indeed still is played today. That film included one of my favorite lines from my films. The group had serious roots in gospel, so we filmed them with their families on a Sunday morning in a little church in South Central L.A. As a big woman led the church choir in song behind the altar, the group's mother, who we were filming, encouraged her by shouting out from her pew, "Put a little *weight* on it, sister!" Good advice to a musician. No wonder she had spawned a hit group. Much of the film dealt with the band's interaction with their Hollywood agent. A photograph of him graces the cover of this book (he's the one with the teeth, not the camera).

On *Horse Latitudes* the network assigned me a Story Editor named Barry Pearson. We hit it off so well that we decided to start a film company together. We named it Rosebud Films after *Citizen Kane*'s famous last word, and began writing projects. We spent a year on a script we called *Stuntman!*, that never got made (more on it in Chapter Seven). One of the first we did get going was a mini-series about explorers and other larger-than-life historic personalities that we called *The Spirit of Adventure*. The first one was a portrait of Marguerite de Roberval—the first European woman in North America. This young girl of eighteen had come over on one of Jacques Cartier's fifteenth century voyages to Quebec, along with her uncle, who in film terms was kind of the Executive Producer of the venture. She upset him by getting involved with a common seaman aboard the ship, and so he marooned her—and her lover—on a desolate island off the coast of Labrador. Her lover died, their baby died, but she survived—eventually alone—for three years on the island, until she was finally rescued. It was another terrific adventure story, and I needed another really good actor for the main role. I lucked out with Céline Lomez, a hot Quebecoise actress at the time. She had begun her career by doffing her clothes in the mildly sexy "Maple Porn" films of the early 70's, and had just done her first big English language film, starring opposite Elliot Gould, Christopher Plummer, and John Candy in Garth Drabinsky and Daryl Duke's crime heist *The Silent Partner*. She was a hot commodity, performing with her exotic Argentine-Quebecoise accent. She was also a trouper, willing to get out in the water and the snow and ice for our shoot, her bodice ripped in the right places, messing with snakes and lobsters, her hair thick with grease and grime, her eyes flashing with passion.

For the second film in the series, we were again on the water, filming the story of renegade explorer Étienne Brûlé and his battles with the Jesuit missionaries on the rivers of what was then New France and is now Ontario. We got another group of skilled actors for this one, including Raymond Cloutier as Brûlé. For his Huron Indian guide, I am honored to be able to have given Graham Greene his first film role. A few years later, Graham would go on to win an Academy Award for his role in Kevin Costner's *Dances With Wolves*.

116

It was plain while he was working with us on *Spirit of Adventure* that he was a terrific actor. He was also just about the funniest guy I'd ever met, keeping us in stitches with his wicked deadpan wit matched with his cigar store wooden Indian demeanor.

The film's climax involved a long sequence of canoeing disaster and rescue on a whitewater river. I learned an important lesson that I would use on future projects with actors in marine, and other potentially dangerous environments. Actors are, almost by definition, dramatic, emotional people. Throwing them into unusual situations and asking them to be dramatic and play scared can often implode into a situation where they amplify things and become genuinely scared and nervously ineffectual. To give them the confidence that they aren't going to be hurt for your movie, you often have to first get them comfortable with the new unusual environment, then add the acting requirements.

For my Brûlé film climax I found a photogenic whitewater river that was exciting, and controllable. It normally had a kind of modest amount of water running through it, but on request the authorities would open the upstream damns and give you an impressive release of water through the rapids. For a high water peak in the middle of the day, when the lighting would be ideal in the canyon, they agreed to turn on the taps ten miles upstream at two in the morning. Unfortunately, though, I did not have an opportunity to introduce the actors beforehand to the dramatic river.

The big crew, including helmeted camera operators, a stunt coordinator, a big prop and art department, marine coordinators looking after our birch bark canoes, plus all the other usual suspects, and our cast of four, arrived early in the morning for an intense day of shooting on the river. Early on I discovered I had a mutiny on my hands. Graham Green, and the young native actress playing with him, and the Quebec actor playing St. Jean de Brébeuf, were all down with getting into the canoes and heading out into the rapids. However the star, playing Brûlé, freaked out at the sight of the now impressive whitewater waves out in the river, and flat out refused to

117

get into the canoe. It was a huge potential disaster. In the end, I sort of shamed him into doing the sequence by saying I would re-write it using the young female actor (who was game to get out on the river) instead of him. Finally, his manhood in question, he agreed to get out and do it. It worked, but it wasn't the greatest way to get a performance out of an actor. In the end, though, we got the sequence and the film. He did a great acting job, and the film was enough of a success that I was asked, a couple of years later, by a new producer in town, to return to the same river and shoot a bigger, grander film on it. This time I was better prepared for the on-water action.

Bill Macadam was an interesting, unique character. He was another transplanted Brit—the son of an Earl or a Duke or a Knight or something, and a descendent of the inventor of the macadam road, which revolutionized land transportation in the early 19th Century. On arriving in Canada he had first started a bush-plane company on the west coast, then ran the Progressive Conservative Party for a while, and now was trying his hand at being a Film and TV Producer. I thought he was great—a breath of fresh air, with big ideas. Eventually he ran into some financial problems, and he is still being vilified today for them. The Writers Guild, absurdly, still prints his name monthly on the "Unfair Engagers" list in their magazine, even though he hasn't been an "engager" for thirty years.

In 1980 he had the idea of filming all of Jack London's stories of the Yukon Gold Rush, with Orson Welles onboard to narrate the dramas. The series would be called *Jack London's Tales of the Klondike*. He hired me to direct the first one—a story (loosely based on fact) of a guy who tried to take 1000 dozen eggs to the gold fields, to make his fortune. Again, there was a major sequence to film on a whitewater river, as the hero tries to make his way with his 1000 dozen eggs through the Whitehorse Rapids on the Yukon River down toward Dawson City. This time, we weren't working with canoes, but in a replica of one of the jerry-built boats built on the shores of Lake Bennett by the naive gold seekers. We actually found a boat builder to build our replica for us, whose great grandfather had himself been a sourdough and had built one of the primitive boats.

Again, we needed to find an actor to play the part and to handle the physical action the script required. I cast Neil Munro—a terrific actor, who later became a major stage director. Again, though, Neil wasn't much of an outdoors kind of guy, and he certainly wasn't a waterman. This time, though, I knew how to deal with it. As part of the pre-production period, I organized to take Neil and the other actor playing with him in the river scenes up to check out the river in advance. No acting required. No lines. No pretending to be scared. No crew, no costumes or make up or any of that. Just the two of them, our marine coordinator, me, and a big rubber raft. At the put-in spot, the actors looked at the waves with some of the same trepidation that had been felt two years earlier. But we all piled in and paddled the waves down through the canyon. Two hours later, at the take out spot, they climbed out, elated, and said they wanted to do it again. I said they could—on shoot day. When that day came, they considered themselves old hands on the river, and keenly showed off their prowess while playing their parts with ease.

Neil Munro was the onscreen star of the show, but top billing went to the off-screen narrator—Orson Welles. I was chuffed at the possibility of directing the great Welles as he recorded the narration—and also a little terrified. He was a bitter, angry man, underemployed and convinced he had more talent than any of the people who were getting opportunities to make films (and reinforced in that view by the press, if not by studio or network chiefs). A popular underground tape making the rounds in those days was a recording of Welles recording a commercial for a winery—with various directions heard from the ad agency director—and either ignored, or contradicted by the imperious Welles, who eventually stomps out, shouting at the poor ad man, "You're a pest, sir! Nothing but a pest!" In the end, though, neither I, nor anyone from our team got to even meet Welles. By then his rule was that if you wanted his magnificent voice, you sent him your script, and your cheque, and he then recorded it in his own little studio, (not that little, I guess, as he weighed three hundred pounds) and sent you a tape of his recording. No direction required, thank you.

With London and Welles and Munro on board, what a great film we made! Bill hired an art department that built us the main drag of Dawson City circa 1898 on the old Kleinburg Studio Backlot. After filming the climax of the film there, we moved to the foot of the Scarborough Bluffs on Lake Ontario, where they re-built the sourdough tent city on the shores of Lake Bennett—the spot where thousands of gold-crazed desk clerks, farmers, and layabouts had assembled, after climbing over the Chilcoot Pass, to boldly, though inexpertly bang together the rafts and boats that would take them down the Yukon River, past heavy rapids, bears and ice flows, to the Klondike. I look on the gold rush as one of the wildest adventures that the world has seen—and so it was great fun re-creating it eighty years after the original event.

Naysayers whined about the fact that we didn't go to the Yukon to shoot the film. My feeling is if you want to wait until conditions are perfect and you have enough money (which is lots more) to shoot everything on location, you may be waiting your whole career. It's not like we were the first filmmakers to shoot a film that was titled with one location and shot in another. *Casablanca* was shot in Burbank and Santa Monica, *Lawrence of Arabia* in Morocco, Spain, and England, and *Chicago* would be shot in Toronto. When I did get up to Lake Bennett and the Chilcoot Pass to shoot *Angry Planet* there years later, I was gratified to see how remarkably similar they looked to the locations I'd chosen to double for them, 2000 miles away.

However I did have a real interest in getting out to film the most exotic parts of the world. Haiti had a lot of interest to me, and, I think, to a lot of people, in the 1970s. The country had just gone through the long dark night of being run by the voodoo- and violence-fueled dictatorship of François ("Papa Doc") Duvalier, and was now being run by chubby son Jean-Claude, "Baby Doc". I put together some financing for a little documentary on Haiti, and learned a good lesson in the process. I organized to get an interview with Baby Doc, and to film a number of other aspects of the island, and then took the concept to the news and features department at a network, which will remain nameless to protect the guilty. They proceeded to rip the idea off me, and just sent off their own crew to do the story on their own. Lesson learned—in the film world, where virtually everyone is freelance, there is a certain amount of respect for the concept that your idea belongs to you. In journalism, where freelancing is less the norm, and the perceived prize is the "scoop", freelancer beware.

However, it turned out okay. I focused our film more on voodoo than on politics, and got it on the new CITY-TV instead of the un-named network that stole the first idea. Filming voodoo ceremonies in remote *hounfours* in the back woods of Haiti was pretty intense. People biting into live doves and chewing on broken glass made for pretty lurid footage. We couldn't really keep up with the energy of the rum-filled, noisy ceremonies. By three in the morning we were usually ready to pack it in—and in any case had filmed all the material we needed. But the hordes of voodoo celebrants didn't want us to leave. Our movie lights meant that for the first time they could see what was going on in the dark forest. Eventually I just left all the blazing lights with them, asking someone who seemed semi-sober to turn them off when the sun came up— and left. Sure enough, I returned at nine or ten the next morning, to find the lights where I left them (but turned off), the *hounfour* now an abandoned site of empty *clarin* (Haitian moonshine) bottles, beaten down bushes, and a few celebrants sleeping off their hangovers. I packed up my lights and we moved on to the next location.

My old friend from McMaster Film Board days, Patricia Murphy, was now a fixture on Znaimer's new station, with two shows of her own, *Sweet City Woman* and *World of the Unexplained*, plus regular appearances on CITY's flagship nightly show, *The Shulman File*, a news, information, and entertainment magazine show hosted by Morton Shulman. Shulman was an extraordinary character. He was first the Chief Coroner of Ontario, and then for many years the crusading Chief Coroner of Toronto, in the news every week as he took on shoddy subway and high-rise construction safety issues, pharmaceutical companies and others, on behalf of

121

people who had died unnecessarily. He became the model for the highly successful CBC drama series, *Wojeck*, which chronicled the trials and tribulations of a big city coroner (*i.e.*, Shulman). He then moved on to host, in his inimitable fashion, his nightly show on CITY.

All the while, he was a daily newspaper columnist, a very active stock market investor, a multi-millionaire Member of Provincial Parliament for the socialist NDP party in the Ontario legislature, a writer (his *Anyone Can Make a Million* was an international bestseller), and also ran his active medical practice in the west end of Toronto. For a while, he was my doctor. While I was shooting *Spirit of Adventure* out on location in the deep woods, I got poison ivy all over my rear end (don't ask). I went to see Shulman about it. There aren't many people in the world who have had their bare butt closely examined by the top television host in town, only a couple of hours prior to his going on air.

Patricia was able to go toe-to-toe with his outlandish behavior as a regular on his show. For the crazier subject matter, she had her own *World of the Unexplained*. The show invited me on to talk about and show my Haitian voodoo film. One thing led to another (the old black magic, I suppose one could attribute it to), and Patricia and I became an item, living together for the next four years.

I wanted to get back and do more work in the Caribbean. In 1977, a Canadian Member of Parliament named Max Saltsman proposed in the House of Commons that the Turks and Caicos Islands, a group of thirty small islands southeast of The Bahamas, should somehow become part of Canada. A lot of people both in the islands and in Canada got interested, but in the end he got flak for it from both the left and the right. The left—specifically Pierre Trudeau—thought it a "neo-colonial" idea, and the right—the Conservatives—fretted about the possibility that all these islanders would soon be up in Canada, seeking healthcare. (A bit of a ridiculous concern, since a) there was no indication that these

122

people living in their island paradise wanted to move to Winnipeg next February, and b) the entire population of the islands was considerably less than the population of Dundas Street.)

Patricia and I thought this sounded like a good story, and headed down to the remote archipelago. This time we did get to have an interview with the political leader of the islands. His title was Chief Minister of the Turks and Caicos Islands—but his card, which he presented us on our arrival at his office, read "Cheif Minister". Hey, typos are hard to correct when the nearest printing shop is 500 miles away. He also surprised us a little by telling us that the political party that got him into office was known as the Junkanoo Gang. All right! Sounds like a party.

My best memories of the Turks and Caicos are those of learning to scuba-dive—which would become a big part of the next ten years of filming adventures. An ex-L.A. cop with a one-man dive shop on the beach gave me my first lessons on the amazing 7000-foot reef wall that lies in front of Grand Turk Island. I got my advanced certifications with a colorful operator back in Canada (colorful? He used to belt out entire librettos from Gilbert & Sullivan operettas en route to the dive sites)—but it all began on the wall off Grand Turk.

When we got back Patricia decided she would do the story nationally, so she got a gig on Peter Gzowski's late night talk show to talk about it. Gzowski was a much-loved morning radio host across Canada, but he was a dreadful, stiff television host. He was actually a perfect example of the Peter Principle (appropriate, given his first name). He was a brilliant writer, and a great radio interviewer, but just as Dr. Lawrence Peter says that everyone in the world is, Gzowski was elevated to the level of his natural incompetence, and there he sat, as a bad TV host. I certainly knew his brilliance as a writer. On my quest to do films about islands, I did a show with him about a group of less exotic but no less interesting islands that both of us loved—the Toronto Islands. As an ending for the film, I had shot a beautiful sequence on a summer Sunday afternoon of a sailboat meandering through the Ward's Island lagoon, with some cat sitting on the bow pulpit of the boat, blowing on a saxophone, as the boat glided though the dappled light of the late afternoon. Only trouble was, it was supposed to have a poetic voiceover wrapping up our film essay running over it—and I couldn't come up with any poetry. Gzowski, in his rumpled, grumpy manner, kicked our editor, our producer, and me out of the editing room, and closed the door. When he re-opened it ten minutes later, we played the sequence and he read us a beautiful piece of absolutely perfect writing he had just composed for it. That was the good Gzowski. Here is the bad:

His television talk show was a big, overblown affair, with too many cooks and too little broth. A number of these cooks—a team of producers and associate producers and the like, pulled Patricia in to a meeting before the show and told her they wanted her to try to liven things up on the rather dull show by wearing one of her most provocative outfits. She certainly had lots of them. She was not only quite good looking but also very...well endowed, and as a personality on all these shows, she had a collection of Yorkville clothing stores and fashion designers providing her with dresses and other clothing to wear on TV. Her fashion signature was the low cut décolletage neckline.

Her most outrageous designer, a flamboyant Jamaican who went by the one-name moniker Winston, came up with a wild gown with the neckline cut to the waist. It was really designed for the red carpet, not the talk-show sofa, (and in fact one of the few copies he made of the dress was worn by Kim Cattrall at the Oscars the following year), but Patricia agreed to wear it for the show.

The Minister of Tourism for the islands, a British colonial type I had connected with while we were down there, and a rep from the Junkanoo Party also in the Turks cabinet, flew up to Toronto to appear on the show with Patricia and Gzowski. It was a crowded set, as our trio was coming on in the second act, following Gzowski's first guest, the loose-cannon British comedian Spike Milligan. Perhaps Milligan's off-the-wall antics had rattled the easily rattled Gzowski, but for whatever reason the rest of the show was a shambles. A cool cat like Johnny Carson or George Stroumboulopoulos would have had a ball with Patricia's wild outfit. Johnny would have had fifteen double-entendres spilling out of him before she had to say a thing. Not Peter Gzowski. It was all a sea of embarrassed, flustered confusion on his part, not helped by the seven-syllable mouthful of a name that the Caribbean colony goes by. Gzowski began abbreviating "The Turks and Caicos Islands" first to just "The Islands", eventually simply to "Them". Unfortunately, whenever he was referring to "Them", his gaze rested on Patricia's gleaming...breasts, until he desperately averted his eyes, searching around the studio for something else to look at. Meanwhile, the story of poor MP Max Saltsman's plan to annex the Turks and Caicos Islands into Canada, and of these earnest Turks and Caicos legislators' enthusiasm for the scheme, all somehow got lost and forgotten in the awkward shuffle.

Luckily for Gzowski's legacy, there is no record of it, so far as I know. There was no home video in those days, though it was introduced two years later. Sony spent a good deal of time developing the Beta format, while JVC engineers worked hard to create VHS. Both formats were released in the late 1970s, revolutionizing how people watched television, and sparking a format war between the two incompatible designs. Unfortunately for Sony, even though Beta was a (slightly) superior format, people cared more about ease of use, length of recording time, and, especially, availability of popular titles than they did about engineering quality, and the VHS format of course came out the winner. That again created another revolution, with Sony deciding never to be beaten again by software, buying Columbia Pictures, a merger that began a long chain of media consolidation that continues to this day.

How did all this affect me? Early on, I was on the home video bandwagon. My first idea was that I should make what I called an *Electronic Aquarium*—a videotape that would turn your television into an aquarium—nothing but fish, colorful reefs, and music. With my new diving skills and underwater 16mm camera gear I went off to Key Largo and then to San Salvador in the Bahamas to film gorgeous fish and underwater scenery. Once I got it shot and finished, I took it off to an early edition of the now-massive Consumer Electronics Show in Las Vegas to try and find buyers for it. This was a year before the American studios had agreed to release their films on home video, so there were only two videos on offer—mine, and Lorimar's *Jane Fonda's Workout* video. Unfortunately for me it was the Jane Fonda tape that lit the world on fire, but mine did sell, and unbelievably is still selling today. It was the first home video that the Eaton's retail chain ever sold (in both VHS *and* Beta); it was sold for a few years by American Express Home Video, and then it was picked up and promoted by my pal Michael Bennett, who has operated for years the world's biggest marine video distribution company, based in my old home town of Marina Del Rey, California.

While living in Marina Del Rey, I came up with a new idea— a video magazine, sold by subscription, called *Ocean Adventure Video Magazine*. A number of us started video magazines that year on everything from golf to flying. Some were garage operations, others created by big media companies, and some, like mine, midway between. We were written up in *People* magazine and all the rest, had telemarketing promoters and venture capitalist investors, but in the end neither mine nor any of them really took off. I did get some good adventures out of it—filming the Single-handed Trans-Atlantic yacht race in England, Michael Fay's New Zealand challenge for the America's Cup, and with a guy named John Walton, racing against Dennis Connor (and beating, on handicap, this most famous of all American sailors) and then cruising around Mexico on one of the super-light trimarans that he was building. Walton was an interesting fellow. Although I sailed with him for two weeks and worked with him for three months on the project, I never learned until much later (and then, from others) that John, in his blue jeans and t shirt, fiberglass dust in his hair, was the son of Sam Walton, founder of Walmart, and thus heir to the richest fortune in America. He died in 2005 in the crash of his homebuilt aircraft. At his death he was worth $18.2 billion—the fourth richest person in the U.S., (tied with his brother). I assume that vast fortune has been or will be inherited by his one son Lucas, who as a three-year-old gave me the worst review of my career. When I had a rough cut of the film I had made for John, he drove up from San Diego to look at it in my home editing room in Laguna Niguel, bringing with him his young son. It was plain from the start that the restless little boy did not want to sit through the film. About half way through it, I heard a tinkling sound that seemed unfamiliar. I turned around to find the boy with his pants at his ankles, brazenly peeing on my new carpet. Fortunately his dad, and others, were keener on my efforts.

Wanting to notch up a few more islands on my growing list, and make a new film, I headed off to make a film titled *Micronesia: The Winds of Change* (more on that title a bit later). That Islands list has grown over the years. It now stands at 163. Just for the record, they are:

Abaco, Algonquin Island, Allan's Cay, Amherst Island, Anak Krakatau, Antigua, Aquidneck, Baffin Island, Bali, Banana Island, Barbados, Bermuda, Berry Island, Bloodletter Island, Booby Cay, Bowen Island, Camelot Island, Cape Breton Island, Capri, Catalina, Cayo Afuera, Cayo de Tierra, Centre Island, Cocos Island, Cozumel, Cuba, Cumberland Island, Curaçao, Cuttyhunk, Deception Island, Dominica, Dominican Republic, Efate, Elbow Cay, Eleuthera, Fenwick Island, Fiji, Flores, Forest Island, Gabriola Island, Galiano Island, Galveston Island, Grand Bahama, Grand Turk Island, Great Britain, Great Guana Cay, Green Cay, Greenland, Grenadier Island, Grindstone Island, Guadeloupe Island, Guam, Heimaey Island, Haiti, Hawaii, Heart Island, Highbourne Cay, Holbox Island, Hornby Island, Hunga Ha'apai, Iceland, Igloolik, Ile d'Orleans, Île du Grand Calumet, Ios, Isla Hermite, Isla Hornos, Isla Hoste, Islamorada, Isla Navarino, Isle of Man, Isle of Pigs, Isle of Wight, Islote Panqueque, Jamaica, Java, Jekyll Island, Johnson Island, Kauai, Kea, Key Largo, Key West, Komodo, Kythnos, Kyuquot, Leek Island, Lido(Italy), Lido Isle (California), Little Abaco, Main Duck, Man-O-War Cay, Manhattan, Marathon Key, Martha's Vineyard, Martinique, Monsoon Island, Montreal Island, Monumental Island, Moon Island, Mount Desert Island, Mugg's

Island, Nantucket, New Providence, New Zealand, Newfoundland, Norman's Cay, North Bimini, Oahu, Oak Island, Olympic Island, Palau, Paradise Island, Paros, Parry Island, Pellestrina, Ponape (now Pohnpei), Prince Edward Island, Prince Regent Island, Puerto Rico, Rat Island, Rakata, Rinca, Rogers Island, Rose Island, Royal Island, Saipan, Saltspring, Sampson Cay, Sandy Cay, Santorini, Shroud Cay, Sicily, Smith Island, Snake Island, South Shetland Island, Spanish Wells, Saint Thomas, Saint Maarten, Staniel Cay, Stromboli, Sugarloaf Cay, Sundown Island, Tangier Island, Tanna, Tierra del Fuego, Tobago, Tongatapu, Tortola, Trinidad, Truk (now Chuuk), Vancouver Island, Venice, Vieques, Virgin Gorda, Volcano, Walker's Cay, Warderick Wells, Ward's Island, Waupoos, White Island, Wolfe Island, Yap.

There it is. A to Y. Haven't been to Zanzibar yet. It's a reasonably impressive list of islands, and I filmed on many, though not all of them. I'm sure there are some people out there who can top my count.

When it came time to find a narrator for our *Micronesia* film, I decided to go with the voice they used to call "The Voice of Doom"—Lorne Greene. Greene's *Bonanza* days were behind him, but he still commanded a hefty fee for his voice-overs. He was producing a show with his son called *Lorne Greene's New Wilderness*. I couldn't afford his high performer's fee, so I traded him—enough of my footage for him to make an underwater episode of his series, in return for a morning of his time in a Los Angeles recording studio. So while I never got to direct Orson Welles, I did get to boss around Pa Cartwright in a recording booth. Greene was by then a solid Southern California Republican, and he took offense to some of the more liberal sentiments in our script, but in the end I wore him down (and he wanted to get to lunch), so he eventually read the lines as written.

Another oversized ego I worked with in that period was a Brit expat named John Stoneman. The British film industry was contracting in the 70s, and lots of British film types were emigrating to

128

Canada—mostly to Toronto. We used to joke that many of them got on to the plane at Heathrow as production assistants, and by the time it had landed at Malton (now Pearson) in Toronto, after five hours of resume-inflation, they climbed off as Executive Producers. Stoneman was not quite like that. For one thing he had actually had a career in England. He was an Assistant Director on some big British movies like Lindsay Anderson's early hit *If...*, the Stones' film *Sympathy for the Devil,* and the Bond spoof *Casino Royale.* But from what I understood his Sergeant-Major manners and sensibility did not really gibe with libertines like Anderson, Mick Jagger, and Woody Allen. In any case, like a lot of us (I did my share of Assistant Directing on other people's movies, too) he didn't want to assist others—he wanted to make his own films—underwater films—and he thought the chances of putting them together were greater in Canada than in England.

By the time I met him he had his own film company and was making a series for CTV called *The Last Frontier.* Stoneman found out about me and hired me as a cameraman and writer for the series. Everyone was either a hero or a bum to John—usually, first a hero, then a bum. I heard from the many other people that worked on the show that in the days leading up to my arrival he was wildly touting me as the Great White Hope that was going to make all the difference at the series. Within a few weeks, though, I was tossed in the barrel with everyone else on the show, subject to his paranoid rants about us. It was very much like working for Commander Queeg, the Humphrey Bogart character in *The Caine Mutiny*—freak-outs about who might have eaten from the tub of frozen strawberries, and brooding discussions about who was loyal to the series—and who was not.

He was obsessed with sharks, and we were always going down to the Bahamas to shoot new shark episodes. In 2004 Wes Anderson brought out a movie with the unwieldy title of *The Life Aquatic with Steve Zissou,* which tried to mine comedy from exactly the same sort of low budget underwater documentary making we were doing on *The Last Frontier.* It was a good concept, and some people profess to be amused by the film, but for me the shenanigans of our filmmaking were far nuttier than anything in the feature.

For a few weeks one winter John took over the editing room of the film company, pushing the film bins out of the way to build a twelve foot papier-mâché   shark around a cage of chicken wire. Once that was complete he put together a lightweight two-man shark cage. We took both down to Long Island, a Bahamian island south of Nassau and the Exumas. The task of getting a semi-realistic twelve-foot faux-shark on to a plane and through customs, into taxicabs, and through the islands provided many moments of glee. When we got to Long Island we loaded everything up on some boats and headed out to a reef notorious for its high shark population. All of our shows had some quasi-scientific theme. This one was supposed to address the issue of whether size mattered to sharks—would six-foot sharks be intimidated by our much larger monster shark? To convince the audience how terribly dangerous our mission was, we tethered our shark cage to the bottom—and filmed the sharks from inside it. Of course, the only way to get to and from the shark cage was to swim to it from the boat—swimming right through the school of sharks, thus completely negating the need for a cage. (We didn't put that part in the film). My concern about filming sharks from cages is not the big ones that might smash it, but the possibility that a little one might swim inside it, get trapped inside it with you, and in its panic take a bite out of you. Fortunately that didn't happen.

Our big monster shark had received a few dents and dings on its airplane travels, but we patched them up and swam it down to the bottom to anchor it in front of the cage. As soon as the shark hit the saltwater it began disintegrating. As it sat on the bottom it appeared to be molting, with hundreds of tiny bits of papier-mâché floating away from its fearsome, toothy visage. Meanwhile the real sharks completely ignored our shark sculpture, blithely swimming around it giving it no more attention than they would a rock or a chunk of coral.

Since that hadn't proved much, we moved on to do some "experiments" on the sharks. The plan was to catch a shark on hook and line, pull it into the boat, subdue it a bit, then do some blood work on it, pull some teeth out of it to check its age, then put it back in the ocean. Trouble was, just like lots of fishermen the world over, we didn't get a bite. John, with the film production clock ticking away, was fuming over the lack of any action. Finally one of the deckhands spilled the beans with a theory as to why we weren't getting any bites. *Another* underwater filmmaker, an American named Jack McKenney, had beaten us to this reef only a month earlier, and had put down a long line of about twenty hooks, hoping to catch one or two sharks for his own filmmaking. Instead, when his team returned the next day, they found sharks on every hook, all caught up in a tangled ball, all dead, with bites taken out of them all by other, un-hooked sharks. It was apparently a real mess, and the deckhand theorized that that misadventure had not only reduced the local shark population, but left the remaining sharks wary about hooks and lines. John had a new villain conspiring to destroy his films. For a few hours he cursed out Jack McKenney, instead of us, for ruining his life. In the end, though, we did manage to catch a seven-footer, and hauled him into the boat. He thrashed around, everyone danced out of the way of his snapping jaws, we did our "experiments" on him and slid him back in, possibly unharmed. It made an exciting sequence for the show. Whether it actually proved any ichthyological truths, I don't know.

We were always blurring the documentary line with a little filmmaking invention. One day in Florida we were supposedly doing a show about the extensive migrations of the bluefin tuna. We first sent a young Norwegian intern we had on the show on a shopping mission to the local Publix Supermarket and Radio Shack. He returned with some gutted but otherwise intact fish, a collection of capacitors, resisters and other electronic paraphernalia, and a television aerial. John, the onscreen host of the show as well as the producer of it, prepared for our sequence of "tracking" the mighty bluefin up the Gulfstream from Florida to Nova Scotia and on to the

Azores. We began by filming him sewing a contraption made up of all these random electronics parts into our Publix bluefish. This was supposedly a tracking device that once consumed by a tuna, would allow us to follow him on his northern journey.

We then got out on the water, filming a sequence of trolling our bait behind the Sportfisher we had hired for the afternoon, first slapping a sign on the side of it announcing it as being part of the fleet of John's "Foundation for Ocean Research". The "foundation", created to give the TV show some faux gravitas, had as its sole assets a box of letterhead and a set of these reusable signs. It did hand out the annual "John Stoneman Award" to various friends of the series—at least one year awarded to John himself. Once the bait and tracker had supposedly been gulped down by the tuna (or so the narrator would tell us—and who could argue, as this was all happening beneath the waves, behind the boat), we filmed shots of John and his young Norwegian assistant nobly tracking the tuna's mighty journey. They stood, dramatically silhouetted by the sun, high on the tuna tower of the boat, holding the TV aerial, its cable running conveniently off-screen, bravely recording the bluefin's every move for scientific posterity. Of course, there was no tuna, there was no tracking device, and the TV aerial was nothing but a goofy prop.

As one internet blog I've found about the series accurately puts it, "Every episode of the series seemed to feature John Stoneman doing something clever, heroic, or more commonly both, to the point that it strained credibility, but I suppose they thought it made for better television." We certainly did—you've got that right.

What drove me nuts was not the fakery but the massive egotism involved. John was always telling anyone who would listen that he had done 11,000 dives. One accepted that as an impressive but presumably accurate number, until actually doing the math and realizing that for someone to do 11,000 dives, they would have to dive at least once a day, every day, *for 30 years*. One morning, at a Bahamian hotel breakfast before a shooting day, I casually mentioned to John that I had heard that he had once met Jacques

Cousteau. He looked at me sourly, and in all seriousness replied, "I didn't meet Jacques Cousteau. Jacques Cousteau met me."

Now, okay, wait a minute. I'm not one for hero worship, but we are talking about *Jacques Cousteau* here. This is the man who invented the device that would make scuba diving possible. This is the man who virtually singlehandedly created one of the coolest things ever—the sport of scuba diving. This is the man who created the concept of the underwater movie—and won three Academy Awards for his films. This is the man who through his television show turned millions of people around the world on to the amazing underwater world—and to the need to conserve and protect it. This is one of the greatest explorers of the twentieth century, a man who received numerous honors, including the Commander of the National Order of Merit, the Cross of War, Commander of the Legion of Honour, Commander of the Order of Arts and Letters, and the Presidential Medal of Freedom. Oh, and just by the way, this is a man who helped win World War II—by fighting as a commando for the French Resistance. And you didn't meet Jacques Cousteau—he met you?

Jacques Cousteau died the summer I was shooting *Treasure Island* on the Isle of Man. He received a state funeral from the French government. I really wanted to attend, and seriously considered it, but as we were shooting early the next day and the airline connections were too dicey, regrettably, I passed. The show must go on.

The show was not going on for me in the early 80s. I had just had a nice payday with a film that will be described in the next chapter, and there was nothing new coming up, so I decided to buy a small sailboat and head off down the Intracoastal Waterway to the Southern Bahamas. I enlisted my *Micronesia* partner Corinne Farago—and her husband—to come with me, and the three of us sailed on a long interesting voyage, getting as far south as Staniel Cay. They say three's a crowd—but it wasn't there. The early 80s were a free-spirited, swinging era. That would all change in a few years when AIDS forced everyone to get a lot more serious, but for a while we all seemed to be having fun. I certainly was—even if the interest rate on my mortgage was at 21%.

Eventually I singlehanded the boat back to Florida and trucked it home, then got an investor to put up some money so I could buy the rights to a great book about another crazy true sailing adventure —also involving a trio of sailors—called *Lost!*. Here's the logline on this one: An obsessed Seventh Day Adventist religious fanatic (didn't drink, didn't smoke, didn't chew—and didn't go round with those who do) wanted to get to Costa Rica to become a missionary. Rather than take a plane or a bus, he decided to get a small sailboat—a trimaran, again—and sail there. He enlisted the help of his brother, and his brother's wife. They went out, got caught in a giant storm. The brother kept the boat upright for 12 hours. Then the wannabe missionary took over, and flipped it within twenty minutes. The trio survived the storm, and once the seas settled down, carved their way through into the hull, and proceeded to live in the overturned boat, eventually for eighty-five days, drifting almost to Hawaii. Unknown to the other two, the missionary began throwing away everything of value, thinking they were being "tested by the Lord", and having food and water with them would be "cheating the test".

It was an intense, lurid tale that worked as an adventure story, as an interpersonal drama, and as a polemic against extreme Christian religious fanaticism. People liked my script, and I got some money from Telefilm Canada to go out and capture a real Atlantic storm on the high seas, to use for the background plates if and when we did get the serious financing to make the feature. Along with my partner on this mad exercise, Tony Hall, I tracked November storms crossing the continent that looked like they could develop into serious Nova Scotian nor'easters. Twice we flew out to Lunenburg to link up with big storms that in the end didn't materialize into anything very photogenic. On the third time, we got lucky (though some might question that word). Early in the morning, we went out into the Atlantic in a thirty-six foot Cape Island fishing boat. I was ready for anything—dressed in a Mustang survival suit, wearing swim goggles, heavy gloves, and boots. My camera was in a special waterproof housing I had gotten a production services company to build me. We screwed an eyebolt to the deck, and chained and turnbuckled my tripod to it. I had a scuba tank of air I was using to blow off salt spray from the lens.

Within an hour the storm got much worse than anyone expected. The wind was howling and the waves were getting bigger and bigger. We didn't realize how big they had become, until the one other boat we saw out there passed us. It was a big ninety-foot scallop dragger, heading for shelter. One moment the front half of the barnacle-encrusted hull would be right out of the water; the next the stern half would be totally exposed, propellers screaming until they dropped back into the ocean. Tony and the young fishing captain were at the bridge; I was on the open stern deck, furiously trying to capture the storm. After shooting each three minute reel, I would have to dismantle the set up, go into the cabin, perch on a tub full of 1000 foot hooked longlines, and change film. The boat reeked of fish guts and diesel fuel, and all three of us were constantly seasick in the maelstrom. Throw up, go back to work; throw up, go back to work. Finally I had shot all my footage, and so went forward to tell them I had got enough and we could go back now. They both looked at me like I was out of my mind.

"Go back now?" repeated the captain incredulously. "I've been trying to go back now for the last two hours!"

Turns out he had been unsuccessfully waiting for a slight lull so he get up his nerve to spin the boat around. He was terrified that in these conditions he would get the boat broadside to the waves and it would be capsized. He also was trying to let the Coast Guard know where we were—but the radio antennas were all ripped off the coachroof. The anemometer peaked at sixty-five knots—then it too snapped off. Finally he got up his nerve, found a lull, and spun the boat around—and we headed back for Lunenburg harbour. Once we were back safely he vowed to us he would never do another movie charter in his life.

We now had the storm, but needed the money for the rest of the film. As usual, I need to get a TV network onboard to anchor the rest of the financing. At that point in time CBC was really the only game in town for that sort of thing. Ivan Fecan was then considered the golden haired boy at the Corp, and as director of television programming, he held the purse strings. He had just returned to Canada from a stint as a vice president to Brandon Tartikoff at NBC, and so everyone kowtowed to his programming wisdom. He would later move over to CTV, and eventually become President and CEO there.

I went in to see him. He went into a long cockamamie speech about how he'd been to Hawaii, and knew that the color of the water was different in the Pacific than it was in the Atlantic, and so none of our shooting would work. Well, excuse me, Mr. Oceanographer, but the only reason the ocean has any colour at all is that it is reflecting the sky above. Scoop up a tumblerful of it from the Pacific, the Atlantic or any other ocean (they all flow from one to another anyway), and they'll be the same color—clear—as the water from your tap. But what could I say—it was obvious he didn't want to finance the film. No point in aggravating him.

So I didn't have a gig—but I still had my little boat. One day I had it moored down on the Toronto waterfront, and was walking along the dock in front of the Harbour Castle Hotel, when I passed by a big, beautiful, powerful looking sailboat—a Cooper 416—called *Zuzu*. A guy—looked a little like Dudley Moore—was sitting on it.

"Nice boat", I told him.

"Thanks", he replied. "Something needs to be done to the diesel. Know anything about diesels?"

A little, I offered.

"C'mon aboard. Have a look. Want a Heiny?"

It was a brief exchange that would lead to ramifications that would change my life—not just for the immediate future, but, as you'll see shortly, forever. Within a minute, I was in the sparkling clean, brand-new bilge of the boat, cold Heineken in hand, inspecting his engine. Within ten minutes, he had told me he wanted to put the boat into charter in the Bahamas. Within twenty minutes, he asked me if I would captain the boat for him. Within a week, I was hired as captain of *Zuzu*, running it for the summer as a party boat in Toronto harbour, then delivering it down to Beaufort, North Carolina, and then out into the Atlantic down to Nassau. For the next season I ran the boat, with a mate/cook with the elegant name of Felicity Barrington, doing one and two week charters through the remote islands and cays of the Bahamas.

If I couldn't make my movie, this wasn't a bad way to spend the winter. We had an interesting group of clients. A few of them were people were people I knew from the film industry. They were in the end my least favorite customers—many of them people with very high expectations, and very low threshold for anything other than absolutely perfect conditions. My favourites were total strangers—for instance, two couples, farmers from rural Saskatchewan. They had never been south before and loved every minute of it. I would tell them I would sail them to "the prettiest cay in all the Bahamas" (somewhat of an exaggeration—there are well over 2000 of them, and I certainly hadn't seen them all)—and I'd sail them to a little desert island I knew of, show them how to free-dive on the reefs, and they'd love it.

Another guy that I found to be a good customer was a very high-end restaurateur from uptown Toronto. As he'd never sailed the islands before, he too was a great client, who loved the Bahamas. He was great for me, not so great for my cook Felicity. She was an okay meat-and-potatoes cook, really more interested in the sailing, which she was good at, than the cooking. Here, she was cooking for this very high-end gourmet chef. Fortunately, one day, we were trolling while we sailed, and hooked into a little reef shark. I had an idea of to help out both of them. I handed our fancy chef the rod. He

137

battled the fish into the boat, and landed it. Sure enough, he took full possession of the fish and announced that he would cook it up for dinner that night—which he did, expertly. The fish was soon off the hook—and so, at least for one night, was Felicity.

The owner of the boat, Peter Michie, was Canadian V.P. of Sales for one of the biggest IT companies of the day, Wang Laboratories. He sent down a lot of his staff and salesmen to sail with us on the boat. Whenever they were there, regardless of wind conditions, we had to fly the big Wang-embossed spinnaker that Peter had made for the boat. We had a lot of crazy afternoons, over-canvassed and booming around the Bahamas with the spinnaker flying in the boisterous conditions. In those days there were quite a few Haitians living in the Bahamas. From time to time I noticed them staring at the name of the boat, and then doubling over in laughter. Eventually I learned why—the word *Zuzu*, I was told, is a also a Haitian Creole word, meaning…well, think of the second rudest four letter word in the English language. With *Zuzu* on the stern, and "Wang" in giant letters on the sail, we must have been quite a sight to these folk.

Between charter gigs, we'd hang out with the locals—mostly the local drug-smugglers who were a fixture on the Nassau docks. There were some pretty amusing characters there in those days. One brazen dude used to drive in from Florida in a black cigarette boat with his logo *Midnight Express*, slogan "Pick-ups. Deliveries" and a Fort Lauderdale phone number emblazoned across his bow. He was a bit much for me, but I did enjoy the company of another Floridian who used to arrive late at night from runs in from Andros or Key West.

He was entertained enough by me, but totally smitten by Felicity. Sometimes she and I would be anchored off one of the outlying islands to New Providence, cleaning up the boat for the next charter, and after he awoke at noon he'd call us on VHF and find out where we were, then zip out to hang out with us in his big cigarette boat. We'd both be glad of an opportunity for a short break in the

138

janitorial duties. She was a big girl, so I'd mix the pair of them gin and tonics, and he would toss me the keys to his gas-guzzling speedster. I'd head off, leaving her to ward off his unwanted advances on her own (I'm sure successfully), while I roared around the banks in his boat. It was a good thing I knew the reefs and sand bars of the *baja mar* ("shallow sea" in Spanish). It is one thing (not that you want to do it) hitting ground in a sailboat at six knots, quite another when you're travelling at sixty miles per hour.

The U.S. Drug Enforcement Administration was pretty seriously patrolling the islands in those years. Their big initiative, which they called Operation Blue Lightning, was quite evident throughout the islands. We would often see their big corvettes and patrol boats, shadowing us on the horizon, as we cruised through the out-islands. Fortunately they never stopped us. Although we, and our boat were completely clean, we certainly didn't need the hassle. I was boarded and searched by the DEA and Coast Guard a few years later on my own boat. It's no picnic.

One of my favorite destinations was Norman's Cay, the beautiful island at the north end of the Exumas that until a year earlier had been the private lair of Columbian über drug kingpin Carlos Lehder. After the unlikely duo of William F. Buckley Jr. and Edward Kennedy both complained to the U.S. State Department about their experiences trying to moor beside the once-friendly island, the Americans demanded the Bahamian government stop taking bribes from Lehder and instead shut him down. Once he and his AK-47-touting guards and henchmen were finally run off the island, we were one of the first charter boats to head back in. It turned out to be a spectacular spot. Lobster and conch were abundant in the picturesque anchorage after being left alone by the dope smugglers, and being off limits to fishermen for four years. There was a certain illicit attraction to exploring the bullet-scarred Lehder Headquarters and airstrip. I was also keen on showing my more adventurous guests the drug cartel's twin engine DC-3 that had crash-landed in the lagoon, and now sat in twenty feet of water on the sandy bottom. We would free-dive into the empty fuselage (the contraband washed away months earlier), and I would introduce them to the large nurse shark that had taken up resident underneath the starboard wing.

Running the big charter boat was great, but I hadn't lost interest in my *Lost!* feature script. From time to time I would check back from the Bahamas to see what was going on back in the film business. I discovered that my pal Peter Pearson, who will get a more formal introduction in the next chapter, was now running Telefilm—and that a terrific new guy, Jim Burt, was now holding the reins of control over drama development and production at CBC. Burt was a really talented writer himself, but he sublimated his own creative urges to shepherd lots of other writers' work through the network. He died a year or two later of brain cancer, but he is still honored with a screenwriting prize that the Academy of Canadian Cinema and TV hands out in his memory. Fortunately for me, he was a fan of my script, and kept me abreast of the status of things. In May he alerted me that the Corporation had finally given the film the green light. It was good timing—the charter season was over. I wrapped up the boat and flew home to get started on the movie.

That didn't mean simply going out and shooting it. Between CBC and Telefilm I had verbal commitments of about half a million dollars, but I still had to rustle together the rest of the financing—about another half million. It was no easy task putting the rest of the deal together. It never is. If you want to produce films, be prepared to master the financing game—and to deal with reams and reams of paperwork and contracts. To help with the months of negotiations ahead, I brought in three very colorful characters.

The first was Don Wilder, an old-time Director of Photography turned Producer. Don had started as a cameraman shooting commercials through the fifties and sixties, but when the feature film game got going he had gravitated into features, shot some big ones, and then began helping people like Johnny F. Bassett get other big pictures underway. He was close to the end of his shooting career when we made *Lost!*. Although he had begun as a sort of mainstream Director of Photography, working with big cameras, big

140

lighting setups and big crews, the older he got, the...well, *wilder* he got. When we finally got shooting the film, after four months of preparatory legwork, he attacked the shooting like a bull. On one occasion the grips were preparing an elaborate camera mount on the hood of a car, in order to shoot a driving shot through live traffic. Our two stars were ready to go, I had my worried eye on the rapidly sinking sun, and the grips were fussing with the rig, worrying about safety straps and padding and this and that. Finally, Don just peremptorily pushed them all aside, ripped all the clamps, suction cups and straps off the hood, threw them on the ground, grabbed his handheld camera, leapt on to the hood, and shouted, "Okay! I'm ready! Let's fuckin' go!" And that is how we shot the sequence, with other drivers on the busy streets looking over in surprise to see this curly-haired, wild-eyed 59-year-old man hanging on to the hood of a car with one hand, while holding a camera with the other—and with two TV stars inside the car, both of them trying to keep a straight face while reciting their serious dialogue about sailing to Costa Rica.

Lost! was one of Don's last films, but after I moved to Los Angeles, and he moved to Vancouver, we did one more feature together, which we shot in Calgary. He caught the religion bug after that and oddly became a convert to the "Born Again" movement. Strange. He used more four-letter words per minute than anyone I'd ever met in show business (and that's saying something), drank his young camera crew under the table, and our *Lost!* is one of the most persuasive polemics ever against religious extremism—and yet he ended up being a squeaky-clean Bible-thumper.

The next person I brought in was Sean Ryerson. He was a guy who had moved up through the ranks from grip to production manager to producer. *Lost!* was one of his first big shows as a producer, and I had trouble convincing some of the funders that he should do the show—but he's since transcended all of them and gone on to become one of the biggest line producers in television, working all over the world on big TV shows and series. He was big in every sense of the world—a physically big guy who reminded people a bit of Sydney Greenstreet in *The Maltese Falcon*, boisterous personality, big heart, lots of smarts, big plans. He not only ramrodded the film through production and completion, but when the last piece of our financing fell apart, he found us some west end sharpies that topped up our interim financing. It was scary, Italian money—they expected 25% interest on it until it got repaid, and told us if it wasn't they'd break our kneecaps—but it got the film into production (and you can bet we paid it off as soon as we could).

The third outsized character that got involved with the film was Peter Simpson. Simpson was another doppelganger of Sydney Greenstreet—and a major player in the film scene as a distributor, producer, and media buyer. He was also heavily involved in the organization and support of the Toronto International Film Festival, though I doubt if any of the popcorn films he produced or distributed were serious minded enough for snooty TIFF. He came onboard as distributor of my film—and he knew how to make that work. He took the film to Cannes and got it into distribution all over the world—on video and TV. He was very colorful guy, and working with him was always fun. Even though he had the appearance and reputation of being a bit of a bandit, I found him to be scrupulously honest. He reported earnings and paid royalties religiously. Eventually, though, he lost control of his company and sold it to Alliance. Once that happened, we never saw another distribution report—or another nickel.

And finally, I needed a straight-shooting lawyer to keep all the i's dotted and the t's crossed, and brought on a very good one, Victor Solnicki, to keep everyone and everything above board.

Along with my financing production partners, I got three terrific actors for the three lead parts. Michael Hogan was just about my favorite actor on the planet—someone I had worked with numerous times before, someone I knew would be great to play the hero of the film—the sensible brother, foil to the crazy religious fanatic. Michael not only plays heroes, but he *is* a hero to the rest of the cast and the crew of the films he works on—a funny and stable pillar of strength that keeps everyone going even on tough physical shoots like *Lost!*. Today, I suppose he is best known for his role as Colonel Saul Tigh in *Battlestar Gallactica*, but he has a long list of credits going back to the 70s.

My long-time filming assistant and cruising companion Corinne Farago came onboard as an Assistant Producer. All through pre-production she kept pressuring me—I had to consider Ken Welsh for the central role in the film of the religious fanatic skipper. We should see his latest films, we should go down to New York and see him performing on Broadway, we should go out to the airport and meet with him while he's on a layover to fly out to another shoot. It didn't take much persuasion—I thought he was a great actor, I'd worked with him twice before, he was perfect for the role. But why was she so adamant that he was the only actor I should consider? I would find out. I did hire him. He was splendid in the part— delightfully wacked out and obsessed and mad. And by the end of the first week, heavily involved with Corinne. By the end of the shoot, they were living together and within a year married and she was having his baby. Unfortunately, it didn't last. Like Don Wilder, she too caught the religious bug (though a different strain), and went off to the South Pacific to join an ashram in Fiji. Ken continues to act in dozens of projects—his credits include *Twin Peaks, The Aviator, Legends of the Fall,* and numerous other films.

For the female lead I was able to get the Canadian star Helen Shaver. Helen and I had done a low budget feature called *The Supreme Kid* together in Vancouver in the early seventies. Helen had starred in that one—and also did the makeup and wardrobe. She got her big break in Robert Lantos's *In Praise of Older Women*, in 1978, playing an "older woman" at the ripe old age of twenty seven—which tells you something about our weird attitudes about what young and old meant back then. She has done some big films over the years, such as Martin Scorsese's *The Color of Money,* playing opposite Paul Newman. I was lucky to get her. She was an intense actress. Her character (spoiler alert) dies midway through *Lost!*, and she actually literally passed out while performing the death scene.

She and I had had a brief fling back in the seventies, and as we were both single while making *Lost!*, we kind of resurrected our affair during the shoot. There must have been something in the water, other than our upside down boat. Ken and Corinne were making out in his dressing room, Helen and I were doing our thing, and there were another couple of instant flash affairs going on among males and females of the art department and production staff. This was getting to be a bit like the shenanigans in Truffaut's great backstage film *Day for Night*. This was supposed to be *Lost!*, not *Love Boat!* Let me bring in Don Cherry for some *Coach's Corner* commentary:

"Awright, youse kids out der who wanna be filum drectors! Lissenup! Dis is jus' not a good idea, see? Ya wanna make movies, make movies! Doan start havin' the monkey business wit' yer movie star actresses! Take it from me, youse kids—doan get offside on dis— it's jus' not a good idea!!"

But it all worked out okay in the end. It was a complex shoot, filming all this intense drama on and in an upside down boat, but we all knew what we were doing, and we got it done. I had a great art department, led by production designer Bill Fleming, a very nautically knowledgeable guy who taught me a technique that was very useful to *Lost!*, and that I used again on *Treasure Island* and other marine films. On a film like this, where the upside down boat is sitting out at sea, you can't just let the boat drift and expect to be able to film that way. The background and the lighting will be constantly changing, driving everyone crazy. So we anchored the boat out in deep water, hiding the line by tethering it under our boat. (Not a simple task—I think we lost six big anchors during the shoot—I can provide the coordinates if you want to go look for them.)

What Bill showed me was the technique of "Nelson anchoring"—so named because it was supposedly invented by Admiral Nelson for the Battle of Trafalgar. What you do is first anchor normally from the bow, then attach another line with a camel-hitch to the anchor rode. (I use the Arabic name for the knot—no doubt the British admiral called it by some other term). Then you run this new line to a winch at the stern of the boat, and then let out your anchor rode until you have made a bridle with the two ropes. Done! Get shooting. Now if there is any problem— Michael is having to squint because he is looking straight into the sun, or Don doesn't like the angle of light on Helen's face, or there is a damn fishing boat deep in the background of Ken's close-up—a simple command to a grip sitting at the stern winch to either crank in or let out the bridle rope—and the problem is solved. You can tweak the lighting or the camera angle easier than you can on a terrestrial shoot.

What I didn't know then was that without this simple but effective technique, I might not have been making the film at all. In 2012 I was doing research for a new marine film about an event that had taken place during the Battle of Lake Ontario during the War of 1812. I discovered that the commanders of the British fleet, students of Nelson's nautical genius, had used the same anchoring technique in a major battle in Burlington Bay. They lured the American ships in, anchored, adjusted the angle of their cannon fire using the technique (which the American captains hadn't yet learned), and won the skirmish. Lake Ontario was the main naval theater of the war—it is conceivable that had the British navy not won that battle, the tide could have turned and the Americans could have taken Upper Canada, and won the war. If they had, I guess there would be no CBC, no Telefilm Canada, no financing for the film, and no *Lost!*

We had perfect weather for the principal photography of the film. It did not hold when Don, Ken, and I went out to Vancouver a month later to shoot some additional material for the opening sequences in the film. It was now November, and Vancouver was performing as it usually does—long stretches of pouring rain interrupted by brief respites of drizzle. We had to try to match the sunny exteriors we had shot earlier. With lighting and a bit of lucky timing we were able to get the shots involving Ken, and after a few days I was able to send him home. Don and I still wanted to get some establishing shots of Vancouver harbour. We dodged the rain and managed to get most of them. There was one last shot I wanted to get—a focus-pull through the famous totem poles of Stanley Park through to the Lions Gate bridge and out to the Salish Sea. We tried a couple of times and got skunked by the horrible weather. Finally we decided he would help me set up the platform we needed for the shot, and leave it for me to shoot on my own when the rain finally stopped. We went out there, dragged four park picnic tables into the perfect spot for the shot, then lifted up another picnic table on top of them. I now had a shooting platform with the camera maybe fifteen feet up—the perfect height for the shot. As the rain pelted down, I drove him to the airport, and he flew home.

The next day, I waited, listening to my weather radio for any news of a break in the weather. Around three, I got one. The weatherman suddenly predicted a lull in the non-stop precipitation. I roared out to Stanley Park, heading for my makeshift camera platform. The weatherman, though, was wrong. I set up the tripod and was all ready to shoot the shot (the damned shot, I was beginning to call it), but it was raining so hard I didn't dare even take the camera from its case. I waited. Now, not only was it raining, but it was starting to get dark. There was no one else in the sodden park. Then, out of the gloom, a limousine pulled around the corner, and stopped. The driver scurried around and opened the back door. A woman got out. She seemed to turn down his offer of accompaniment, or an umbrella, and began gingerly walking through the puddles. She was a strange sight—looked like a bag lady. Frizzy hair, a ratty dress, a frayed ugly cardigan. Once she saw me, she began to walk towards me. As she got closer I realized she was... iconic Hollywood movie star Katharine Hepburn.

"Hello, young man," she said, in her distinctive, quavering voice. "What are you doing here?"

Well, Miss Hepburn, I told her, I'm trying to shoot a shot for a movie—but I'm waiting for the rain to stop.

"Certainly does rain a lot here, doesn't it?" she said. "We're making a movie too, but I gave up on it, today."

146

We talked a little more; I told her about my film, she told me about hers, then she decided the rain was too much, turned around, and walked back to her limo. The driver ran around to open the door for her, and they drove away. I never did find out if the ragged clothes she was wearing were costume for her film—or just her own super casual style of dress. A brief, likely forgettable incident for her. Memorable for me. I did think this doyen of American cinema had inadvertently given me good advice. I decided I didn't really need the shot, packed up, and left the rainy town.

A month later I took Michael down to Fort Lauderdale, and along with a group of sailors we picked up a big new boat for Peter Michie's charter fleet, and sailed for Nassau. Once out in the islands we shot the last of the pick-up shots we needed for the film. So (you'll remember the claim that we couldn't shoot in the Atlantic because it was a "different color" to the Pacific) we ended up shooting the film in the Atlantic, the Pacific, Lake Ontario, a water tank filled with hydrant water, and the Caribbean. Did the shades of blue all match? In the end, yes, of course—that's why they invented color correction. Not that the audience really cares—as Sam Goldwyn wisely said, when a finicky director was trying to convince the studio chief to allow him to go off to shoot some B western in Montana, "Hell, a tree's a tree. A rock's a rock. Shoot it in Griffith Park."

While we were on a brief hiatus from the post-production of *Lost!*, I went back to the Bahamas to finish my charter-skippering gig. One of my final guests on *Zuzu* was the boss's star, top-performing saleswoman at his big computer company, Carolyn Fonso. While I was running the boat I didn't talk filmmaking, so she thought of me not as a film director on hiatus, but as a seaman with a weird obsession to become the first person to sail around the Americas— and a cruise director working hard to keep everyone entertained. But I was smitten, one thing led to another, and within eight months we were married, she had changed her name to Carolyn Rowe and we were heading off to live together in Los Angeles.

147

Only by going with her was I able to move to California, and get the Green Card needed to work there. The fact that she was successfully launching a major Canadian software company in the U.S., and using her credentials, degrees, and years of experience in education to teach Americans how to use and sell the company's complex products got her, and me with her, the coveted Green Cards. We both had some success down there, and also had a ball exploring Southern California—sailing our new boat out to Catalina, Ensenada, and other sunny playgrounds, and most importantly, starting our family.

Before heading south, though, I had to deal with some major issues, like promoting and releasing the film—and minor issues, like figuring out how to get rid of garage-fulls of detritus from the *Lost!* shoot. The biggest thing I had to deal with was the multi-ton floating set of the upside down boat. Sean and I didn't know what to do with the damn thing. We'd used up our thin budget on more important things. If we wasted a lot of money hiring a team to tear it all apart and somehow dispose of it, we wouldn't have any money to hire a composer for the film. I remembered, though, that there was a tradition on Toronto Island that people used to leave derelict boats in one of the lagoons—and any trapped in the ice there would be torched by the residents as part of the New Year's Eve skating and drinking parties. What a cost-effective way of getting rid of it! We hired someone to tow the now-useless, cumbersome boat to the lagoon.

For reasons we never discovered, the New Year's Eve skaters never did burn the boat, and so it was still there the next summer. As the theatrical run of the film approached, we got a call from the harbour police. They had spent months trying to identify the owners of the weird looking craft, and had finally located us. We had to get rid of it, they told us.

But by now we'd spent the entire budget, except for—a few bucks in the publicity department. So that's what we decided to do—turn it into a publicity stunt. On the afternoon the film was going to open, we'd tow it out in the lake, and…blow it up. The local tabloid, the *Toronto Sun*, was always down with covering something crazy like that. We got six big wine barrels, half-filled each with gasoline, tied them to the boat, got a special effects friend to wrap them all up with cordite, and towed it offshore. (There are about five reasons why this is all illegal, but let's get on with it.) Sean and I took my new wife and a *Sun* photographer with us on my new boat *Blade Runner*, and once he was all set, buddy lit the fuse. Kaploee!—an unbelievably huge fireball cascaded high into the sky. Apparently the fire department's phone system was deluged with calls from worried citizens. The remains were sunk in deep water, along with all the other thousands of shipwrecks in Lake Ontario. If archeologists find it hundreds of years from now, they'll wonder at the odd "upside down" nature of the boat's design.

The Photo Editor at the paper asked me to call him that evening so he could tell me how the picture had turned out. He was ecstatic. He thought it was a riot—from the angle it was shot at, the fireball looked higher than the CN Tower. He was going to run it in full color on the front page the next day. Trouble is, a Pakistani airliner was hijacked later that evening, made the front page and booted us back to page 48—in black and white. Oh, well. Onward.

I wanted to get to Cannes, to help my distributor Peter Simpson promote it to his international buyers in the nitty-gritty *Marché du Film* that runs simultaneously with the Competition. I wasn't going to be able to get to the extremely expensive Riviera town from the film's budget, as we'd long ago run out of money. Only through the largesse of my new fiancé was I able to attend the world famous event. She had just become the top North American sales rep for another major new computer software company, and they rewarded her with a prize of a trip anywhere in the world. She chose Cannes in May, and so I was able to show off not just my new film, but my new wife-to-be, on the storied Croisette of the famous French town.

Lost! got great numbers on the network—slightly over three million people saw it over three telecasts—an impressive number then and one you would be hard-pressed to duplicate in today's splintered television landscape. Helen and I both got Genie nominations, for her acting and my script. I think she was at the awards ceremony (neither of us won) but I was in Los Angeles, shooting a new feature. Next!

As a working filmmaker, I think it's best to be both a specialist and a generalist. That is—develop some specialties where you can claim some ownership of the niche, but don't get so identified with that niche that producers won't hire you for anything else. After several years of these marine films culminating with *Lost!*, I got a few chances to direct some very different kinds of films. First I made a gory horror film called *Splatter: The Architects of Fear.* I had some trepidation about doing the somewhat sleazy film, but in the end most films are fun to make, and something good comes from all of them. In this case I met a cool new guy named Allan Levine who A.D.'ed that film and has worked with me (as my Lieutenant, as he likes to call it), on numerous other projects since then. I still get calls from aficionados of the 1980s direct-to-video genre about the film (in fact a film crew flew up from Texas to interview me about it recently), but it's probably best forgotten. If it really interests you, go hunt it down on the *Fangoria*-style corners of the Internet. There are even a number of good reviews of it you can likely dig up. No accounting for taste.

Right in the middle of shooting our post-apocalyptic horror film, in April of 1986, our Executive Producer came on to our blood-spattered set to tell us the big news about Chernobyl—one of the closest things the world has ever had to a real apocalypse. Twenty-three years later I'd be filming inside the dead zone of Chernobyl myself—but you'll have to read on to the final chapter to hear about that.

Then I shot a thriller, *Take Two,* in Hollywood, and then a comedy (about the IRS, of all things) called *Personal Exemptions.*

Lame script, but fun to work with the star, Nanette Fabray. It was the only film I've ever made that was cast by watching *Hollywood Squares*. The first-time producer (more an accountant than a producer) was a big fan of the dumb game show, and she cast the feature by going through the aged contestants in the colored boxes until she found someone that she could afford. Although Nanette had done a fair bit of television, she had done just three feature films since her only hit *Band Wagon* (1953), but she was full of beans and a trooper to work with.

The tax department comedy (sounds like an oxymoron—and perhaps it is) also featured the dumbest move I've ever seen a producer make on a film. I had already fortunately talked them out of what would have been the *second* dumbest producer decision ever. The script called for a major pie fight (it was that sort of script—full of ridiculous set-pieces that had nothing really to do with the plot—but sounded to me like they'd be fun to shoot, so I didn't object) What I did fight them on was their plans for shooting the scene. They wanted to shoot in a real kitchen, and had convinced one of their friends—a suburban housewife, with a nice sparkling suburban kitchen, to let us shoot it there. "It won't make too much of a mess, will it?" she naively asked me. I put the kibosh on that nonsense, and told the producers they had to build me a set. There is no way you can shoot a proper, old-time silent movie pie fight in a real kitchen, without destroying it, receiving a lawsuit, and, in this instance, losing a friend. They acquiesced, got a set built; we brought in forty or fifty lemon meringue pies, I had the actors throw them all at each other, we made a glorious, giant mess, and walked away from it. I assume the carpenters dismantled the sticky set and threw all the flats in the garbage.

As for the *dumbest* move, that also started with another ridiculous piece of business that the writer had dreamed up for no other reason than it would be cool to shoot and perhaps cool to watch on screen. This was going to be a car that was going to spin a collection of donuts through a supermarket parking lot. Part One of Stupidest Producer Move Ever was that our producer in question volunteered his *own* car for the gag. Now, stunt drivers are not known for the gentle way that they handle automobiles, particularly old clunkers like this first-time producer drove, but okay, if he wants to save some money, we'll do that. So we get to the location. The stunt driver looks the car over, fiddles around with the emergency brake, gets it ready for action. We clear the area, and he goes out to practice a little with the car. Very impressive—screeching tires, spinning wheels, smoking rubber. He brings it in—it's all good. He's ready to do it, whenever we are. We send him off to wardrobe, to get suited up in the appropriate costume. Now, while we set up the cameras, the producer decides that this all looks so cool that *he* wants to try the gag himself. Normally, this is a complete no-no. Just for instance, I did the racing-themed series *Fast Track* with Keith Carradine some years later, in which we had a stable of about twenty-five NASCAR stockcars, and where it was absolutely *verboten* for anyone other than the authorized drivers and actors even to sit in, let alone drive, the speedsters.

On *Personal Exemptions*, I wanted to, but couldn't very well tell the *Producer* that he couldn't drive *his own* car—so off he went, merrily trying to emulate the stunt driver's skill, spinning donuts in the lot while we set up the reflector boards and tripods. Unfortunately he hadn't picked up quite enough tricks from the stuntman, and so at high speed lost control and drove the car straight into the side of a Safeway supermarket. He was okay (pride a little damaged), but the car was destroyed. We had to find another scene to shoot that afternoon—and he had to get a ride with the Third A.D. to the set for the rest of the shoot.

Enough of these wacky terrestrial films. It was time for me to get back to sea. Twelve years after *Lost!*, I got a great opportunity to get out on the water again, and make another feature. I did it with three of the wildest producers in the business—and one of the worst.

Harry Alan Towers was a hell of an amusing old duck— almost a throwback to another era, and a guy who managed to produce over a hundred features in a career that stretched from the forties till his death in 2009. He always had about thirty projects on the go. He was working on a new version of *Moll Flanders* with Ken Russell during the weeks before his death; I'm sure he was coming up with a new financing scheme for it on the day he died. He was virtually the inventor of tax shelter financing. He was also big on turning public domain titles into films—some of which he made over and over again. He made three versions of *Ten Little Indians* (aka *And Then There Were None*) (1965, 1974, 1989), each with an 'all-star' international cast, and when he approached me about doing *Treasure Island*, he had already made one before.

In 1961, Harry and his then girlfriend Mariella Novotny were charged with operating a call girl ring in New York City. Rumors flew around that he was a Soviet agent, using the call girls to compromise American diplomats, and was somehow involved with Stephen Ward, society osteopath and accused pimp at the center of the Profumo sex scandal. Harry jumped bail and returned to Europe, and because of his issues with the American authorities, basically single-handedly invented the concept of Euro-pudding tax shelter film financing, finding distant corners of Europe to live and make movies in. Among the jurisdictions that Harry helped get feature film industries going were Spain, Bulgaria, Malta, Liechtenstein, Canada (during the tax shelter years of the late seventies), Zimbabwe, and, in my case, the Isle of Man. Where did Harry live? Well, he had a place in Toronto, and he had a place in London, but really—Harry lived in the Carlton Hotel on the Croisette in Cannes, and the Sunset Marquis in West Hollywood. (Must have been an incongruous sight. I made one of my rock and roll films out of the Sunset Marquis, and know that it was then almost entirely populated by metal bands like Motley Crue and Poison. How Harry, with his old-school British style fit in, I don't quite know)

Harry's first crack at *Treasure Island* had not gone well. He planned to shoot it in Spain, with Orson Welles as Long John Silver, and a British sailing vessel doubling for the pirate ship. Unfortunately on the sail from Britain to the Spanish shoot, the ship sank in a storm on the Bay of Biscay. As they all waited for a replacement to arrive,

Welles decided he hated the script they were using, and proceeded to write his own version. In the end, they shot the original (you can only imagine all the fights on this one), and Harry inherited (or thought he inherited) the rights to Welles' version. Twenty-five years later, I met with him, first in his crowded Toronto home, awash in faded elegance, then later at his similarly decorated London flat, on the roof of which he'd produced Edward R. Murrow's famous radio broadcasts during the bombing raids of the London blitz. Dressed, as always, in the height of 1958 formal fashion, although usually with a few food stains on his Peckham Rye tie, Harry rummaged around his giant piles of scripts and pulled out the Welles *Treasure Island*. He wanted me to give it a bit of a re-write—for starters in all those years the first two pages had been ripped off and lost, so at very least I'd have to do something there. Once I had the re-write done, he wanted to hire me to come to the Isle of Man with him to help him convince the local authorities to put up thirty percent of the budget. Meantime, he was going to raise the rest of the money in Canada with his partners Pieter Kroonenburg and Gary Howsam.

Pieter Kroonenburg ended up being the real hands-on producer of the film. He was the guy I turned to when some of the actors went on strike over their hotel accommodations, the guy who helped me resolve script and casting issues, the guy who inspired great loyalty and passion for the project, not just from me but from the Québécois and British crew he assembled for the shoot. Unfortunately, like all three of these producers, he had 25 balls in the air at any one time, and he couldn't really keep them all juggling. Before my film was even wrapped he was off to Kenya to make what turned out to be a very nice film—and a financially disastrous production—called *To Walk With Lions*. It seemed to be the beginning of the end. He has spent much of the last fifteen years trying to get a huge film about Paul Watson and the Sea Shepherd underway, and although millions have been spent, it has never gone into production. Fortunately he has another passion—tennis—so I guess he keeps himself sane with it.

154

The third musketeer in this effort has had an even rockier row to hoe. Gary Howsam was not hands-on at all on *Treasure Island*—he was never even in the Isle of Man. In fact, I've never ever seen him on a film set. Although he looks and dresses like a grip or a cameraman—pony tail, blue jeans—he is strictly a financial guy, working arcane aspects of film financing to make the deal happen. He was a very important part of the *Treasure Island* financing, as he was on dozens of films in the nineties and early 2000s. People like Robert Lantos get all the press and attention, but guys like Howsam and Towers made way more films every year than the better-known producers in town. Gary had a pretty major setback in 2007, though, when the FBI charged him with using forged distribution agreements to defraud investors. He had to wear a GPS shackle around his ankle for eight or ten months, until he went to trial and eventually was cleared of all charges. I met him three years later at the Gemini Awards in Calgary, where he was up for *The Tudors* and my host George Kourounis was up for *Angry Planet*. He spent twenty minutes telling me the story in detail, and convinced me he was innocent and it was a set-up. I'm glad he's back in the game.

I read the Welles script and discovered it was pretty awful. I think his secretary wrote it while he drank sangria. I figured, though, that no one had probably read it in twenty five years—if ever—and so no one would notice if I just went back to the Robert Louis Stevenson source material, and did a page one rewrite. I didn't mind sharing credit with Orson Welles, even if I wrote every word of the script. Turned out, that was a good plan. Welles' estate—notoriously litigious—caught wind of the new film, and started waving lawyers and lawsuits around. Harry and Pieter told me to forget about the Welles script—and instead write a new one from scratch. No problem—I was doing that already.

They all liked my script but I still had to convince them I was the guy to direct it. A lot of the financing was coming from Quebec and they wouldn't be getting the tax credits on my salary, since I was not resident there. On the other hand, I had applied for and received a British passport years earlier, and so it was thought I could qualify as part of the British spend on the co-production. But I think the deciding factor was that I convinced them they didn't want to hire a landlubber for a complicated marine shoot as this was.

In the end the marine aspects of the film went very smoothly. I scoured England for an appropriate ship; we found one in a tiny Devon port, they sailed it up to us, didn't sink it, and we did two weeks of complex shooting on it off the Isle of Man. It's an interesting relationship, working as a director with the captain and crew of a big vessel like that. The captain of the ship is the ultimate authority, ultimately responsible for the safety of the vessel and of everyone on her—the ship's crew, and the film's crew, and cast. As director, though, you're ultimately responsible for getting the film shot, getting the job done. You're putting much stiffer demands on the ship and its crew than most of their clients do. Everything is in flux—the boat is moving, the weather is changing, the sun is going in, or coming out, you're wanting to mount cameras high in the rigging, or stage swordfights across the deck. One actor is ready, another is not. Let's tack, so we can shoot this scene, instead. We just did, they complain. Too bad, let's do it again. I know there are 14 sails to swing across. That's what we're paying you for. You've got to know as much about it as they do, so they can't bluff you. And you can't get too precious about it. You're not there to make friends—you're there to make a movie. You know what they say—you can't make an omelette without breaking some eggs.

The locals loved it. They thought having the big tall ship sailing in their island waters was wonderful, and they flocked down to our base at the south end of the island to see it, and to try and catch glimpses of the North American, British, and Irish movie and TV stars we had working on the film. Working with the ship actually proved simple compared with the problems we had finding an Admiral Benbow Inn to shoot in. Much of the early part of the story takes place in and around this old inn that Jim Hawkins runs with his old grandmother, before he heads off to sea searching for treasure.

156

The Art Director, Location Manager, and I kept scouring the island, unable to find a building that could be transformed into the 18th Century inn. Finally we came upon a guy named Steve Christian. We learned, to our surprise, that he was a descendant of Fletcher Christian, the leader of the famous mutiny on the *Bounty*. We further learned that not just Christian, but his antagonist in this most famous of naval misadventures, Captain Bligh, was also from the Isle of Man. Fletcher Christian's descendent told us that he owned the three hundred year old stone house that his great-great-great grandfather had been born in, and he thought it might serve our purpose. Steeve Henry, the Art Director, and I went out and found the abandoned old building. The doors were sealed shut, the windows boarded over, weeds growing everywhere. We pried off the cover from a second floor window, and shimmied inside. It had last been used as a crack house. There was graffiti on the walls, garbage strewn around, rats running about. Hard to believe—it had never been electrified, so it was dark inside, but as we peered around, we realized, this would make a fantastic set for the Benbow Inn. Steeve and his crew did a great job tearing down some three hundred year old stone walls, restoring others, and turning it into a country inn, perfect for the period pirate film.

For the part of Billy Bones, the boozing pirate who gets the story rolling by passing on the map of the treasure island to Jim Hawkins, we brought in the Irish actor Patrick Bergin. Patrick behaved as I think people feel movie stars should behave. He was great to work with, seemed to enjoy every minute of performing in the classic old tale. He had recently had some good paydays from films like *Robin Hood* and *Sleeping With the Enemy*, which he did with Julia Roberts, so he bought himself…a castle in Ireland. Now that he was wrapping up *Treasure Island*, he was looking around for something else to buy. I was (still am) in love with the Jaguar XJ-S. While I was being driven to the set one day in one of the production vans, I noticed an XJ-S convertible in baby blue in an Isle of Man used car lot. It wasn't for me—for starters it had right hand drive—so I mentioned it to Patrick, on his last working day on the picture. He stuck around for another day, wrapping his things up with the production office while we shot other scenes with Jack Palance and Kevin Zegers. That afternoon, he came by the shooting location to say goodbye to us all. He told me he would drive me back to the hotel. He hung around craft service until we wrapped. When I found him, I discovered he had gone out and bought the Jag. The two of us put the top down, and went roaring around the island on the famous Tourist Trophy motorcycle racecourse. We went zipping through one of the best known features of the track, known as Church Bends—a tricky chicane past two churches, where numerous motorcycle riders have flown off the course and straight into the churches' graveyards—thus saving their relatives several steps in the post mortem wrap-up to their lives. Fortunately, it didn't happen to us, and in fact I remember Patrick, impressed with how his new Jag was performing, turning to me at one point on our drive and observing, "It's not a bad life, is it, Peter?"

The production went swimmingly. The post-production started well—then ended badly. The editing was fun. I enjoyed working with Ion Webster, a good, creative editor, and for both of us, it was the first time we got to use the new non-linear Lightworks editing system, which was quite revolutionary. Both of us had started with film editing (which, like digital, is non-linear), and then had, like everyone else, lived through eight or ten years of linear off-line/on-line tape editing. In my case, I had been approached four years earlier by a Vancouver promoter to create a complex DVD called *Adventure USA*. For that project I made fifty mini-movies about adventures around America, using the then new Apple 7100 computer running a very early non-linear system called Edit DV, so I had learned digital editing on the early prototype. Lightworks was a huge step up in horsepower, the first system that could handle the demands of a big 35mm feature in full resolution. Still, it was utterly primitive—and incredibly expensive—by comparison with what we have today. Final Cut Pro today is perhaps one hundred times more sophisticated than the 1996 Lightworks was—and sells for $320. Lightworks came installed on a dedicated computer that sold for over

$100,000. I hope whoever owned the model we used got their money out of it—because within four years it was obsolete—and the lunking computer it ran on would only be useful on a film like *Treasure Island* as a very inefficient boat anchor.

We cut the picture, and then I moved on to what I believe to be one of the most important stages in filmmaking—scoring the picture. Around this point all three producers abandoned the film. Pieter was in Kenya, dealing with serious financial problems on his *To Walk With Lions*. Harry was also in Africa, rustling up some new project funding in Zimbabwe. Gary was back at his desk, working the phone, raising money for a new collection of action films and thrillers. *Treasure Island* was handed off to a fourth producer—a woman, who began her work by unraveling much of the editing Ion and I had worked on. Anything that she thought might possibly upset the sensibility of a delicate five-year-old girl had to go.

While Ion tried to save our film, I worked hard to find a composer who could save the picture with a great score. Two talented composers wrote and recorded demos—both of them very good. She rejected both, came up with someone she knew— someone who might possibly have come with something okay, except that she forced him to write and record it in one week. That week happened to be the first week following the infamous Quebec Ice Storm of January 1998. For his entire period of composition, he had no electricity. Then she demanded that the music be recorded and the film dubbed and mixed—again in a week. The key mixer had not only had no electricity during the storm, but no heat, and had come down with a severe case of the flu. He should have been in bed—or in hospital. Instead, she was driving him to finish it, regardless of quality. Poor dubbing, slapdash mix, poor music recording. What was the need for all this rushing around, during the worst weather crisis in the history of Montreal? She told me the film had to be finished, so the distributors could take it to Cannes. Then she barred me from the mix. I called the distributors in Los Angeles. They thought I was crazy, talking about releasing the film at Cannes. They had no screening slot there, no poster ready, no plans to release

159

the film until the American Film Market, six months later. All her rushing round and forcing people to do things quickly, and badly, was pointless.

She damaged the film, but she didn't ruin it. We had some positive screenings of it at film festivals, and then Columbia TriStar released it as a "Family Classic". I think that families around the world have likely got a kick out of it. It's a pity though—it could have been a lot better, without her meddling.

If in 1990 you had predicted that documentary and reality programming was going to become wildly successful and popular in ten years time, spawning documentary festivals and reality channels and pushing drama to the back burner, people would have said you were nuts. And yet, that is what happened. Once this doc bandwagon stared rolling, I was quick to jump onboard. As the century turned, I turned away from drama and moved instead toward nature and historical docs—still with a marine theme. I shot a film about the cute but beleaguered sea otters of the west coast for Canadian Geographic, helped make a Discovery Channel film I named *Sharks of the Great White North*, then wrote and directed biographies on Joshua Slocum, the first man to sail alone around the world, and Sir Samuel Cunard, the creator of transatlantic steamship travel, and the ocean liner.

For both of those, I was back out on the Atlantic. Prior to his small boat adventuring, Slocum was a preeminent sailing ship captain at the height of the Age of Sail, so I recreated a bit of that by racing aboard a similar vessel to his *Northern Light* with a fleet of Tall Ships from Boston to Halifax. For the Cunard film, the producer and I sailed across the Atlantic aboard the *Queen Elizabeth 2*. There was always a strong connection between the Cunard liners, especially the two *Queens*, and the World Trade Center towers and the Statue of Liberty. As we left New York harbor, I filmed the ship passing between the statue and the Twin Towers—all of them iconic symbols of the links between America and Europe. The date was September 6, 2001. I wasn't the first person to take that shot, but I would be the last.

Five days, and two Atlantic gales later, we arrived in Southampton, to hear the news that the World Trade Center had just been destroyed. It was a piece of news that would influence everyone's lives for the next four or five years, and to some degree, probably, forever.

Future generations will find it hard to comprehend how shaken everyone was by the events of September 11. That afternoon, though, I did go off, as planned, to Brompton cemetery in London to get some shots of Cunard's gravestone. Even though we were 3500 miles from Manhattan, I remember that I, and the other people around me, looked up to the sky with irrational fear every time a jet went overhead, setting up its landing pattern for Heathrow. And it got sillier. On Friday of that week, which was the day of mourning for the victims, I was in Liverpool, wrapping up a couple of days of filming in the old port. In the early afternoon, I checked out of the hotel, called a cab, loaded all my (suspicious looking), black camera cases inside, and headed for the train station, in order to return to London. En route, though, I asked the cabbie to make a quick stop at the Beatles gift shop on the Mersey, so I could pick up a couple of souvenirs for my two daughters, back home. The incompetent young clerk in the gift shop could not seem to operate the Visa machine, and the "quick stop" became a not so quick one. When I finally got out, I walked to the waiting cab, to find it had been moved to the middle of an empty parking lot, and that the driver was no longer in it. I looked around, to see him standing in the rain on the far side of the parking lot. I waved to him, to indicate I was ready to leave. Slowly, tentatively, he walked over, climbed in, and drove me to the train station. As I paid him my fare, he told me, in his thick Scouse accent "Ad me worried back there, mate. Thought you might be Al-Qaeda, gonna blow me up." Right. Al-Qaeda's plan for world domination—Part One—the Twin Towers of the World Trade Center. Part Two—A random Merseyside taxi.

The Liverpool cabbie was by no means the only person to over-react to the crisis. I can't say I was immune to the spreading paranoia. I found the anthrax–in–the–mail crisis that quickly followed on the heels of 9/11 to be even more unsettling than the jet attack. At the time, I was Chairman of the Ontario wing of the Directors Guild of Canada, and in mid-September had to make a trip to Los Angeles on some business for the DGC. After I completed that work, I planned to do some filming aboard the other famous Cunard ship, the *Queen Mary*, now moored as a hotel in Long Beach harbor, for the documentary. Seems crazy now, but I remember serious soul-searching about whether to make the trip into Anthrax America (and I guess I wasn't alone—the flight was almost empty). I know, as well, that I was not the only guest at the hotel worrying about whether the iconic—but very low security *Queen Mary* might be a terrorist target while we were inside, especially as Britain had just joined in on George Bush's fallacious and off-track "war on terror" against the Middle East.

Along with directing these marine-themed shows for others, I began producing a new series myself in the mid-nineties for a string of Canadian and British TV outlets called *Exploring Under Sail*. I worked with two veteran sailors-turned-sailing-videographers Paul and Sheryl Shard filming a series of ocean adventures in St. Maarten, Antigua, and around the Atlantic.

Then came my biggest and longest-running production. The thirty-nine episodes of *Angry Planet* were mostly terrestrial tales of exploring deep caves, chasing hurricanes and tornadoes, and climbing volcanoes. The last chapter of this book will be dedicated to the best of those yarns. However we also undertook some serious marine adventures, which belong here. Two of them fulfilled long-held ambitions of mine—to dive with great white sharks, and to sail around Cape Horn.

Fortunately, I don't have many great tales of derring-do or adventurous mishap to tell about either. Instead, we filmed both with good people who knew what they were doing, got the job done, and came back in one piece. Diving with great whites, though, is certainly an intense adrenaline-pumping experience. I considered a couple of locations to film the big sharks before settling on Guadalupe Island off the northwest coast of Mexico. The south coast of Australia and

162

the east coast of South Africa are better known for great whites, but both have fairly cold, murky water, and South Africa is a bit of a zoo with many boats converging on the sharks whenever they show up. Guadalupe, by comparison, is a remote island 250 miles southwest of Ensenada. It's a two-day boat ride to get there from California, but once you're there, you're on your own, with the only feeding frenzy coming from the sharks, not from competing photographers. The water is clear and fairly warm, the location protected and calm, and most importantly, the sharks are, in my experience at least, abundant.

We wore dry suits (it isn't *that* warm), breathing with an octopus rig, wearing a heavy vest with about forty pounds of lead in it, filming from floating shark cages at about six feet underwater. The most important people in the operation are the deckhands above on the boat, who are chumming the water with buckets of fish blood and guts, and then luring the whites in to the cameras by hurling out long lines baited with tuna and albacore. They have to then pull the bait in at exactly the right speed to bring the whites right in front of the camera. Pull too fast, and the sharks lose interest. Pull too slowly, and they grab the bait.

Trouble is, you need eyes in the back of your head to catch everything that is going on. Wearing a facemask and pressing it up against a viewfinder, you get tunnel vision and with the sharks coming in from all over, can miss important parts of the action. You really need a dedicated assistant to keep his eyes peeled in all directions while you keep your eye to the camera. Fortunately for me (not for him), I had one. There was another photographer on board, from New Jersey. He had a very fancy Nikon rig, which flooded on the first day we were there. With his camera ruined and no opportunity to do any more shooting himself, he bravely ignored his grim misfortune, volunteered to be my underwater backup eyes instead, and did a great job of it. With help from him and the chumming deckhands above me, I was able to get good sequences of the sharks coming in from the distant gloom and then swimming right up and interacting with my show host, George Kourounis, in another cage beside us.

163

George and I enlisted two sailors to join us for our episode rounding Cape Horn to tell the story of the wild weather of the Southern Ocean. We met up with them in Ushuaia, Argentina—the southernmost city in the world, and took a most circuitous route to get to the boat that we'd use to sail around Cape Horn. The rest of the world would think that Chile and Argentina would be two countries that would get along with each other, but in fact they are at each other's throats for reasons that elude the rest of us. They have carved up their national boundaries through Terra del Fuego, Cape Horn and the Beagle Channel in a most convoluted manner, and the sharply defined ports of entry, heavily patrolled waters, and complicated exit permits, make passaging through the area messy and difficult. In order to land at Cape Horn (which is in Chile), we had to pick up the boat in the Chilean town of Puerto Williams. In order to do this, we had to load all our filming, sailing, and diving gear on two small planes, and take two ridiculously short flights through Argentina in order to properly clear through customs and immigration between the two uncooperative neighbours. The first flight—wheels up in one airport to wheels down in another—took less than five minutes. Then everything was unloaded, inspected, loaded onto another plane. Then a sixteen-minute flight across the channel from one country to the other—more customs, immigration, inspections.

We finally linked up with our boat—a fifty-four foot steel expedition sailing boat, originally built for famed polar mountaineer and sailor Bill Tilman, now sailed by a couple just as tough and hardy as he was. She was from northern Ontario; he was from New Zealand. We sailed down towards Cape Horn, then found an anchorage where we could lie low until the weather changed. We wanted to round the famous "Everest of the Seas" in rambunctious conditions, not in survival conditions. It was currently blowing fifty knots. With an ocean fetch of thousands of miles, all the way from Australia, and with a wicked, rocky lee shore, you don't want to be trying to round Cape Horn in fifty knots if you can avoid it. We waited it out, on the hook. In Patagonia you always have to use three point anchoring—a bow anchor down through the kelp to the bottom, then two long sturdy thousand foot lines to shore, to tie off to trees or rocks. The winds are predictably unpredictable down there with the chance always there of hurricane-force williwaws ripping down from the mountain peaks, able to capsize a boat even while at anchor. Even with all our preparations, our skipper would sometimes decide at three in the morning that we needed to re-anchor, and we would have to pull all our lines in and move to a different, better protected part of the harbour.

The winds fell to twenty-five knots, and we weighed our various anchors and shorelines, and took off for the notorious cape. Our show host, more at ease beside a tornado than on the deck of a bouncing sailboat, gamely hung on and did his TV hosting thing. He did make a few unplanned offerings to King Neptune, including his Nikon, which slid off the deck and now sits eight hundred feet below the waves, but he made it. For me, and the other sailors on board, it was a major milestone. One hundred years ago, a rounding of Cape Horn allowed you to put an earring in your left ear. These days, with every second thirteen-year-old sporting an earring, none of us bothered with that, but we did celebrate our accomplishment with drams of naval issue rum.

Once around the cape, we tucked into the lee of the mighty bulwark. It is impossible to anchor at Cape Horn, but there is a dock where it is possible to land a dinghy. Our skipper relinquished the helm to his mate, and while she took solo command of the boat, he drove us into shore by Zodiac. We climbed up the long steep path to the top of the cape, where a Chilean naval lieutenant has the lonely job of maintaining the tiny sentry post at the southern tip of the hemisphere, and looking after the massive Chilean flag that flies from it. I filmed an interview with him. In cases like this, where the interview subject speaks limited English, I always do the same thing—ask the questions, and let them answer, in their own language—then add sub-titles later. It's much better than having them struggle with trying to tell me their story in fractured English. So it was much later, after getting his interview translated, that I understood the things he told me, one of which was that he had to replace his flag every week, because that is all the time it would take for the wind to tear it to shreds. I couldn't believe this, and went back to the translator. She listened again, and then confirmed it—in less than a week, the national flags were destroyed, ripped beyond salvation by the ferocious winds of the Roaring Forties and of Cape Horn—one of the most extreme, desolate—and windy—places on earth.

Before leaving Patagonia, we sailed up the Beagle Channel to film and climb on some of the glaciers, which, even though receding due to global warming, are still some of the most impressive on earth. We sailed deep into a remote fjord, then hiked for about four hours though beaver bogs to the foot of the Holanda Glacier. In 1946 beavers were introduced to Patagonia from Canada (fun fact—by the bush plane-flying uncle of the editor of this book), in order to try to create a fur industry. The industry didn't take off, but the beavers did—propagating like crazy and turning thousands of acres of forest into damned up swampland. We were frequently up to our thighs in mud, and on at least one occasion had ours arms buried to the shoulder, searching for boots that got pulled from our feet by the sticky muck. Eventually, we made it to the spectacular blue glacier. Our guides were amazed how much it had receded since they had last seen it, but it was still an impressive sheet of ice. George and I strapped on our crampons and began climbing up the lower edges of it.

During the four years of filming *Angry Planet* I was often asked what was the most dangerous situation I had encountered on the series. I usually gave a flippant answer that the most dangerous part of the job was driving the thirty-five miles to the editing studio. The show's editor, Gary Vaughan, had his studio in Ajax, accessible only by driving on the 401—the massive (twenty-two lanes, at its widest) freeway that is considered the busiest highway in the world. I don't like the road, and so used to jest that driving on it during post-production was more dangerous than any hurricanes, wild animals, or volcanoes that I filmed during production.

166

The answer to that question changed in Patagonia. George led up the glacier, with me, delayed as usual by photo opportunities, maybe thirty paces behind him. At one point he slipped on a glare patch, and began sliding down the steep face of the glacier. I will always remember the sight of him, sliding out of control, the sharp points of his crampons aimed straight for me. We were on a ridge, with a giant crevasse immediately yawning down eighty foot deep beside me. If he had hit me, we both would have gone flying down into the crevasse. We had no ropes with us. The best we might have been able to hope for (assuming we survived the fall) would be that our skipper would have hiked the four hours back to the boat, got some ropes and snatch blocks, and been able and willing to hike back four more hours in the dark, to try to pull us out. It was an unpleasant scenario to consider.

The last thing you should do in a situation like that is to use your crampons to try to stop, for they are only likely to send you ass-over-teakettle on top of yourself. Fortunately, George knew that. Fortunately, we had filmed an episode on top of Mount Washington the previous January (with its claim of having "the world's worst weather" and for many years the highest wind speed ever recorded— 231 miles per hour). On his climb up the mountain on Tuckerman's Ravine, he had been well trained in the techniques of using an ice axe to make what mountaineers call a "self arrest". He used it here, finally came to a stop, and my heart stopped pounding.

We got into another weird, potentially dangerous situation while filming an episode about the monsoons of India. I had linked up with a terrific local line producer named Kartikeya Singh and the three of us were winging all over the sub-continent filming swollen rivers, washed out bridges, flooded streets and torrential rainstorms. We decided we wanted to film the 1017-foot high Dughsagar waterfall, which turns from a trickle to a torrent in the summer monsoon. We flew to Goa and then drove south towards the remote waterfall. En route we came upon a filming opportunity that you could only find in crazy India. A mahout was washing his elephant in a flooded stream by the side of the road. Never one to pass up local color, I filmed this for a while, then asked Kartikeya to ask the guy if George could participate. Without a good fixer you're out of luck in India. I certainly didn't speak this guy's tongue (there are over 400 languages in India), and I don't think even Kartikeya did, but he made himself understood, handed over a few rupees, and we had a new little sequence going. George, always game for a new experience, waded in to participate in the monsoon clean up, and eventually even climbed on the animal's back. The elephant got into the spirit of things too, sucked gallons of water up into its massive trunk, arching it back, and giving George a powerful shower.

At one point on the rapidly narrowing road to the falls, we needed to ford across a river. We were warned that we might have problems in the flooded monsoon conditions, and indeed, we discovered the river was running at high speed, two feet over the road, and impassable. We were about to turn back when we noticed a strange emergency unfolding out in the rapids. Out in the middle, a young guy seemed to be pinned against the trees by the force of the water. His friends, on shore, seemed to be laughing about it—and drunk—and it was unclear whether it was a real emergency, or a fake one. There seemed to be some indication, as well, that he was naked, and so was staying submerged more by false modesty than necessity. However, when one of his friends went out to try to help him, he himself was swept away down the rapids, never to be seen by me again—so it was beginning to appear more and more like a genuinely serious situation.

By now I had the camera on sticks and was filming the incident, and of course thinking of how I might integrate it into the storyline of the show. I looked over to George, hoping he might decide to volunteer to go out and help the guy. Perhaps it crossed his mind, for it would of course made for better television had our star saved the day, but instead I saw that he had pulled out another of our cameras and had begun shooting the drunkard in the rapids with it himself. In situations like these, you can't demand that other people risk their lives for a shot in a TV show. Incidents like this raise the question of how long you as a photographer can stay behind the camera and when one should forget photography and instead lend assistance. Over the years there have been many incidents where photographers have been censured for taking pictures rather than assisting people in trouble—one of the most notorious being the New York Post photographer who shot stills of a man pushed in front of a subway train, rather than try to help him. My experience is that these situations are complicated and confusing, and it is wrong to try to judge or second guess the actions of people in emergencies, without being there to witness all aspects of them.

In the end Kartikeya decided to strip down, wade out into the fast moving river, and throw the guy a ripped sari that he found on the bank and pull him to safety. All worked out well, the dazed guy lived to tell the tale, and unwittingly was seen around the world in a short sequence in our show. However, we still needed to get to the falls, so now commandeered three motorcycle riders to take us on a different set of paths up to some railway tracks, then walked for an hour carrying the camera gear through the pouring rain, with freight trains roaring past us. Only one motorcycle accident; my rider crashed into the rear of George's bike. Broken lights—no broken bones. By the time we completed the long, wet trek, our feet were covered with leeches—but our Indian hosts were prepared, pulling out little packets of salt to kill the blood-engorged critters, which quickly fell off us.

Eventually we made it to the falls, which performed admirably for us. I commented to Kartikeya how impressed I was with both the waterfalls, and all the sidebar adventures we had getting to them. He smiled and addressed my camera, saying, "India never disappoints."

A year later we had similarly nutty adventures filming the Catatumbo "Perpetual Lightning Storm" on Venezuela's Lake Maracaibo. This is a little known and seldom filmed phenomenon that we were keen to capture for the show. I don't pretend be an authority on the science behind it, but the theory seems to be that vast amounts of cool air swoop down from the Andes and mix with equally enormous quantities of methane gas, created by rotting plant matter in the huge, shallow lake, but somehow this gaseous mixture creates a situation where for 160 days of every year, for 10 hours a day and up to 280 times per hour—and for every single day during the fall period we were there, furious lightning storms break out over the lake. Amazingly, geophysicists claim that the vast amount of lightning on the lake is the world's biggest creator of tropospheric ozone—and makes a major contribution towards replenishing the massive hole in the ozone layer sitting over Antarctica—8000 miles away.

It was a major adventure getting out to the tiny villages built on stilts in the middle of the lake, where we could witness and film the perpetual lightning storm. En route we encountered two of the notorious aquatic creatures that are synonymous with the rivers and swamps of South America. First, we hunted for an anaconda—the world's biggest snake. We finally found one in the jungles of Los Llanos—a big female, about seventeen feet long, curled up in a thicket. It was so heavy that it took four guys to pick it up, with George taking the pointy end—grabbing it just behind its huge head, its mouth open and displaying its large, sharp—but non-venomous—fangs. We pulled it out into the open, inspected it, and released it. It smoothly swam past me and back to its home in the swampland.

We had less problem finding piranhas, for the notoriously ravenous fish seem to be common throughout the waterways and ponds of the Orinoco basin. Our theory was that the piranhas would not live up to their fearsome reputation. George and I swam in a remote pond filled with lots of the fish, with me filming him—and them—with a housed underwater camera. Foolish? Maybe—but we came out unscarred. They didn't eat us—but we did eat them. After swimming with the toothy critters, we threw lines hooked with rotten chicken into the pond, and pulled up enough for a fish fry. Verdict? Bony—but tasty.

Our destination for the lightning storm was the village of El Congo—a cockroach-infested community on stilts out in Lake

Maracaibo. There were once many of these marine communities in Venezuela—in fact they gave the country its name, for they reminded explorer Amerigo Vespucci of the city of Venice, so he called his discovery Venezuela—little Venice. It was a long ride by motorboat out to the tiny village. Venezuela is a remote country; Lake Maracaibo is in a remote part of Venezuela that few other Venezuelans visit, and El Congo is in a remote part of Lake Maracaibo. Families occupied most of the shacks in the village, except for one bachelor pad that doubled as a guesthouse for the very occasional visitor. It's no wonder this guy didn't have a wife. Of all the crappy third world bug-infested accommodations we used in the four years of filming our angry planet, this was the worst. Maybe second worst—a squalid Radio Moscow repeater station (also an all-male operation) in the middle of the Uzbekistan desert that offered us rusty uncovered bedsprings to sleep on and chipped unwashed cups of vodka to drink was also a contender for the title.

In the early evenings in El Congo, we'd comb through the nearby mangrove swamps in our boat, searching for and finding snakes hanging from the overhead branches. By 10 p.m. we had to be back at our aquatic abode, as the storms would start in earnest then, and continue through into the next day. The sky would light up with electricity, the winds would pick up, and the torrential rain would begin to pour down, making an insane din on the corrugated iron roofs. At one point during the worst of the storms, so much rain fell that it filled our large motorboat, and threatened to sink it. The wind was blowing the boat around so violently that no one could get to it to bail it, so our boat captain eventually stripped down, dove in the water, swam around to the other side of the boat, clambered in and began to furiously bail. They say there is no better bilge pump than a frightened man with a bucket—and this guy, shivering in the cold rain, proved it.

One of our wildest marine adventures began on frozen water—the ice of Frobisher Bay, in the Canadian Arctic. We were on a two-part journey—first using skis to traverse the ice, then dogsleds to cross the Akshayuk Pass in Auyuittuq National Park, through

171

Baffin Island. It was early March—still the dead of winter, and extremely cold, especially at night in the thin-walled tents we were using.

It wasn't my first time filming in the Arctic. In 2003 I had gone even further north to Igloolik to film with Zacharias Kunuk, the maker of the feature *Atanarjuat: The Fast Runner* for my feature doc *Popcorn With Maple Syrup*. I went far out on to the frozen Arctic by snowmobile with Zacharias and his Inuit filmmaking pals, and learned a couple of things about the North while out in the -40 temperatures (probably -60 with the wind chill). The first is that if you can use your boots or clothing in the South, they aren't warm enough for the Arctic. The second is that the Inuit take the cold very seriously. After dragging me in a komatik (sled) for miles behind a snowmobile while searching for seals, they stopped and found that I was very chilly. You might think they would just laugh at the dumb southerner not dressed properly for the conditions. They didn't. After briefly checking me out, they immediately told me they were going to build an igloo for me to warm up in. While they set to work building it, they told me I was to run around in large circles to try to get my blood moving again. It took fifteen minutes. I ran; they built. Once finished (it was actually a day shelter, half moon shaped, not a full igloo for overnight use), they carved out blocks of snow to serve as seats and a table, pulled out an ancient Coleman stove, and melted snow to make tea. That began to warm me up, and we kept going. They threw two caribou skins over me for the next part of the journey.

In Baffin Island, six years later, I was better equipped. Minus-100 Baffin Boots on my feet, the most heavy-duty polar parka that Canada Goose makes on my back. On my head, my ski helmet—and a good thing too, or you wouldn't be reading this. Travelling north from Pangnirtung, I picked up a father and son team of Inuit guides to allow me to film our dogsled teams from their snowmobiles. I filmed from the komatik that they towed behind the snow machine. At one point my driver lost control on the glare ice, spun out and the centrifugal force hurled me from the sled. I hit the ice head first, and went flying across the ice. My camera fell from my hands and slid another forty feet from me. Dazed, I got up and went to retrieve the camera. The footage still exists of my walk to it, as even though the camera got a little dinged and dented, it kept running (and still runs today). Good ol' Sony. In 1957, I bought their very first product (a baby-blue, nine-volt six-transistor AM radio), and I've stuck with them ever since.

Once I got the camera turned off, I turned my attention to myself. No broken bones, it seemed, but when I took off my helmet, I discovered a big chip out of the top of it. Presumably had I not been wearing it, that chip would have been taken out of my skull. And then, hey—you'd be doing something boring right now, like reading Quentin Tarantino's memoirs, instead of mine.

One really strange aspect of filming on frozen Frobisher Bay was that, as the bay has an extreme seventeen-foot tidal range, at low tide we were standing on a thick sheet of ice sitting unsupported by the ocean, with fifteen or so feet of air beneath us. It was a freaky thought. Just as freaky, once we got into the Akshayuk Pass, was the fast moving river we were travelling on. Sometimes I would get my guides to drop me off and ask them to go on far ahead and conceal themselves and turn off their machines, so that I could record clean sound. I would set up my camera on the magnificent landscape, all alone, with the Inuit guides far ahead and the dogsled team far behind. I would be standing on the frozen river, in the shadow of towering Mount Asgard, the site of the famous Union Jack parachute ski stunt that opens the Bond film *The Spy Who Loved Me*. I could see for miles down the pristine pass, and there was utter silence. Except…for the gurgling of the white water river below me. The ice was holding my weight—but it wasn't solid. If it ever cracked, I too would need some fancy geegaw from Q to save my life.

Under the extraordinary northern lights, we camped in the frigid temperatures every night. I had a little dynamo operated shortwave radio with me. One night I wound it up and brought in Radio Canada's northern service. At the end of their news broadcast was one of those oddball items that editors like to end the news with describing a brand new island in the Tonga archipelago that had just been created by an exploding undersea volcano. I told George the news. He was as excited as I was, and I know wanted to jump on to a laptop for more details—except that the nearest Wi-Fi connection was a hundred miles away. We had long had an ambition to be among the first to step on "the newest land on earth", wherever that might present itself. When another new island had been created in the South Pacific a year earlier, I had gone so far as to charter us a yacht to sail to it. That island had unfortunately slid back under the waves. This one might not last long either—but we couldn't do much about it right now. We were on the other side of the world, with only dogsleds for transportation.

On our last night in Auyuittuq, we were camped at the very appropriately named Windy Lake. In the middle of the night a massive storm came up, ripping all the carefully set guys out of the ice, and blowing down all the tents. George and our expedition companions ended up in a tiny extreme emergency shelter, while I bunked in with our Inuit guides, who had sensibly found a heated wooden hut to sleep in. The next morning we searched unsuccessfully for one of our guide's sleeping bag, which was completely blown away by the storm. (See, my concerns about being blown into a volcano—as related in Chapter One—weren't so irrational, after all). Helped along by the fierce tailwinds, we hiked out, flew out, re-grouped in the South. I logged all our Arctic footage, handed it over to our editor, and within two weeks, we were on a plane headed for the South Pacific.

Of course, getting to the brand new piece of planet earth was far from simple. I was able to find and charter a skipper by phone and email who agreed to take us from Tonga's capital, Nuku'alofa, to seventy miles out to the remote new island. It was impossible to find out if he knew what he was doing or if the boat was seaworthy, but he did agree to try to get us there.

We flew first to New Zealand. Given the last minute nature of the planning for this film, we did not have a carnet for the equipment. After a twenty-seven hour flight to Auckland, we got off the plane to find the New Zealanders demanding a $30,000 cash bond for the equipment. This idea—that people would fly half way around the world in order to sell their used camera equipment to the locals, thus screwing the government of their import duties, is, in our current age of the internet, eBay, international mail order suppliers, and free trade, a completely stupid and archaic concept. In my experience, the only two countries that continue with the 1950s absurdity of bonds and carnets are the United States and New Zealand. Unfortunately, they were the two countries we needed to pass through in order to get to Tonga. I rustled up the $30,000 for the bond, and they gave us our equipment back. Next problem…

The next problem is we found there was a typhoon blowing through Tonga. Now normally, on a show called *Angry Planet*, that would be considered good news. In this case, though, we wanted to film the newest land on earth, not a typhoon. It was very unlikely we could film both, because even if we could fly into the island at this point (doubtful), we almost certainly wouldn't be able to put to sea in a small fishing boat. We waited in New Zealand, instead, for the typhoon to pass. We filmed a couple of New Zealand volcanoes. White Island, a few miles off shore on the easy coast, was quite spectacular. Mount Ruapehu in Tongariro, at the bottom of the North Island, fortunately, was not. When it gets spectacular, it tends to also get deadly, throwing lava bombs all over the roads, destroying the ski resorts on its flanks, burning down the towns and killing people. We didn't need that. We did, however, film a cool sidebar story, rappelling fifty meters down into a cave system, to see if I could get an image of a cave lit only by the thousands of glow worms that hang from its roof. Verdict—stills, yes; video, no. Very impressive sight, though, and an exciting sequence of George traversing the underground rivers and waterfalls.

Finally, the storm abated, and we flew to Tonga, arriving at two in the morning. The skipper was to meet us at the airport. He wasn't there. He didn't answer his phone. By three o'clock, the officials told us we had to wait outside, then locked up their airport, and went home. Finally, at four o'clock, he breezed in. Sorry he's late, he told us. He was busy. O-kaay. Who's busy at three in the morning? But we didn't push it. He drove us across the island to his boat. Ninety percent of Tongans are overweight, with more than 60% considered obese—the highest percentage in the world. I was glad to see that our skipper was part of the 10% minority. He looked quite fit—and so did his small crew, once we met them at the boat. On the drive across the island, the radio played *My Heart Will Go On*, the theme song of *Titanic*, sung in Tongan by a local Céline Dion wannabe. I didn't want to take it as an omen, but as our sea cruise would begin at daybreak, it was hard not to think of it as one.

The boat was a rusty old Hawaiian fishing boat, transformed into a local harbour booze-cruise party boat. I wouldn't want to try a circumnavigation in it, but it looked like we might make it out to the new island of Hunga Ha'apai and back. Regardless, there were no alternatives, so off we went. Once we got outside the harbour, we immediately discovered that while the typhoon was over, the seas were still unsettled. We'd be rocking and rolling all the way to the new island. George immediately took what he calls his "normal seafaring position"—face down on a bunk, wishing he weren't there.

After about an hour, I heard the engine sound change, and went to investigate. One of the two engines had stopped working. There seemed to be little we could do about it, so we continued, at two-thirds speed, on one. Now, we'd be lucky to get there by dusk. An hour later, the skipper called the Tongan coast guard to report our voyage. They came back with a new rule they claimed to have just instituted—the new island was considered off limits. We were not to go there. I began to see this long, expensive, and complicated trip ending in disaster. My skipper signed off with them, and then, seeing my long face, reassured me. The Coast Guard would never know where we were, he told me. We kept going.

Their news did seem to indicate we wouldn't have any competition at the newly minted island. We weren't going to be the first to visit—we'd already heard that three others had set foot on it—but we would be numbers four and five—still pretty good. One of the first three, apparently, was an extreme golfer, who'd fired off some balls from the new volcanic fairway. I understood the goofy passion, being a bit of an extreme golfer myself. I have golfed at midnight in the Yukon, inside a volcanic crater in Iceland, on the world's most southerly golf course in South America, and likely the most northerly one in Greenland, in the immediate ragged aftermath of a hurricane in Jamaica, and on a war-ravaged course in Rwanda, with only one flag left, and an extra caddy to run it forward from one hole to the next. But I wasn't going to waste time golfing on this spot. We had a film to make—and not much time to make it in. The island might sink back into the sea at any minute—and so, it seemed, might the boat we were on. I returned to the cabin to find all the floorboards up, and one of the crew down in the deep bilge, sloshing around in two feet of water, and handing up bucketfuls of it to be thrown over the side. I'm not sure that anyone knew what the problem was, but the intermittent bailing continued for the rest of the trip.

Not wanting to think too deeply about the whole issue of the fact that the ship was sinking, I returned to the stern, where I discovered that the painter towing the motorboat we'd be using to get in to the island had severed. The little boat was still visible, but now bobbing far behind us. I returned to tell this news to the captain, who spun the boat around, and we steamed back to get it. After a lengthy delay we got it re-attached to the boat, with a somewhat stronger line, and the decision was made to put the youngest crew member in the dinghy, "for safety". He climbed in, and we cranked up and got back on course. It was an idiotic, pointless, and dangerous thing to do, but I wasn't going to argue it. The kid could easily have lost his life, but in the end, other than being baked, unprotected in the hot sun for six hours, he came out unscathed.

Unlike George. I rousted him up to do some filming on the top deck. As we were shooting the boat lurched badly and he crashed off his seat, striking his head on some sharp edged part of the boat that shouldn't have been there. A fraction of an inch lower and he would have taken his eye out. Thank God, it was instead only a blow to his temple. There was blood streaming down across his face, but that always adds a little *je ne sais quoi* to an adventure TV show. He patched himself up, and we carried on.

The island finally showed in the distance, and after a couple of more hours steaming towards it, we arrived beside it. Sure enough, it was there in front of our eyes, but not on either the electronic or paper charts in front of us. We had a few more issues before getting to our destination. The first was not unexpected. Being a brand new island in the middle of the Pacific, there was no shallow water around it to anchor in. We searched around for some for a short while, but the depth sounder gave us nothing but 2000-meter soundings, so the captain decided he'd just have to bob around off the island while we went in to film it.

The second issue probably shouldn't have been unexpected either. Why is it that with all the improvements made in technology in the last fifty years—the wildly improved autos, airplanes, and appliances, snowmobiles and helicopters, and everything else, outboard motors still act like the ones I remember from 1957? Of course, they couldn't get the damn outboard started. Naturally, we had to wait around for another half an hour while they fussed around with it. Finally it coughed into life, and we headed in to the newest beach in the world.

Only one more mishap to go—this one, a biggie. Once we got close to the beach, we discovered the surf was too high to risk going in with the boat. The crewman running the motorboat told us we'd have to swim through the surf to shore. He got no argument from me. If we had ever capsized the motorboat, we would have had a serious disaster on our hands. We (or our bones) might still be there today. In any case, I was ready for it. I was wearing a bathing suit, and my cameras were in bulletproof, leak-proof Pelican cases. George, on the other hand, was wearing his on-camera duds, and his still camera and microphone and other bits and pieces were in a large "waterproof" backpack. Now those bags are waterproof when you buy them, and continue to be waterproof if only used on your back or the bottom of a canoe. Airport baggage carousels are not so good for them—and his had gone through a few of those. Somewhere along the line, it had picked up a few tiny rips and holes, almost invisible to the eye, but not to the ocean. George striped down to his underwear, put his *Angry Planet* hosting outfit into the bag, and jumped in. I followed, with my cases. We both swam through the surf, and stepped on to—the newest land on earth!

That was a high, immediately followed by a low, as he opened his bag to find his clothes soaked, and his camera and our radio microphone ruined. Okay, Plan B. He's going to be doing his stand-ups in a Tongan life jacket, and Stanfield's gotch. There won't be any stills. As for audio—well, we'll figure something out. I had some backup gear in my case. Let's go explore this island. You never know—it might start exploding again. The fresh lava was still warm, and we soon found a large inland pond of water too hot to touch. The sun was going down. We had to move fast. Even in his crazy get up, and with all our setbacks, George as usual came through in the crunch and did some great bits to camera. I got some good shots of the island, and we were done. We returned to the beach, and waved to the distant motorboat crew to come in to get us. They came in close, and shouted to us that they wanted us to come out one at a time. Understood. They didn't want to get caught broadside by the surf while fussing about pulling two swimmers and all the gear into the boat.

George went first. I volunteered to stay behind. You can always use another shot of "the island sun setting in the west", as the old travelogues used to call it, and I wanted some shots of him swimming away from the island, in case they proved useful in the cutting room. He swam out, and they came in and, with some difficulty, helped him board. I quickly threw my gear in the cases, jumped in, and began to swim out towards them. They gunned the engine to get out of the surf line, and it promptly...died. Of course, they began yanking on the damn starter cord, and of course, it wouldn't start. "Probably flooded," as everybody always says in these all-too-frequent occasions.

As they yanked away, they began drifting away from me. It was then I discovered that, as I had suspected, there was a rip tide running past the island. Only trouble was, it was taking me, mostly submerged in the water, in one direction, and them, sitting on top of it, in another. To be more specific, they were headed for Fiji (400 miles to the southwest), whereas I was headed for the Wallis & Futuna Islands (500 miles to the northwest). Now maybe our mothership might have picked us both up, once we drifted further offshore—except for the fact that it was now really starting to get dark. Would they be able to find us? As I drifted away from the island, as the "motor" boat drifted further and further away from me, as the sky continued to darken, I began thinking about...sharks. Tonga is famous for its substantial shark population. Sharks like to feed at dusk. Sharks are attracted by noises, such as—oh, say, volcanic explosions. Oh, and, perhaps—guys trying to start outboard motors. Well, you know the end to this story, so we won't prolong it any further. There perhaps were sharks, but I didn't see them—and there were certainly no shark bites. My boatmen finally got the motor going, came in, searched in the dark for me, finally found me, pulled me in, and we eventually made it back to Nuku'alofa, back to New Zealand, back home, with another show in the can. It had been an adventure, but not our craziest marine accomplishment. That would, instead, be the traverse of Dominica's Boiling Lake.

Tony Hall, who you met in Chapter Three, when he co-produced my first feature, and again at the beginning of this chapter, when he filmed with me in Haiti and on the stormy Atlantic, and produced my film *Horse Latitudes,* moved on to become a prominent Production Designer, art directing all kinds of major features through the eighties and nineties. He never really loved the film business, though, and by the mid-nineties, he gave it all up, moved to a remote corner of the most remote and wild island in the Caribbean, Dominica, where he designed and built a boutique hotel called

Zandoli Inn. He also smoked a lot of Gauloise cigarettes, and after smoking one too many, one Saturday night at his hotel, he had a heart attack. His wife Linda Hyland tried to drive him through the mountains to the hospital, but she got trapped behind a drunk driver who was driving very slowly so that he didn't crash off a cliff, and by the time she got him there, Tony was dead. I went down to give a eulogy at the funeral, and while there learned about this wild volcanic feature—a lake of violently boiling water on top of a volcano deep in the middle of the island.

Years later, I considered the idea of visiting the boiling lake for *Angry Planet*, and proposed the story to our network boss, Patrice Baillargeon, who loved it, and to George, who topped it. Instead of just climbing to the lake, and filming it, he proposed that we shoot him making the first ever traverse of the lake on a rope. It was a grand idea, and one that would take a bit of planning. Following our expedition rounding Cape Horn, the pair of us made a circuitous journey through Buenos Aires and Miami and San Juan to Dominica, where we went to Tony's old hotel to organize a climb (a "recce", as the Brits and South Africans call it) to the lake, and to enlist Linda's help in introducing us to the various government ministers who might be able to give us permission for the wacky stunt. All worked out well, and we organized to come back a few months later to do the shoot.

We enlisted the help of a professional rigger and before returning to Dominica first went out to the Canadian Rockies to get training and equipment advice from him. He turned out to be a great guy who sold us all the climbing rope, wire slings, pad eyes, turnbuckles, prusiks, and ring clutches we'd need, and then set it all up, stringing it across Johnson Canyon outside of Canmore, Alberta, and getting George to try it out. The rigger impressed us so much we thought we would take him with us down to Dominica, but then— another heart attack. He died, too, and so we were on our own. Fortunately George is a fast learner, and he felt confident with the advice and information he had gleaned from our training trip. He went off to his day job as an Oklahoma tornado-chasing tour guide, and I returned to Toronto to set up the rest of the shoot with our guides, riggers, and the permit-issuing government officials in Dominica.

The Caribbean and Latin America always get a bad rap as being inefficient, lazy places—the land of mañana. My experience is mostly quite the opposite. Two quick examples. In 1983, I singlehanded my sailboat from Nassau back to the US. In the middle of the Great Bahama Bank, a steering ram snapped on my autopilot. It was an essential part, and I was a bit devastated by its failure. I self-steered the boat through the night and went in to Bimini soon after daybreak, fully expecting, on a Sunday morning, that everything would be closed, no one would be able to help, the obscure part would be almost certainly unavailable, and I'd probably have to hand steer across the Gulf Stream to West Palm Beach to replace it. But I asked around, and the local mechanic at the reverse-osmosis desalination plant was rousted out of bed, and offered to come in and meet me at his shop, where he proceeded to skillfully fabricate on a lathe and milling machine a replacement part which worked better than the original. No charge—just helping out. Within four hours I was on my way. Would that happen on the mainland? I don't think so.

Second story. While we were surveying the volcanoes of Dominica with Linda Hyland, our rental car suddenly developed a horrible whine. It was 5:55 p.m. on a Friday—a bad time for a car problem. The car rental company was at the other end of the island, closing in five minutes. We called them—they instantly diagnosed it as a likely brake problem—and since they couldn't give immediate help themselves, they directed us to a garage that they hoped could. We whined our way there—again, closing time, the workers already washing up and changing into street clothes. In most shops in North America or Europe, they'd have told you to come back Monday. There, the dreadlocked mechanics put their work clothes back on, quickly pulled the wheels off with a smile, confirmed that brakes were the problem, pulled replacements from the shelves, and had us out of there, humming, by 6:30. Again—no charge. They'd sort things out later with the car rental company, they told us. It was quite amazing service.

So I was sanguine about the local assistance we would get on the difficult shoot, and I was not disappointed. There were a few documents and indemnities to be gotten through, but generally the local bureaucrats were completely helpful, and a group of local riggers and guides calling themselves Extreme Dominica proved themselves totally up for the extreme challenge.

There was another dilemma we had to figure out. How were we going to get the rope across the lake, in order to rig it on the other side? I brought another storm-chasing adventurer named Mark Robinson on to shoot second camera at the boiling lake, and the two of us experimented with using a high-powered bow to fire a line that would pull the rope over the lake. It seemed to work, so we added it to the growing collection of rigging gear, ropes, and tools, packed everything up with an array of cameras, and headed back down to Dominica. There were a few adventures getting a bow and set of arrows through American customs during their famous "War on Terror", but we won't get bogged down in details.

Commandeering an army of porters, guides, and riggers, we climbed through the Valley of Desolation to the top of the mountain and the boiling lake. It was a four-day task, with the first two getting to the summit, setting up our camp, anchoring and setting up the complex rigging system, and triple-testing it with heavy bags of rocks before George went out on it.

Camping on top of the rugged volcano was difficult. There were almost no flat spaces, so I brought only one tent, to store the camera equipment in and to keep it dry at night. For all of us, I brought a new kind of hammock that is completely enclosed by mosquito netting and a rain fly. We rigged them in the trees that grew from the volcanic rock. They proved to be unsuccessful. It poured with rain every night, and they all seemed to develop leaks. Mark's somehow ripped in half, dumping him unceremoniously on the mud below in the middle of the night—amusing for the rest of us, less so for him. I found mine uncomfortably claustrophobic, so ended up lying on the ground beneath it for the first night, squeezed in with the gear in the camera tent for the rest. It was probably while lying on that ground that first night, unprotected, that I was bitten by the mosquito that gave me dengue fever.

Once we had everything prepared, we didn't want to wait. Volcanoes produce sulfur dioxide and hydrogen sulfide gases, which combine with water vapour to produce sulfhydric acid. Nobody really thought in the short term the acid would weaken and degrade the Kevlar ropes we had stretched across the lake, but nobody really knew—and nobody wanted to risk it. It was time for George to step up, and step up he did. The rest of us had played our secondary roles in this drama, and would continue to, filming his traverse, and muscling him across into the cauldron, and back. It was now time for the featured attraction to take center stage. It was extremely dangerous; he knew it, and nonetheless, he did it.

Not only did it, but did it with style, and courage. Hemingway defined courage as "grace under pressure"—and George certainly exhibited that. Not just style and cool in the bits he would do to my camera, while hanging above the deadly, lake (boiling a bag of eggs in the water!), but class before and after, in the way he would deal with everyone who had participated in their minor way in his adventure. Never the diva, never the prima donna, never the privileged, demanding SOB that the television camera turns so many people into. I lucked into a good one, this time.

It wasn't, of course, the first time I'd dealt with showbiz personalities. It wasn't even the first time I'd dealt with death defying highwire performers. Eight years earlier, I made a film about the amazing tightrope walker and aerialist Jay Cochrane. I was totally lucky to be able to climb to a slender tower atop the Niagara Falls casino, alone, the only other person up there being Jay, walking towards me on a tightwire, with hundreds of people watching him from the streets below. A few weeks later, though, I was at the Georgia State Fair, filming him doing another wire walk. This time I had a Chicago-based cameraman named Max Miller shooting with me. Following the wire walk we set up a scene filming Jay as he walked through the fair. Now, both Jay and Max were great, but neither was what anyone would call easygoing. Max didn't take guff from anyone (not even fellow Chicagoan Oprah, with whom he'd had, apparently, one or two differences of opinions over the years). Jay was walking too fast. Max asked him to slow down. Jay flew into a rage, and stomped off in a huff. Suddenly, as director, I had to go into damage-control mode, trying to patch our shoot back together.

Now, I believe that when someone has just risked his life crossing a highwire, or is about to perform live in front of two million people, you should cut them a lot of slack. That stuff ain't easy. My point, though, is that George didn't require any mollycoddling—and I found that admirable. He'd just crossed a boiling lake (or, on other occasions, wrestled an alligator, rappelled down a waterfall or navigated past a tornado). He didn't see that as a reason to engender a sense of entitlement, to lord it over others, or to fly off the handle.

There was no time to dwell on that then. Another storm was coming in, and we'd all had enough of breathing sulfur dioxide fumes and sleeping rough on top of the volcano. We were planning to stay another night, but we all agreed—let's get out of here. We all went into high gear, dismantling the rigging, packing up the camp and kitchen and cameras, and preparing to leave the rugged mountaintop. Unfortunately, we were carrying more weight down the hill than we had carried up. Our long ropes were now all soaking wet—and so weighed perhaps three times as much as they did dry. Our porters now struggled with very heavy loads, as we descended the slippery volcano, in the rain. My own load—the precious camera and even more precious shot tape from the shoot—hadn't got heavier, but it felt that it had, as I was starting to weaken from the dengue fever that was beginning to course through my body. I wasn't the only one. Most of our Dominican assistants charged on ahead of us down the mountain, planning to try to come back up (another four-hour climb) before nightfall, to bring down the rest of our gear. One of them, though, collapsed at the bottom, and had to be taken to hospital. Perhaps he too had been bitten by a dengue mosquito—I never found out. I did give him my rain jacket before leaving the island as minor compensation for his misfortune, as I knew he had been lusting after it all through the shoot, and I also knew my next major shoot would be in Death Valley. I wouldn't need a rain jacket there.

We couldn't make it down the mountain before nightfall. As darkness fell, our guide told us of an emergency shelter the government had built on the trail. We headed for it in the pelting rain, and spent the night there. Not the most comfortable spot, but we couldn't complain, after we discovered what happened to our favorite number two guide. He had made it to the bottom with his extremely heavy load, returned to the top to pick up another, and during his second descent been caught in the pitch black darkness and rain, and had to sleep unprotected on the side of the steep hill in his t-shirt and shorts, rain pouring down on him, his machete driven into ground as a pillow to sleep against, to prevent him rolling away down the slippery slope into the volcanic valley in the middle of the night. Think about that next time you're considering complaining about the thread count of your hotel room sheets.

By the time I was at the bottom I was in full dengue fever sweats. I thought perhaps I could get a volcanic cure, and so headed for a hot sulfur spring spa. Worked wonderfully for half an hour, then the fevers were back. Not good. I had organized a follow-up session to shoot before we left the Caribbean. Every summer in late July whale sharks (the biggest fish in the world) show up in large numbers in the waters of Holbox Island—a Mexican island off the Yucatán peninsula. They only stay for two weeks, then disappear for another year. The timing was perfect, and I had chartered a boat to take us out to film them. Now, I was in bad shape. My partner was still good—although he too had been bitten, and would eventually succumb himself.

We flew out of Dominica and island hopped back to Florida. From there, I dragged my sorry ass down to Cancun, and then, lurching in and out of consciousness, I was driven across the Yucatán, bundled on to a ferry boat, then into a golf cart and into a tiny three-room Holbox Island hostel. I promptly fell into bed. Fortunately, there were two beds in the room. Once the sheets in one were soaked through with my feverish sweat, I would laboriously make the big two-foot move to the other, using it until it was soaked, then flop back into the first. A day passed, then a fitful night. The next morning, my show host banged on my door. Ready to go film the big fish? I shook my head—impossible. I sent him off to check out the whale shark operation on his own, asking him on his way to send up the hotel manager to look into my health. We filmed for just under four hundred days on *Angry Planet*; this was the only day I had to beg off.

There was one young doctor running a tiny clinic on the remote island. The hotel manager, a wildly eccentric and funny character—but also a very efficient one, rolled me into his golf cart and took me to see her. At the miniscule Mexican clinic I again got a taste of the efficiency of the distinctly non-mañana Caribbean. Concerned that I might have malaria, she took a blood sample. She told me she'd have an answer for me that afternoon, and sent me back to the hotel, to sleep. She then organized to get the blood sample to the ferry dock, by boat to the mainland, somehow overland the sixty miles of dirt road to Cancun, into a laboratory, in for analysis, and then the results gotten to her some way or another. While the vial of blood was making its convoluted journey, I was back in my twin beds, sweating out the toxins. Late that afternoon, she made a personal visit to the little hostel, with good news. I did not have malaria. Instead, she told me, I possibly had dengue fever. She handed me a vial of Tylenol, and told me a major dose of the drug would probably be a big help. What she did not hand me was a bill. The Mexican healthcare system would cover the expenses, she told me. Imagine the bill I would have received for that kind of service had I asked for it in Florida, instead of Mexico. As she left, George arrived, returning from his day with the whale sharks. You've got to get better, he told me. The sharks are incredible—thirty-five footers, ready to be filmed.

So I popped Tylenol through the night and by the next morning seemed much improved. I certainly wasn't a hundred percent, but I was good enough to go out diving and filming with the sharks. Or so I thought. We took a long boat ride out in the Mexican waters, searching for the big fish, who like to cruise just below the surface, their dorsal fin cresting the light waves. With them, frequently, were massive manta rays, flying through the water like Klingon battleships on the wingtips of the Starship Enterprise.

Once we found them, the boat would motor directly ahead and then George and I would leap into the water and I'd begin filming them, and him. They are slow moving fish, so with some strong swimming you can just keep up with them. I had a couple of reasonably good encounters with the huge fish, but on one, my fever-muddled brain didn't react as quickly as it needed to. The shark was heading straight at me. I had eye contact with it, and remember dumbly thinking it was going to veer right. So I moved left, and so did it. The twenty-ton giant seemed to try to make a last minute correction to avoid the moron it was about to bump into, but it was too late. It crashed into me, and I bounced off its mouth, head, and pectoral fin. As it swam away I saw it turn back to glance at me with what looked like disapproval, shake its head in disbelief at the dumb creatures it has to contend with, and swim off.

After the traumatic event, my health started to improve, just as George, apparently also bitten in Dominica, began to come down with a worse case than I had of the disease. Back in Toronto, he was in and out of the Tropical Disease Clinic several times, trying to kick the debilitating effects of it. Unfortunately, though, we had another shoot booked to begin only six days after returning from Mexico. I had long wanted to film an episode contrasting the hottest and coldest places in North America—Death Valley, California in July, and the Yukon in February. We were going to focus the show on extreme athletes—runners participating in ultra-marathons through the desert heat and the winter cold.

In order to get out to the Kiehl's Badwater Ultramarathon, in which several hundred über-athletes run (or stagger) from the lowest spot in America, Badwater, through Death Valley and up the slopes of Mount Whitney through the scorching 120° F heat (49° C), we first had to fly into Las Vegas. We were quite a pair, sitting forlornly on the side of an empty baggage carousel, waiting for our missing film gear, sweat dripping from our faces as we shivered uncontrollably in the over air-conditioned, neon lit, garish gambling hall that is Las Vegas airport.

Maybe the dry, scorching conditions of Death Valley burnt the virus out of us. It was no picnic for the first few days, but slowly we began to return to good health—unlike some of the road warriors we were filming, many of whom fell to the wayside with dehydration and exhaustion.

Six months later, we were back on the water—the frozen water of the Yukon River, filming another group of crazies running the 300-mile 2008 Yukon Gold Ultra (some skiing, some snowshoeing—your choice of weapon—run what you brung, as they say in Baja auto racing). This time we were both healthy and well dressed for it—good thing, too, as it was -50° for the start. We all had to wait until the temperature rose to -40° before it was felt to be safe enough for George to wave the starter's flag and send the athletes out on to the trail. We followed them as they forged their way north along the river and through the woods towards Dawson. By the first night we were filming dropouts and casualties—including a pair of crack British SAS paratroopers who couldn't handle the extreme Yukon cold. By the end of the 300-mile race, all but two had dropped out. The eventual winner was a forty-eight-year-old woman from Colorado named Diane Van Deren. A decade earlier she had had a lobectomy (removal of a lobe of the brain) to prevent epileptic seizures, and was left with an inability to judge the passing of time, which curiously aided her long-distance endurance. We left them after a few days to film another ultramarathon happening at the same coldest week of the year—the Yukon Quest 1000 Mile International Sled Dog Race. We returned to search for the remaining contestants in the Yukon Gold a week later. We found Van Deren still out on the cold trail near the village of Carcross. Sleep deprived and frost chilled, she looked like she had aged ten years in the brutal contest.

Chapter 5
Ripped From the Headlines

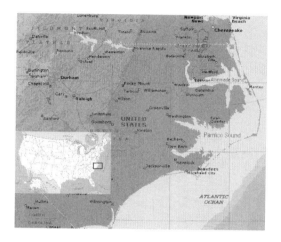

Concurrently with the production of my marine adventure films, I was, from time to time, making films that were either investigative, or dramas ripped from the day's headlines, or else docs and dramas that for one reason or another were themselves *making* headlines. The first of these was a film called *Backlot Canadiana* that I made for CBC. Throughout the sixties and seventies I began to be intrigued by the many references I found to Canada in Hollywood films of the thirties, forties and fifties. I began compiling all these dozens and dozens of weird, oblique references to Canada on little typewritten file cards. Eventually I began investigating and discovered that the reason for all this Canadiana was a program set up in Hollywood in the late forties to attempt to thwart the development of an indigenous Canadian film industry. Called the Canadian Cooperation Project, the plan was an agreement between the Motion Picture Producers Association and the Canadian government, whereby the Hollywood studios agreed to insert references to Canada into American movies, in return for an agreement that the Canadian government would drop their proposed legislation supporting indigenous Canadian feature film production.

After uncovering the story, I got the support of CBC to turn it into a film, and went off to New York and Los Angeles to interview the retired engineers of this nutty scheme. I cut these together with examples of these politically inspired bits of screenwriting. One of the favorites was Jimmy Stewart, from the 1952 western *Bend of the River*, telling co-star Arthur Kennedy, for no apparent reason, that the birds flying overhead were "red-winged orioles…from Canada" "Yeah", Kennedy agrees (just in case the audience missed Stewart's identification of their homeland), "From Canada."

Backlot Canadiana caused a bit of a stir. The early seventies was a period of active nationalism, and many of us were actively campaigning for a screen quota system similar to those existing in European countries, and similar to the one that had been already instituted in Canada for television and radio. My film, chronicling an earlier failure of will to attempt to get Canadian films into Canadian theaters, struck a nerve, and kept the dialogue going. In the end, though, it had little effect. The theater chains, then fully owned by American and British studios, fiercely fought the government on any proposed quotas or levies, and they never were instituted.

There was another weird controversy regarding the little film. Another Canadian cultural icon got his nose knocked out of joint by our production. Pierre Berton was a celebrated and very prolific writer, newspaper columnist, television and radio personality, and producer with big shows on both CBC and CTV, as well as a radio talk show and various other ventures. Unknown by me or by CBC, as I was making my film, Berton was researching and writing a book on the same subject. He called his *Hollywood's Canada*. I'm not sure whether it was the fact that I had scooped him with my discovery and interview of the Canadian Cooperation Project founders that bugged him, or whether it was that my film meant he was not going to be able to sell the television rights to his

192

book, but he let the network brass know that he was not pleased. He demanded to see the film before it was aired, and so a special screening was set up—just him and me in a screening room. He was obviously not happy that I'd made the film, but in the end couldn't find fault with it, so he just harrumphed about the Jimmy Stewart clip. Along with his many other skills and interests, he was a expert birdwatcher, and so sniffed that *Bend of the River* screenwriter Borden Chase had called the bird a "red-winged oriole", rather than the correct "red-winged blackbird".

Borden Chase had more pressing issues than ornithology to deal with. His career as a Hollywood screenwriter began with a cinematic re-telling of his career as a goon and getaway driver for Brooklyn gangster Frankie Yale. A major league tough guy, Chase barely escaped the hot lead as his boss Yale was rubbed out in a gangland shootout by rival mobster Al Capone. He ended up, after writing a string of gangster flicks and western gunplays, on the board of the ultra right-wing Motion Picture Alliance for the Preservation of American Ideals, ratting on fellow screenwriters. Is it any wonder he wasn't cross-examined in story meetings too closely on his choice of bird names?

The next controversy I got involved in was a good deal more serious. The political struggle to get a theatrical film quota going was heating up, and got me connected with a very political and pugnacious filmmaker named Peter Pearson. Peter, a relative of former Prime Minister Lester Pearson, ran at least three major organizations—the Council of Canadian Filmmakers, the Directors Guild of Canada, and most importantly, the Broadcast Fund of Telefilm Canada. In 1978 he got an opportunity to take on the Alberta government and their development of the Athabasca Tar Sands. He brought me on to write the script for the drama with him and Producer Ralph Thomas, and to work as Second Unit Director on the show. The controversy over the oil sands in those days was not, as it is today, about the environmental impact of the massive development, but rather over political questions about whether

Canadians and Albertans had been ripped off by the oil companies (and their partner, the Alberta government).

It was a difficult, complicated script to write, and we ended up trying to make the story understandable to the audience by consolidating numerous players in the story into single, fictitious characters, and creating cabinet room and boardroom dialogue that was, by necessity, invented. The film also tended to diminish the role and image of Alberta Premier Peter Lougheed. He was a colossus of Alberta politics, much loved by many in the province from his early days as a quarterback for the Edmonton Eskimos to his powerful stand against Pierre Trudeau and his National Energy Policy. The westerners did not take kindly to a bunch of eastern filmmakers lifting the curtains on the backstage machinations of Alberta oil and politics. Even the guy who commissioned the film, dyspeptic CBC drama boss John Hirsch (himself a westerner from Winnipeg, though born in western Hungary) disowned the film. This is how director Peter Pearson remembers Hirsch's response to the rough cut:

"Peetaire, I hate telling you dis," he said, delighted at telling me this, "but you haff no firkin' talent. Dis piece of shee-it should be flushed down the toilet. You cunt write, cunt direct, cunt cast, cunt anytink."

This absurd outburst shows one example of why many of us in the film and television community felt little of the adoration that members of the theater community had for the dour Hungarian.

Once our film was aired, the CBC's disclaimer about the fictional composite aspects of the script was not enough to prevent Lougheed from suing for defamation of character. The law suit named Peter Pearson, Ralph Thomas, and me, along with the CBC itself. The network's lawyers handled the defense for the three of us, but in the end the judge ruled in favor of the Alberta Premier. He won the case, received one dollar in damages, plus $82,000 in court costs, which the Canadian taxpayers ended up paying (so every

Albertan had to pay for their Premier's petty vendetta), and an agreement from CBC that they would never air the film again.

Through the 1970s a number of big city newspapers closed across Canada, and, with suspicions of collusion between the big ownership chains when two papers owned by competitors closed the same day, a CBC producer named Sam Levene decided to make a drama based on the event. I was brought on as director, and *Final Edition* turned into a sweet shoot, with an excellent cast, that ultimately received good reviews and got great numbers. That led to a TV feature I did with Sam called *Takeover*, and *that* led to my directing the first three episodes of a series based on the characters and situations in the film, called *Vanderberg*.

Final Edition and *Takeover* combined forces to create an interesting moment for me that was more an *Adventure in Filmscreening* than an *Adventure in Filmmaking*. The fee I received for directing the newspaper film was burning a hole in my pocket, so I decided, after many years of sailing other people's boats, to go out and buy my own. I got a ten-year-old twenty-four foot boat, fixed it up, and renamed it. At the time that I bought it, it was stuck with the lame moniker *Gloria Too*—named after the *ex*-wife of the *previous* owner. I considered painting *Final Edition* on the transom as a nod to the film that had paid for it, but that sounded a bit morbid for a boat, so instead I called it *Rosebud* after my film company (perhaps also so that people would think I was working hard when I told them I was "at Rosebud"). As described in the previous chapter, within a month of getting it I decided to sail it with two companions down to the Southern Bahamas. While we were about half way through the trip, sailing down the Great Dismal Swamp Canal through Virginia and North Carolina, my producer on the two films, Sam Levene, learned that both of them had been accepted by the Banff International Television Festival - *Final Edition* in competition and *Takeover* as the Opening Night Gala presentation.

If this were today, of course, I'd have learned the news within minutes via cell phone, text, or email. In those days, the only way to communicate from a boat was by using a phone link on VHF radio. Over. Limited range, cost quite a bit of money, you had to have the right channel turned on to receive calls, other people listening on that channel could hear every word you said, there were rules about the kind of language you could use, and you had to use proper radio lingo and etiquette. Over. Sam placed a number of calls to me to try to tell me about the festival screening, but I guess I never had the radio on to Channel 26 when he called, and so he was never able to get through. Fortunately he wasn't one to give up easily, so he called the North Carolina Coast Guard and told them he had an emergency message for me. I did eventually get that message from the Coast Guard, and I called him back on the radio to get the news. He told me that the network was willing to put up the cash for a bunch of us—him, me, our star, Michael Hogan, and some of the executives in the drama department—to fly out and attend the opening night gala. Could I make it? I began to investigate, and found that if I could get to Raleigh, North Carolina, I could then get a flight to Chicago and on to Calgary and then on to Banff.

The question, though, was what to do with the boat, and with my two crewmates. I couldn't just abandon them on anchor in the middle of the Great Dismal Swamp to wait for me for the five days I'd be gone. I looked at the charts. The best place to try to get to seemed to be the charming harbor town of Beaufort, North Carolina. Trouble is, it was 140 miles away, on the other side of both Pamlico and Albemarle Sounds, two notoriously rough pieces of water. Sailing is easy—if you do it when the conditions are good, and lay low when they're not. So far on this long trip we'd been sailing without a schedule, moseying along, exploring America's waterways, not driving the modest little boat too hard. Suddenly, we'd have to crank up into high gear, if I wanted to make it to the Alberta festival. I called Sam back, and told him I'd be there. He organized the airline tickets, and asked for my shirt and pant size. Knowing I had nothing with me but shorts and Top-Siders, he'd rent me a tux, and take it with him to Banff.

196

Off we went, travelling from dawn to dusk in our quest to get down to Beaufort. Ignoring the cruising guides that recommend you wait for a good weather window before crossing the often rough, choppy waters of Albemarle Sound, we charged off on a wet, windy day. Gentlemen don't sail to weather, they used to say, but, hey, we weren't trying to be gentle. We were on a deadline. We made it across Albemarle and Pamlico Sounds, but the boat took a beating. Not designed for these tough conditions and pounding seas, the boat's coachroof hogged down, caved in by the tension of the rigging. By the time we got to Beaufort, it was concave, the mast now wobbling, though still held by the now slack stays. Oh well, no time to worry about that now. I got the boat safely tied up, bid my crew goodbye, and jumped on a bus for a long overnight ride through the massive forests and sprawling Marine Corps bases of the state, then on to a plane in Raleigh, another in Chicago, a pick up in Calgary and drive on to Banff.

The western audience loved our sprawling story of an Alberta oil and cattle tycoon, and the attempted takeover of his business empire. We didn't remind them of my involvement in the less-popular *Tar Sands* exposé. The film got a standing ovation. We were feted, wined and dined, and Sam and I, and Michael and his Oscar-winning co-star John Ireland did a lot of press interviews. After two days of excitement I made the return trip back to resume our sailing trip on the east coast. Before continuing, though, I had to do some work on the boat, slackening off all the rigging, pushing out the hogged roof with an auto ram jack, then reinforcing it with a new post mounted under the mast. It must surely be the first time ever that a film festival invitation has resulted in the need for that kind of boat restoration. Before getting back into the long cruise south, I learned that our other film, *Final Edition*, had won the Best Drama Special award at the Banff Festival, and that the network, pleased with the performance of *Takeover* there, had green-lit a mini-series based on the film. The writer, Rob Forsyth, got to work on the scripts, while I continued south, knowing there would likely be a big gig available for me when I returned.

The demographics of Canada was changing fast in this period, with huge numbers of immigrants and refugees now coming into the country from Southeast Asia, China, the Caribbean, and Africa. There were frequently stories in the press about racial incidents and altercations between the new arrivals and the redneck end of the white majority. I decided to try to make a film about it, and got some financing from TV-Ontario to write and produce a drama about an Indian teenager targeted and harassed by a gang of hockey players. It turned out to be another contentious film, not because hockey-playing louts objected to my portrayal of them, but because Sikhs did. Co-writer Barry Pearson and I decided to make the boy and his family Sikhs, because the group face additional discrimination. Not only is their skin brown, but the turban that most of the men wear is another inflammatory sore point for the bigoted and prejudiced. I knew very little about Sikhism, but Co-Producer Tony Hall and I brought a Sikh advisor on board, and pretty soon I knew more than I really wanted to about the demanding religion.

Sikhism originally began as a spin-off of Hinduism, set up as a militant wing to protect the gentler Hindus from Muslims. Some factions of Sikhism have become fairly testy (sometimes a bit more than testy, such as when a couple of militant Sikh extremists blew up Air India 182 flying from Vancouver over the Atlantic killing all 329 people on board—still Canada's worst ever mass murder). They are zealous on the physical aspects of their religion – the so-called "Five K's" that the devoted must always wear – *kacchera* (a special drawer type of underpants), *kangha* (a wooden comb), *kara* (a round steel or iron bracelet), *kesh* (uncut hair), and the *kirpan* (a ceremonial sword or dagger, worn at the waist.) They are also very particular, as we would find out, about the way that the turban, wrapping up their long, uncut hair, is worn and folded.

The problems began with the casting of the film. There were only a handful of East Asian actors in Canada at the time—hardly any of them Sikhs. In fact, some elements of the religion disapprove of the whole nature of fiction, and of the concept of portraying a character other than yourself. Which is pretty much what acting is.

198

So there were few Sikh actors available, but so what? The film was about discrimination, not about Sikhism. And who cares what religion an actor is? Don't they all essentially worship the limelight, not some god or another? If you were going to make a film about Margaret Thatcher, you'd hardly demand that the actress playing her be an Anglican. (In fact, Meryl Streep, who won an Oscar for her portrayal of Thatcher in *The Iron Lady*, was raised a Presbyterian, but now follows no religious doctrine. No objections were heard from the Anglicans.) But the various Sikh Temples and anti-defamation groups that caught wind of our proposed film thought differently.

We found a terrific actor to play the teenager, and another to play his mother. Trouble was, he was a mixture—mostly East Indian, some Trinidadian genes. Typical modern mongrel Toronto kid, but not approved by the Sikh racial purity police. I thought I'd really lucked out when I was able to get Mujarrat Majeed to play his mother. She was a big name actress, star of many feature films. Trouble is—they were Pakistani films. Also—not approved. It was not the last time I'd have to deal with racial purity in casting decisions. The next time, as you'll read in the next chapter, it was the Japanese, who were even more demanding than the Sikhs.

An even bigger problem than casting turned out to be wardrobe. The lead boy was to wear a turban. We had Lynda Kemp, the best wardrobe mistress in town on the little film, but she and I agreed we should defer the issue of tying the turban to our Sikh advisor. He was a great guy, but new to both Canada and showbiz. Our first day of shooting, I've always remembered, was December 11, as we got a massive snowstorm that morning – first of the season, and unusually early. Nonetheless, everyone showed up, ready to shoot at the 8 a.m. call time. That's what film crews do—and that's what Canadians generally do. Not him. He assumed that the snow would mean everything would be cancelled, so he stayed home. I wasn't, on our thin budget, about to wait for him to finally show up, so Lynda and her team tied the turban. Looked good to me. Let's shoot.

Not good enough for the Sikh community. We finished the film, and had a screening of it to which a few of them were invited prior to the telecast. Suddenly everything went into an uproar, mostly about the fact that the turban was not sharply tied. There were demands that TVO not show the film, threats of boycotts, thundering community newspaper editorials, and even, to everyone's amazement, a bomb threat on my co-producer Tony Hall's house. And all this from the people who we thought were the heroes of the film. Given that TVO was an arm of the Ontario government, they took it all pretty seriously, and organized a big screening/meeting at a big room at the Ministry of Education. They brought in the Deputy Minister and some other big guns, the Sikhs brought up a bunch of religious activists and advisors from New York City, and Tony and I brought our lawyer. George Miller was the most experienced entertainment lawyer in town at the time, a guy who had put together many high-powered deals, and litigated lots of high-stakes courtroom dramas over the years. After this hot and heavy showdown, he told me, with his usual wry smile, that he had never enjoyed a meeting so much. It was the wildest, most heated piece of histrionics he had experienced in his thirty-year legal career.

In the end TVO agreed not to show the film, and the Sikhs agreed to make sure their more hotheaded types cut out harassing my co-producer with bomb threats over the shape and design of the turban, and the other issues they found offensive. I guess what I learned from the incident is that indeed the devil *is* in the details. Your heart and sympathies may be in the right place, but details that you didn't think mattered matter very much to other people.

The irony was that after the dust settled, a year later I sold the film to CBC—and so in the end it was shown across Canada instead of just across Ontario. The sky didn't fall, I never even heard that there was single complaint to the network, and maybe, just maybe, it helped convince some kid to stop bullying East Asians—which was supposed to be the point of it in the first place.

Four years later my producer pal Sam Levene and his new partner David Pears asked me to direct another film about racial problems and violence against the Sikh community. This time I'd get a more substantial budget and a better developed script, and the experience of making the previous film might help me avoid some potential pitfalls.

This time the story, based on a real event, was about an East Asian woman in the Fraser Valley of B.C. who had to defend her children and farm against bunch of local louts harassing her and trying to burn her house down. She ended up shooting one of them to death, and was charged, but then acquitted on the defense of *Reasonable Force*—which became the title of the show. We prepared to shoot the film in the farming lands south of Vancouver, close to where the original incident had taken place. It was a lively script with car action, burning crosses, gunplay, and fiery emotions.

Casting was as usual the first big issue. I came up with the idea of having Deepa Mehta read for the part. I'd known her since she'd arrived in Canada twelve or so years earlier, and in fact had directed three films for the company she and her husband Paul Saltzman ran, in Sweden, Yugoslavia, and Los Angeles. But I didn't know her well, and she had never acted before. I convinced her to read for the role. I've recently heard her on *George Stroumboulopoulos Tonight* while she was beating the drum for *Midnight's Children*, telling Strombo that the only reason she got the part was that there were no other East Indian actors around back then. Not true. We read other people; she gave the best audition, and she was great in the lead role as the feisty Sikh farmwoman.

It was a bit like *Two Weeks in Another Town* for the two of us. Both staying in Vancouver's Blue Horizon Hotel, and working together intently on the lurid drama, one thing led to another and soon we were in the midst of a torrid affair. I was also enamored with the continuity girl on the film, so my social life was pretty active. But that affair ended. The one with Deepa continued, even after we both returned to Toronto.

It was an intensely crazy affair, lurching from hot to cold, full of secrets, abandonment, and revival. At one point on the crazy roller coaster ride we went off for a week to one of the world's most remote and (I suppose) romantic getaways, where I was doing some writing and photography for a California adventure-travel company. Cocos Island is one of the world's largest uninhabited islands, three hundred miles off the coast of Costa Rica. It has a wild history of treasure-hunting, with everyone from Errol Flynn to Franklin Delano Roosevelt to speed king Malcolm Campbell, treasure hunter August Gissler, and dozens of others searching for the vast hoard of Peruvian gold and emeralds that the pirate Benito Bonito stole on the Spanish Main and buried at Cocos. No one has ever found the treasure (or admitted to doing so), so people keep looking for it.

Deepa and I flew down to Costa Rica, and then sailed out of the sleepy port of Puntarenas with a bunch of Swedish guys and a few other people on their big steel schooner. No one knew what to make of the pair of us. I was into a Keith Richards look in those days—rings and bandanas and sunglasses, and Deepa looked like an exotic rock and roll moll—a mélange of saris and bindis, blue jeans, scotch, and Rothmans cigarettes. Given that it was Latin America, many people assumed that we were rich drug dealers. We didn't bother disabusing them of the notion.

The whole sailing on the high seas thing was new to Deepa. She was a very urban sort of woman, but she took on the outdoor marine life with cautious and guarded enthusiasm. At one point on the three-day sail to the island, one of the Swedish sailors asked her if she'd like to try her hand at fishing. She was negative, saying she'd never done anything like that, but eventually we convinced her to give it a try, and he pressed a stiff ocean-trolling rod with a big Penn reel on it into her hands. They let out a few feet of line behind the boat, and to everyone's amazement, within less than five minutes she had a huge eight-foot black marlin on the hook. The giant fish was tail walking and exploding from the ocean, Deepa was screaming and the rest of us were in hysterical turmoil watching the ocean drama unfold. My greatest fear was that she was going to hurl the rod in the

202

ocean to get rid of the creature she likely feared would pull her over the taffrail. Before we could get her quiet and settled down into trying to set the hook and fight the massive fish, the marlin threw the lure and was gone. Deepa huffily handed back the rod, and returned to her novel.

Our affair ended in a Queen Street courtroom, where I appeared as co-respondent in her divorce proceedings. At that time in Ontario, unbelievably, divorce proceedings were handled by ecclesiastical law. Both of us were amazed at the almost medieval tone of the proceedings. It wasn't done in Latin, but it may as well have been, with the weird archaic fifteenth century religious language being used. I played my part in the arcane proceedings, then ran off to the wilds of Micronesia to make my film there. Deepa changed her mind about the divorce and re-married her husband. Her career as a feature film director was starting to take off. A couple of years later, according to her daughter Devyani Saltzman's memoir *Shooting Water*, Deepa and her husband had a major row in Cannes while she was there supporting her film *Sam & Me*, and that was the end of their relationship.

Our relationship ended in 1984. In 2012, I discovered she hadn't entirely forgotten it. During the press buildup for her film *Midnight's Children*, I heard her describe the harassment she received from the Iranian Islamist radicals while filming Salman Rushdie's novel. In order to protect the cast and crew from trouble during production, the Sri Lankan filming authority demanded that she and her team come up with a phony title to shoot the film under. She told her interviewers, with relish, that she came up with the "most boring film title she could think of"—*Winds of Change*. Back in the 80s, while Deepa and were in the throws of ending our torrid but acrimonious affair, I was coming up with the title for my new film *Micronesia: The Winds of Change*. I never thought of it as that boring a title, but apparently it was.

In the early nineties I began to think about leaving Los Angeles and returning to Canada. I'd had some luck there, making a couple of features and some other films, but I began to see not just me but others around me down there caught up in the side eddies of filmmaking. There's an analogy I use when people ask me for career advice (if I had a nickel for every person who's asked for my suggestions for their son or daughter who wants to get into filmmaking...) The film business is like a river. There is a main current running down the middle, and there are interesting minor currents running on either side. The trouble with them is that there are eddies attached to them, and it is very easy once you get to either side of the main river to get stuck in an eddy—maybe for a very long time. On the left side of the river is the always-alluring stream of big budget theatrical feature film production. Of course, almost everyone interested in filmmaking would rather be making fancy features with A list stars, but the casualty rate in that end of the business is extreme. It is so easy to be delayed, deluded, and ultimately disillusioned in the spinning whirlpool eddies of big budget feature filmmaking that I recommend staying away from it. However just like the Sirens that Homer warned against thousands of years ago, the femme fatale of big budget feature filmmaking will lure you into the rocky shoreline, then more often than not break your heart.

On the other side of the river is another stream—the not-so-alluring but for most people more lucrative backwater of industrial and corporate films, commercials, YouTube videos, event cinematography, and the like. You can make a living in the racket, and for some people it can be quite satisfying. You can dabble in it to pay the mortgage, but it can be a tender trap, and a swirling eddy that's often hard to spring from.

My recommendation is to try to keep the kayak of your career (to stretch this metaphor to its maximum) in the main stream of the river—and, for me at least, the main stream is television. New television production was booming in Canada in the early 90s. When I got an offer to come back to direct episodes of the new drama series *E.N.G*, I packed up my life into the biggest truck Ryder rents, and with my two-year-old daughter Ashley riding shotgun in a child seat, our sports car attached to the rear bumper, Carolyn with two-month-old daughter Brianna driving our Chrysler New Yorker behind (communicating by CB radio), we crossed America and returned home. It was Brianna's first trip ever, but she has gone on to many more, and has assisted me on volcano and underwater shoots. Ashley now works as a TV Reporter in the very same offices at CTV that we used to shoot *E.N.G* in.

    E.N.G is in my opinion the best dramatic television series ever made in Canada. The only other contender, *Flashpoint,* had a much more sophisticated look, and equally good acting, but essentially was just another police procedural. *E.N.G,* with its stories emanating from a big city TV newsroom, was an original. It had great producers starting with Robert Lantos and Jeff King, a really hot writing team, a large strong cast, a decent budget and, if I may say so, really good directors.

    The *E.N.G* writers took on many stories that were "ripped from the headlines", but handled them in a different way than we'd tried to years earlier on films like *The Tar Sands.* By changing all the names and fictionalizing everything, we were able to tell much more contentious stories that would never have passed muster if we'd named names or presented them as being true. For instance...Emanuel Jaques was a twelve-year-old shoeshine boy raped and murdered above a body rub parlor on the Yonge Street strip in 1977. His murder shocked the city, and precipitated the cleanup of the sleaziest elements of Yonge Street. The Jaques murder, (although remembered to this day), was old news by the time we got to make *E.N.G.* What still lingered, though, was an unsubstantiated street rumor that Eaton's, stymied in their efforts to buy up the old Yonge Street strip clubs and sex parlors in order to replace them with their planned megamall the Eaton Centre, was somehow involved in setting up the circumstances that led to the murder, in order to change the attitudes of the public and of City Hall towards the Yonge Street Strip. We never heard any proof that would suggest that this was anything more than a salacious and inaccurate urban legend. It did, though, make for a lively and provocative theme to hang a plot on, and by changing all the names and all the details we were able to make a really compelling hour of television, without outing or embarrassing anyone, or getting into any legal hot water over the show. It was a much better way to make "ripped from the headlines" television, without the show getting into the headlines itself.

E.N.G was produced by Alliance, one of four giant publicly traded entertainment companies in Canada that exploded in size in the 1990s. I worked for the other three as well—Atlantis, Nelvana, and Cinar. Cinar was a particularly interesting place. I did a TV movie for them, then numerous episodes of their version of the classic old chestmutt (uh huh), *Lassie*. More on those films in the next chapter. In those years the company was busting out at the seams. I remember seeing a pair of $70,000 mixing consoles just sitting in a hallway for months, the company so busy that no one had the time to take them out of their crates, let alone install them. The two founders of the company, Micheline Charest and Ron Weinberg, had squeaky-clean reputations, and the company seemed above reproach. That would all change in the new millennium. Six years later, I was involved in an investigative piece into machinations at the company, for my feature *Popcorn With Maple Syrup*.

Several factors contributed to the downfall of the Cinar empire. Ron and Micheline were very well connected with the federal government, and major fundraisers for Prime Minister Jean Chretien and the Liberal Party. So when a separatist Bloc Quebecois MP uncovered proof that the company was playing fast and loose with the Canadian Radio-television and Telecommunications Commission (CRTC) and Canadian Audio-Visual Certification Office (CAVCO) rules that they were supposed to be operating under, he gleefully released the information to the press and police. Then the shareholders discovered that the pair had illicitly invested $122 million into a numbered Bahamian company. It was also discovered that they had created a pen name "Eric Alexander", for Micheline's sister, Hélène Charest, and had thus illicitly collected over a million dollars for royalties on scripts supposedly written by a

Canadian, but actually written by American writers. I got involved telling the story of a Quebec animator, Claude Robinson, who discovered that Cinar had completely stolen a project he had created for a kids series, and who doggedly investigated the company for years. I enjoyed working with Claude, a guy who had had to virtually abandon his career as an artist for five years in order to become a fiscal detective, probing the corporate secrets of the company that he believed had stolen his project. After much resistance, the government and police took on his case, and eventually the once-hyperactive company went down in flames. Then, in a tragic and bizarre twist of fate, Micheline went into a Montreal clinic for a plastic surgery operation, and died on the operating room table at age 51. Talk about bad karma.

While shooting *Popcorn With Maple Syrup* and my docs for Discovery Channel and History Television on B.C.'s sea otters, and on Joshua Slocum, I was frequently in and out of Vancouver. At that time I was one of the founding board members of the Whistler Film Festival, which also took me out west and through Vancouver numerous times. Whenever I would drive into the city from the airport I'd pass the big Chinese Consulate on Granville Street, where there was always a group of protestors marching beside it. Day or night, rain or shine, they would always be there. Who were these people, I wondered. When *Popcorn* premiered at the National Library in Ottawa, I walked past the Parliament Buildings, and then the Chinese Embassy, and discovered them protesting there as well. I discovered they were members of Falun Gong, a huge self-fulfillment group that had over seventy million adherents in China, until it was made illegal, forced underground and persecuted by the Chinese government.

Thinking this might be interesting subject matter for a film, I began researching the group. I discovered what I thought to be a huge story, largely ignored by the mainstream press. Falun Gong was an exercise movement and belief system that sprang from the ashes of the Chinese Cultural Revolution. Although the Chinese government originally supported the movement, they began to fear its massive

207

popularity, and cracked down on it. In 1999 they outlawed it, and began harassing and jailing practitioners. Over 200,000 have been sent to Chinese jails and forced labour camps, many of them brutally tortured, and at least 2,000 killed.

After researching the sordid story I took it to CBC to try to convince them to commission me to make a doc about it. I wasn't alone, apparently. A couple of other filmmakers had the same idea, and I had to compete against them for the gig. In the end I got it, and began shooting the film, which I called *Beyond the Red Wall*. It soon became clear that the Chinese government was obsessed with crushing Falun Gong, and suppressing any news or information about it. Any attempts to shoot material for the film in China would have been pointless, unsuccessful, and dangerous. Instead, I filmed across North America with the huge diaspora of Falun Gong practitioners, victims of the torture, and lawyers, politicians, and academics who had investigated it. I also managed to get a good deal of secretly photographed video of beatings, arrests and torture, smuggled out of China, to use in the film, and reported on gruesome stories of jailed Falun Gong practitioners having their kidneys and eyes removed for sale in Chinese organ mills.

It wasn't an easy film to make, and there were edits, and re-edits, and re-edits of the re-edits. I wanted to make a hard-hitting Michael Moore-style exposé of the persecution. The network wanted "balance"—on the one hand, Falun Gong *claims* this. On the other, here's a mealy-mouthed spokesman from the Chinese Embassy, who denies everything they say. That sort of editing tends to water down the argument and thus the film, but I did understand the reality of their position—even though they never stated it to me or anyone else. The Beijing Olympics were coming up the following year. The CBC had the Canadian broadcast rights to the Games. Had the Chinese government got sufficiently exercised about my Falun Gong film, they could have done things that would jeopardize the CBC's huge investment in their Olympic broadcast. As it turned out, they did.

We finally got a cut of the film that the CBC approved and endorsed. We dubbed it into French and it was shown across Quebec and New Brunswick on Radio Canada. We also licensed the film in Spain, Portugal, and New Zealand. Finally the CBC set an airdate, November 6, 2007. Five hours prior to the scheduled 10 p.m. broadcast, I was in a TV studio doing some press for the film, when I got a phone call from the head of the documentary unit at CBC. She told me that they would not be running the film. She claimed that there was some big news coming out of Pakistan, and so they were going to *re*-run a doc profile of the country's President Pervez Musharraf. My film would be shown some time in the future, or maybe never, or maybe would need to be re-edited.

Naturally a bit devastated by this, I talked to a few people, they talked to others, and soon political columnist Peter Worthington at the *Toronto Sun* was on the story. He began investigating, and discovered the real reason for the last minute yanking of the show. The Chinese government, never happy about any media revelations about their treatment of Falun Gong, asked the network to pull the show—so they did. The fact that the nationally funded broadcaster would cave to the demands of China's communist government was big news. The story was picked up by almost every newspaper and radio station in the country (except for the CBC). There were full pages of letters to the editor about the issue in the National Post, continuing coverage in all the Canadian papers, and reporting on the story in over a hundred international papers, from the Jerusalem Post to the Los Angeles Times.

It is an extraordinary change of pace being suddenly thrust into the center of a swirling controversial news story. Last week you couldn't get a local entertainment reporter on the phone to tell them about your upcoming film; now, the phone is ringing off the hook with requests for interviews, quotes, reactions. In the midst of an interview with the Ottawa Citizen, the New York Times rings through. While on a live radio talk show, AP is on the other line, wanting a quote. In the midst of all this, the CBC gave a list of the changes they wanted in the film, and editor Gary Vaughan and I were back in the cutting room. After a week of editing (interrupted by calls from the press), we gave them a new version—with every one of their demanded cuts met. They then decided they wanted more cuts, and went off (without Gary and me) to trim more bits they were worried about—some damning accusations of organ harvesting of Falun Gong prisoners (made by former Canadian Secretary of State David Kilgour), and an analogy made by a human rights lawyer between the Berlin Olympics of 1936 and the Beijing Olympics of 2008.

After the last round of cuts, the film was finally aired. The *Toronto Star* did a lengthy story analyzing the differences between the original version, and the revised one. TV Critic Vinay Menon concluded, "Unless the CBC has gutted it over the past 72 hours, Rowe's film remains a searing indictment of China's treatment of the Falun Gong." The *Globe's* John Doyle called it "a fine and hard-hitting doc...galvanizing" and stated what everyone wondered— "Exactly what spooked the CBC bosses is beyond me."

In the end the Chinese did retaliate against the network, jamming its internet feed cbc.ca across China for the first three months of 2008.

There was an amusing cultural touchstone that arose from the controversy over the show, when the story was covered by the voice of the (arguably) best known newscaster in the world—Kent Brockman, the unctuous local news anchor seen by many millions of people on the longest running animated series in television history, *The Simpsons*. American comic Harry Shearer, who voices Kent Brockman, also has his own weekly radio program, called *Le Show* on Los Angeles station KCRW. Soon after the controversy exploded about *Beyond the Red Wall*, Shearer picked up the story for his show, riffing on various aspects of it, including his thoughts on how the Canadian Broadcasting Corporation would be now called the Chinese Broadcasting Corporation, and how convenient it was that China began with a "C", allowing the CBC to retain its logo and branding. Even if removed by one small degree of separation, my shallow ego was naturally stroked and my pop-cultural sensibility greatly amused by having the story of my film covered by the all-time king of glib and shallow, Kent Brockman.

The Simpsons is a family show (perhaps the ultimate *dysfunctional* family show). I have never worked on it, but I have worked on many other kids' and family shows, and offer a few thoughts on the genre in the next chapter. As for *The Simpsons*, I did try to make a behind-the-scenes doc about the making of the series. The story of that abandoned project, and many others like it on the Boulevard of Broken Filmmaking Dreams, is chronicled in Chapter Seven.

Chapter 6
Kids, Animals, and Mickey Rooney

   Adding another arrow to my filmmaking quiver, I became experienced at directing shows for teens and families, especially ones involving animals, in the eighties and nineties. By the time I wrapped up working in the genre, I had done a lot: *African Skies, The New Addams Family, The Edison Twins, My Life as a Dog, Lassie, Ready or Not, Rin Tin Tin K9 Cop* (aka *Katts and Dog*), *Spread Your Wings, Heart of Courage, The Campbells, The Adventures of Black Stallion, Pit Pony, Saltwater Moose* (as marine special effects coordinator), *Treasure Island,* and *The Best Bad Thing.* I think I'm the only person in the world who can claim to have directed the three family-friendly mega-stars originally created in the Golden Age of Hollywood: Lassie, Rin-Tin-Tin, and Mickey Rooney. The genre also got me working on shows with modern stars—indie film darling

213

Ellen Page (on *Pit Pony*), world figure-skating champ Kurt Browning (*Ready or Not)*, and *Jeopardy* quizmaster Alex Trebek (hosting *Heart of Courage,* on which I was the master of marine mayhem.)

The Edison Twins was the first of the lot for me. Right away I learned that if you embrace the genre (many scorn it, of course) it can be a lot of fun. Kids are naturals—many of them, at least. Playing, pretending, imagining is what kids do. Handle things right and it is very easy to transfer that into getting them to help you make a film, and put their natural energy on the screen. Many of them also take to the technicalities of filmmaking in a flash. While prepping my first episode of the series I dropped by at the set to meet everyone, especially the young leads—the two budding-scientist twins of the tile, and their rambunctious younger brother, played by a precocious squirt of a nine-year-old. (Most child-actors are squirts. Nobody wants to work with a five-year-old when you can find a tiny seven-year-old who can play two years younger, so in the child-acting racket, it is much more lucrative to be short and tiny.) As I watched the shooting from the sidelines, I heard this little second-banana kid debating with the director over whether the proposed next shot was going to be crossing the axis. The issue of film axis is a somewhat arcane subject that many adults on a film set shy from, fearing they'll be lost in its often confusing geometry. It was pretty amusing to hear this little pipsqueak debating the subject, especially as I thought he was right, and the director wrong. I of course kept my clam shut, but thought to myself I'd better be on my toes when it was my turn to work with these kids the following week.

The series was also where I first created—invented!—something that I hope won't be remembered as my greatest contribution to filmmaking, but was, certainly, my most concrete one. *The Edison Twins* was produced by Nelvana. Being primarily an animation company, it had all the latest in office, art, printing, and graphics equipment. It was the first place I had ever seen the newly invented feature of copying machines being able to reduce a page down to 50% (or less) of its original size. Until those days, I, and everyone in production, used to carry our full-sized copy of the

214

script around on the set with us, usually in a three-ring binder. It was awkward, there was usually never a place to put it, it took both hands to read it, and it would often get misplaced in the cables, cases, and other detritus of a big film set. It was a pain.

When I saw the newfangled reducing copy machine, I had a brainwave. Why not reduce my copy of the script down to just a little bigger than playing card size, and keep it in my pocket? I tried it, and found it worked like a charm. It was always there, I never had to worry about it—it was great. I never thought of it as anything more than something I was doing for myself—but when other people on the set saw it—especially the kid-actors, who loved its pint size—everyone wanted one. Soon we were making the mini versions for many of the cast and crew.

Within less than a year, the miniaturizing idea exploded. People migrated from our series to others, and began making themselves, then soon demanding that the production office make for them, the pocket editions of the scripts. The sizes of them varied over the first few years, but they eventually standardized at about five by eight inches, and somebody gave them a name which stuck: "mini-sides". Actors loved them—suddenly they had their lines on small enough bits of paper that they could be surreptitiously stuffed into the skimpiest of costumes. So did boom swingers, who would paste them on their mike poles, and focus-pullers, who would tape them to the side of the matte-box, to remind them who was going to say what, when. Everyone liked them—except the office staff, which suddenly had a big new job to do every day—printing, cutting, and attaching these sides to the day's call-sheet, for everyone. And soon, the little pages moved on around the world. The American crews who arrived in Toronto in large numbers in the nineties had never seen them before, but they took the idea back to L.A. with them, and eventually it took off there. By the mid eighties they were in Vancouver, and when I arrived in Johannesburg in 1991, some Canadian co-production or another had already popularized them there.

Eventually, like Victor Frankenstein, I would come to curse my creation. In the early nineties I enlisted the help of two other filmmakers, Allan Levine and Richard Rebiere, and in a production lull we sailed my boat *Blade Runner* up the Atlantic from Florida. Fifty miles off the Georgia coast we were caught in the most extreme and lengthy lightning storm I've ever experienced. The night went from pitch black to violent explosions that would light up the entire sky, back to black, over and over again. It was not fun having the only metal object (my big forty-five foot mast) sticking up for miles around, but we, and the boat, survived the storm. My eyes did not. Almost everyone loses their close-up vision at the age of about forty-five, but in my case it was dramatic. When we sailed out of Jupiter Inlet in Florida I had 20/20 vision. Three days later, as we sailed into Morehead City, I couldn't read the buoy numbers on the chart.

Mini-sides were soon a thing of the past for me—and now are for many. Aging population, and all. Not much point using tiny type on small pages if you have to fumble around with reading glasses to decipher it. In any case, people are starting to read scripts on their smart phones today. But mini-sides are still around—a good invention that's now lasted twenty-five years—all because of a pipsqueak kid actor who loved the little pipsqueak-sized script his director had created.

One of the best family shows I got attached to was a complicated international co-production made with Canadian, American, German, and South African producers and networks. We shot *African Skies* in South Africa—mostly on a studio-ranch north of Johannesburg. Catherine Bach, best known for playing Daisy Duke in the original *Dukes of Hazzard*, played the lead, along with a teenaged Canadian actor playing her son. The pair of them ran a big ranch on the veldt, and got in and out of adventures every week with the help of a ranch manager, played by a German TV star, and a number of very good African actors playing continuing or guest roles in the show. On top of that, famous Hollywood tough guy Robert Mitchum, playing the family patriarch, advised them on their screen problems from his corporate headquarters that was both set and shot

216

high in a downtown Toronto office tower. Mitchum's character spoke to the gang in Africa via a video phone hook-up that looked remarkably like Skype—very prescient of us, as we made the series prior to the birth of the World Wide Web, and eleven years before Skype was created.

We needed the yet-to-be-invented Skype, YouSendIt, and email to make the international series, but had to do things the old way—relying on parcel express and phone calls across nine time zones. The brilliant creator of the series, Phil Savath, was in Vancouver, and his partner Larry Mollin was in Los Angeles writing *Beverly Hills 90210* during the day as he wrote episodes of *African Skies* at night. We shot in the wilds of Africa. Our processing lab and our editors were in Toronto, our composer was in Montreal, and we were getting notes from network executives in Los Angeles, Toronto, and Munich. And, surprisingly enough with that wild mélange of interests and egos, it all ran like a charm. I loved the experience of Africa. The climate was easy to film in, the crews were among the best I've ever had the privilege to work with, we had two excellent producers running the show, the scripts were well-written, and the local politics were…interesting (we were there in the heady two-year period following the fall of apartheid but before the election of Nelson Mandela.)

There was also lots of interaction with African wildlife, to add to the challenges I had directing the shows. We had lions and cobras and rhinos and crocodiles involved in one way or another in the stories. Some of the animals were trained, others were wild, some halfway in between. Three stories stick out in my memory. On one episode there was a need for a pair of elephants. While prepping the show, I went out to a remote piece of the jungle, where our animal guy was training the pair for the work they had to do. Oddly, I found that one of the elephants had been born at the Bowmanville Zoo, outside of Toronto, and had been eventually returned and repatriated to Africa. Even the wildlife was international on this Euro-Afro-Americano show!

When I found the elephants and their trainer out in the deep woods, I discovered there was an ostrich hanging out with them. The trainer showed me what the elephants could do, and we figured out how to fake some other things that they couldn't really do, to meet the requirements of the script. He also told me of some of the dangers of working with elephants. Since they are not aggressive animals, people get lulled into thinking it is safe to be around them. On a shoot the trainer had been on the previous year, an assistant cameraman had been standing beside an animal's backside. Not realizing the guy was there, the elephant shifted its back legs slightly, pinned the guy against a wall, and killed him. I promised to pass on the trainer's warnings to our crew.

He also told me about the ostrich hanging out with us. Ostriches have been around for millions of years. They are the closest relatives we still have on earth to dinosaurs. They are not the brightest birds around. (They never even figured out how to fly, for one thing) This particular ostrich, the trainer claimed, was so dumb he actually thought he was an elephant—and would hang out only with elephants. (Sounds like a Dr. Seuss yarn, doesn't it?)

Suddenly things turned ugly. I had separated a bit from the trainer, the biggest elephant, and the ostrich, and was standing over beside the young, smaller elephant. Suddenly, the ostrich, deciding I was a threat to his happy little family, ran at me, ready to attack. With its big size (200 to 300 pounds), sharp beak, and powerful dino-like claws, an angry ostrich could kill you.

"Grab a rock!" shouted the trainer. "Grab a rock!"

I reached down and grabbed a sharp edged shard of rock from the ground. As I raised it to try to defend myself, I saw that the trainer had also grabbed one, and hurled it past the animal's head. That got Big Bird's attention, and it came to a stop. Breathing heavily, I retreated slowly from the riled bird, and it too seemed to calm down, and turned and strutted off.

I had a similar incident with an eland—the largest antelope on the continent. The morning light in Africa is spectacular, and I used to like to get to our outdoor sets really early, long before the rest of the circus showed up at call time. One morning I was walking through one of the open sets. I thought I was alone, but then realized a big eland was with me. They're usually not dangerous, but they are big—about the size of a caribou—and have long sharp horns that could do serious damage if the animal set its mind to it.

This particular one suddenly decided that *he* wanted to direct this week's episode. (It's a common problem on series, but it is usually the stars or DOPs that want your job, not wild animals.) The eland charged me. The only weapon I had with me was my—35mm camera, so I turned it in my hand, holding it now like it was a hammer or axe, by the long zoom lens. Fortunately there was a thin tree nearby, so I dove behind it. The tree protected me, and flailing the camera-axe scared the eland, so eventually, after a few runs at me, it gave up. Pretending nothing had happened, it stopped, dropped its head down to the grass, and began eating.

In the most memorable of *African Skies* mishaps, no animals charged, which was a good thing, as it could have ended in disaster. Phil Savath wrote an excellent script—the best of the series, called *Wild Child*—a well-crafted yarn about a feral child, the sole survivor of a wilderness small plane crash, brought up by a troop of baboons, until discovered by the principals of the series. I was assigned to direct it, and got passionately involved in bringing it to the screen, even playing a part in it as the kid's father—the pilot of the airplane.

While I was merely adequate in my role, the guest kid playing the feral child was great. Dressed in a rough loincloth, with a wild mane of matted hair, the boy threw out his guttural dialogue grunts like he was born to be a baboon. We filmed most of the show in a week.

In most cases, if we needed special animals for episodes of the series, we brought them to our studio location. That wasn't going to work here, though, as no captive baboons were available to us.

219

Instead, following the principal photography of the shoot at our ranch, a small splinter group consisting of a cameraman, two assistants, an associate producer, the young boy playing our feral child, his mother, and me, all headed north, almost to the Zimbabwe border, where there was a sanctuary for wounded and abandoned baboons.

A lot of the local farmers in southern Africa hate baboons, thinking they are dangerous, and because they come onto the fields and eat the crops. Many are harassed or shot at, and some of the lucky ones who are not killed end up being protected in the sanctuary. Often wild baboons, knowing that there is food inside the multi-acre compound, hang around outside the fence.

Once we finally got to the distant location, we set up to film a sequence of the kid alone in the wilderness with some baboons. We got the kid wigged and dirtied up, and ready in his ragged loincloth to shoot these important opening scenes of the film. Unexpectedly, Rita Miljo, the primate protector who ran the place suddenly decided that only one of her baboons was placid and trained enough to be allowed to film with our young guest star. The rest were too unpredictable and dangerous. Well, disappointing, but one was better than none, so we set up the kid on a rugged hillside, prepared him to film a scene with the one baboon, and began shooting. As we rolled, not one but an entire troop of a dozen big baboons came down over the hill, and surrounded our young actor. We were all frozen with anxiety—where had they come from? What were they going to do? Thankfully, though, no freezing from either our cameraman, who kept rolling on the wild scene, or our boy, who, although petrified, stayed in character, kept acting, and did his job. After we got some great, unexpected shots, the baboons ran off down the hill.

We immediately investigated and found that these had not been not her semi-tamed sanctuary baboons, but a completely wild troop, from outside the fence. A warthog had ripped open and dug up the fence, and all the wild baboons had run inside. How did the

220

movie-savvy warthog get its cue that this was exactly the right moment to rip open the fence? That's something we never found out, although I wanted to hire him as a Third A.D. to handle background traffic on future shows. (I'm not sure the young boy's mother shared my enthusiasm.)

After shooting eighteen episodes of *African Skies*, and many episodes of other kids and family television series, I began to start to think I knew something about the genre, and started to try to live by a number of rules that I thought ought to be followed. My first rule was this: In kid shows, the kids in the show must be the ones who get themselves into, and out of trouble, without help from adults—and especially without help from authority figures like parents, teachers, or cops. Seems commonsensical enough, doesn't it? Not so. Many times, I had to re-write, or plead with writers to re-write the material so that the kids central to the story ended up being the ones who saved the day.

Treasure Island was a good example. As I wrote that script, I discovered that Jim Hawkins, the kid that is ostensibly the hero of the story, drifts completely out of the original book about half way through, and the old guys who are presented somewhat as twits at the beginning come in and take center stage away from the hero we thought we were following. Even worse, the pirate Long John Silver is presented in the original book one minute as a loveable cad, the next minute as a bloodthirsty villain. How is a ten-year-old in the audience supposed to know where his or her affections are meant to lie?

Robert Louis Stevenson wrote the yarn in installments as a magazine serial. He didn't have a hard drive—or even carbon paper. He wrote in longhand, and sent the originals off by mail to his publisher. Is it any wonder he sort of lost the plot once his ship of characters got down to the Caribbean? Since I had the opportunity to solve these problems, I did, defining clearly who the good guys were, and who the bad, and telling the story very clearly to the young audience from the point of view of the young teenage hero. Doing this also allowed me to bring a modern contemporary sensibility to the genre, in a similar manner to the way *Pirates of the Caribbean* would, in much grander fashion, four years later.

The people I made the film with were pleased with how I had clarified the themes and structure of the story, but not everyone in the audience was. Diehard traditionalist aficionados of the original posted many of their semi-literate "reviews" on internet sites, slagging all of my changes (some with the bizarre claim I had made them so that the Americans (*i.e.* Jack Palance) came out looking better than the Brits). Internet reader reviews, whether of movies, hotels, or restaurants, are dangerous, and, it seems, permanent. It is unfortunate that the reasoned, intelligent, and stylish comments of great film critics like Andrew Sarris and Pauline Kael are now lost and forgotten, but the tossed-off half-baked rants of Internet amateurs will live, apparently, forever. Can't mess with the traditions they remember from their long-ago youth. Lucky for them I didn't get my way with the producers when I wanted to change Jim Hawkins to Jane Hawkins, a girl, disguised as a boy, on the high seas. They would have had conniptions.

On *The Best Bad Thing*, a TV feature I made in 1996, I had exactly the same sort of problems with the original source material— a novel written in 1983 by Japanese American writer Yoshiko Uchida. The story was that of a young teenage girl who got into an interesting set of problems that stemmed from anti-Japanese racism, poverty, and immigration, in an intriguing plot set in Depression-era rural California. Trouble was, instead of finding a way for the young central character to find a solution to these big issues, and resolve the plot, the novelist had copped out by having the girl's father show up to save the day. Instead of the girl being the hero, suddenly the father was. Fortunately I was able to convince the screenwriter and producers that we had to find a way to keep the young star at the center of the drama, and we did. I had nothing against the actor playing her father, Robert Ito (best known for his roles on *Quincy M.E.* and *Star Trek*), but by the time we had finished re-working the script, he had one day's work on the production, not the originally planned seven.

I had some interesting issues with the casting and performers. George Takei, of course also a *Star Trek* veteran, playing spaceship helmsman Hikaru Sulu in the series and movies, was splendid in his part, as was the young Los Angeles actress Lana McKissack in the lead—although she was not, frankly, our first choice for the role. We had great difficulty casting the part. We started the search in Montreal, and then moved on to look at possibilities shown us by casting directors in Toronto, New York, Vancouver, Seattle, and Los Angeles. We found several, truth be told, who gave great auditions. Our Japanese co-producing partners at NHK Television, though, turned down every one of them. Reason? They didn't like the slant of their eyes. It was a reprise of my Sikh turban problems described earlier. Problems invisible to us dumb *gaijin* (and even to Japanese Americans like our friend George Takei) were huge issues to the racially stringent Japanese TV executives. I doubt they could tell a good English-language audition from a bad one. They could, though, tell us whether the eye-slant of our potential casting choices met their stringent standards of appropriate ethnic purity. Fortunately, things turned out fine, with Lana giving a terrific performance that was possibly better than any of the other girls would have.

The star of the film for the Japanese market was Kirin Kiki, a sort of variant of Yoko Ono, famous as the wife of one of Japan's biggest rock stars of the sixties, Yuya Uchida. She had starred in various Japanese TV shows, on one of which, as a loser on a game show, she was obliged to give away her name Chiho Yuki, and take on this new one. (WTF!?) She showed up in Montreal with a contingent of handlers. One of them, a young son of some NHK vice-president, had been told in Japan that he would be the "co-director" of the film. My producers and our PBS network execs disabused him of that notion within hours of his arrival in Canada.

223

We soon learned that Kirin Kiki literally didn't speak a word of English. I came up with a novel solution to the problem of how she could speak her English dialogue convincingly. We had a good Montreal actress cast with a small part in the film. I gave her the additional job of recording all of Kirin Kiki's character's lines, which she did well. Then I got the young Japanese wannabe director to go off with the Japanese star, and endlessly go over her lines, working with her as she mimicked the Quebec actress's delivery. I didn't have the time or patience for the lengthy task, as I was focused on the most important task—working with the three kids who were the central characters in the film. The four of us were rewarded by having the opportunity to spend a day playing together—jumping on and off antique steam trains for the action Act Two climax of the film, where one of them is badly injured in a train accident. Kiki's hard work paid off—she won "Best Actress" Award at the Montreal Children's Film Festival (and I won the "Best Film" award.) The film played across North America, and then, apparently, in Japan, where they re-worked the opening credits to finally give the NHK vice-president's son his "co-director" credit. The Canadian and US producers found it amusing, if somewhat appalling, but what did I care—the production company was happy enough they handed me the reins to their next series, *Lassie*.

People would always ask me about W.C. Fields's famous line—that you should never work with kids or animals. I would always say the problem wasn't working with kids or animals—it was working with stage-mothers and animal-trainers. That was certainly the case on *Lassie*, where the owners of the dog's pedigree, who handled and trained the various offspring of the original collie that played in the series, gave the producers no end of grief. After the ornery dog trainer hassled the producers over all kinds of issues for the first season, they decided they would replace him, and his dogs, with what *Lassie* fans refer to as "non-line" collie dogs, and a new trainer. They apparently had no idea what fury the passionate dog-lovers, and the Internet, could create. The giant, acrimonious molehill turned into a mountain of a debate about the lineage of the

224

new *Lassie* dogs, a debate that played out first across the web and then in newspapers around the world. In the end Cinar, the production company, acquiesced to the irate fans, and returned to using "line" pedigree dogs in the show, though not to using trainer Bob Weatherwax. It was only the first, and least serious, of the many problems that would drag Cinar down from the heights to the gutter.

There were somewhat similar problems on the production of *Rin Tin Tin: K-9 Cop* (aka *Katts and Dog*). In the twenties and thirties, Rin Tin Tin was one of the biggest stars in Hollywood. The famous rumor has it that the dog received the most number of Best Actor votes in the first Academy Awards in 1929, until the Academy secretly overturned the vote. The dog almost singlehandedly turned Warner Brothers into a major studio. So it is perhaps not surprising that the owners to the rights to the *Rin Tin Tin* name were demanding and difficult partners for the producers of the new version of the franchise. The shoot was plagued with legal and contractual problems, not least when the American network on the show, Pat Robertson's Christian Broadcasting Network, demanded script changes to assuage complaints from their very conservative religious viewers about the fact that the widowed mother in the story was living with the brother of her late husband. As a result of this brouhaha, the producers and writers decided they had to kill off the mother character part way through the first season. The actor playing Rinty's handler also lost some perspective during the 106-part series. The feature film *I Love a Man in Uniform*, about a TV actor playing a cop who starts to think he is a real cop, was partially based on stories that came out of the shooting of *Katts and Dog*.

I moved on from shooting dogs to horses with *The Adventures of Black Stallion*. Each animal has unique problems one has to deal with. With stallions, it was always an issue whenever one of the uncastrated horses would decide to show off his maleness in the background of someone's close-up. The horse training staff, led by veteran Vancouver animal trainer Danny Virtue, always assigned the task of running out to deal with the over-sexed horses to a little middle-aged woman with a riding crop. I would have to call "Cut", and the entire operation would come to grinding halt as we all watched, with some in fits of hysterics, as this little woman ran out and furiously shouted at and spanked the horse with her riding crop into retracting his over-sized symbol of stallionhood, so that the shoot could get going again and the show could keep its family rating.

Of course, the most lively and high profile element of the *Black Stallion* franchise was Mickey Rooney. I had a grand time working with this diminutive icon of the Golden Age of Hollywood. He had literally had a lifetime in show business. Within two weeks of his birth in 1920, he was already on the road, travelling the vaudeville circuit with his comic father and chorus-girl mother, living in a tray in a backstage baggage trunk, gurgling at the colored klieg lights, the and the roar of the audience. At the ripe age of seventeen months he made his onstage debut at the Haymarket Theatre in Chicago, playing the harmonica, wearing a silly costume, cracking little jokes, and enchanting the audience. He has continued to do it ever since. By the late thirties, still a teenager, he was the biggest box-office star in the world, making more money for the biggest studio in Hollywood, MGM, than all their other stars put together. In the 1938-1939 season, his pictures accounted for more than seventy five percent of MGM's profits, in the best season Loews Inc. ever had. He even, apparently, inspired the name of another famous movie star. In his delightfully risqué memoir *Life is Too Short*, he tells of Walt Disney adopting his first name as the moniker for Disney's famous mouse.

Of course, he was no longer a star of that magnitude when we shot *Black Stallion*. However a poll in *People* Magazine once found that his was the third most recognizable face in the world (after Richard Nixon and Muhammad Ali), and he certainly hadn't been forgotten. He had had many ups and downs in his long career, eight marriages (starting with a brief one to Ava Gardner, when he was twenty-two). He used to joke that he kept a marriage license with him at all times, made out to "To Whom It May Concern." He's a ball of fire, coming up with a string of crazy inventions, schemes, and musicals, put on in barns with Judy Garland. At one point he tried to

226

market spray-on hair for bald people, later "Tip-Offs" (disposable bras) for women, and "Rip-Offs" (disposable underwear) for men.

He told me once that he had over his lifetime spent twenty million dollars at the racetrack. After our shoot days I would accompany him out to the racetrack in Vancouver, so he could drop a few more on the local ponies. He travelled everywhere, as many big stars do, with his "Friendly", a guy named Kevin Pawley, who served as all-purpose aide-de-camp, both on and off the set. For instance, while shooting, if I was ready to get Mickey to the set, I would tell the first A.D., who would tell the second A.D., who would tell Kevin, who would tell Mickey. Sounds overly elaborate, but it actually worked very well. Of course, once we got down to the actual filming, all the intermediaries stayed out of the way, and it was just Mickey, me, and the other actors. However Kevin served another purpose. He was almost exactly the same size as Mickey, and so could double for him. We'd always have duplicate wardrobe he would wear, so that if the Mickster (as we called him) got bored with the proceedings, we could shoot long shots, driving shots, light stunts, and sometimes even over-the-shoulder shots of the other actors, with Kevin.

It was fun, but it wasn't simple, shooting with Mickey Rooney. For one thing he never bothered to read the script in advance. He'd just show up on set, ask Kevin or me to show him the sides, run the lines once or twice, and go for it. He had no problem remembering his lines, but we would often have problems with last-minute meddling he'd do with the script. The trouble was, his script complaints were usually completely valid. He knew way more about the intricacies and machinations of the horse racing world than any of us did, and so it was often impossible to argue with his eleventh hour discoveries of script flaws.

For instance, on one episode, I set up a long tracking shot down the jockey's rooms of the racetrack. Mickey, playing the trainer, and the teen playing the young jockey were to have a long scene—the kind I call a walk-and-talk heart-to-heart—just prior to a big race. Normally, an actor would have read the scene weeks or days in advance, or at very least would have shown up for a blocking rehearsal prior to the lighting and dressing of the set. Mickey didn't like to do either of those things, so we spent perhaps an hour lighting the set, laying the dolly track, lacing in the background extras, rehearsing the camera moves, so that we were all set to shoot when Mickey arrived on the set. He showed up, and, as usual, looked at the scene—for the very first time. Almost immediately he found serious fault with it.

"This is impossible—this could never happen," he exclaimed. "No way a trainer would be allowed in a jockey room right before a race, with all the kids in their silks. The guy would get kicked out, or fined, or…it would just never happen! We can't play it like this."

Oh, great. So the entire setting of the scene, premise of the scene, content of the scene—all of that is wrong. And nobody has noticed this until Mr. Mickey Rooney pointed it out, with the production clock ticking overhead. And the trouble is, he's right. Why wouldn't he be? He's been playing the ponies since before many of our parents were born. He was one of the original investors in Santa Anita long before the Second World War. He's been doing horse racing pictures since they were in black and white, and silent. He made one of the greatest ones, *National Velvet*, with Elizabeth Taylor, back in 1944, and lots of others, amongst his 147 (!) feature films.

And so, Mr. Director, how are you going to deal with this little conundrum, while over sixty people stand around, waiting for you to tell them what to do next? There's no point in arguing with your star that it is a bit late in the game to be bringing up these complaints. There is no time to go running for advice from your producers, or writers. The time for a solution is right now.

Perhaps one might suggest that the entire premise of *The Adventures of Black Stallion* is a bit fanciful. How realistic is it that an under-age kid (looked to be no more than thirteen in the movie, maybe fifteen in our series) would be allowed to jockey a wild undocumented Arabian stallion, found on a desert island, on the professional horse tracks of North America? But that's hardly a useful argument to lay on Mickey Rooney at a delicate moment like this. Best you come up with a more elegant solution to the issue.

They don't teach you how to deal with problems like that at film school, but then as you've learned I never went to any film school other than the seat-of-your-pants, figure-it-out-as-you-go film school, so I used that past training to help me come up with some novel solution to the problem. I found a way, without antagonizing the old pro, compromising the thrust of the screenplay, or wasting an hour of production time to make it work, get the shot, and move on. Done. Another show in the can.

Chapter 7
The Films that Never Were

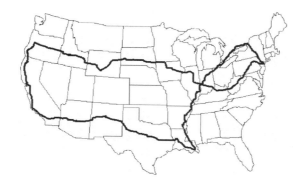

You'd be forgiven if reading this memoir you came to the conclusion my life was just one shoot after another, an exploding volcano followed by a pirate movie followed by a new TV series. No. That's only what the memoir is like. It's not what life is like. The truth is, there are many more misses than hits, more failures than successes, many more old scripts in the dusty trunk that were never made, than those that were.

If your interest is in adventure and derring-do, you should probably just skip this chapter and move on to the next. I've saved the best for last—there are lots of good yarns there. If, on the other hand, you want the brutal truth of a life trying to make movies, then stick around. Welcome to the Boulevard of Broken Dreams. If you are keen on *schadenfreude*, this is the chapter for you. Here we have all the projects I wasted months and years on. In these pages they'll have their last brief whiff of life, before sinking into oblivion forever. Unlike the rest of this book, which as you've discovered has had only the most tenuous grasp on the concept of chronological order, these orphans and black sheep are presented in the order in which they were born, struggled, and died.

Love or What?

I wrote this one in 1968, about the hippy/underground/student milieu of the time. Probably not a bad idea—there was a lot of interest in the subject back then. But how to finance it and get it made? I took the risky and fruitless route of buying an ad in one of the city's big dailies, searching backers ("Angels", as they were called back then. Still are, on Broadway). It is a technique I have never used again, and would never recommend. The few calls I got were mostly from weirdos looking for a get-rich-quick scheme. The rest were from unemployed actors, looking for parts in it. The worst were from the actors I had *already* cast in it. The guy I wanted for the lead, Martin Lavut, was a stand-up comic, writer, and filmmaker. I would later edit a brilliant little film for him called *At Home*. Martin is Jewish—from Montreal. He used to call me up, disguising himself as a variety of potential investors. Once, for instance, he put on a thick German accent, telling me he wanted to put up all the money for the film. Only one thing—there wouldn't be any Jews acting in the film, would there? Bastard. I've never forgiven him. (Yes I have—years and years ago.)

King of the Wild Frontier

In the early seventies there were a lot of very successful films about conmen. There was of course *The Sting,* plus *The Gambler, Paper Moon, The Flim-Flam Man*, and others. My father told me a story about a crazy character he knew named Jimmy Carleton—a two-bit con artist/colorful street person who used to hang around the city hall and newspaper offices in Winnipeg in the late forties and the early fifties. Great character, so I wrote a movie about him. The Davy Crockett-refrain title was a bit off the wall, but people liked my complicated script. Trouble is—a bit too complicated, and way too expensive with all the forties cars, costumes and sets required. I also spent way too much time searching for great period locations in

Winnipeg, and not enough time searching for the money to make it with. Oh, well, lesson learned. (Or maybe not—see next item.)

Kim's Game

Great title. Great story—the wild tale of Kim Philby, the head of the British Secret Service who was really a Russian agent. Modest little story, yes? My gawd, was this one ambitious. Set in Moscow, Washington, Beirut, and London, and spanning the years 1930 to 1960. Oh, sure, Pete, you're definitely going to be able to pull this one off. But I did get some development money and spent a year writing it. When it came time to raise thirty million to make the movie, well—that didn't happen. I was approached by a big theater company to turn it into a musical. But that didn't happen, either. At least by now, I'd learned my lesson about massive ambitious projects. (Or maybe not—see next item.)

The Kennedy Film

I don't think I ever had a definite title for this, but I did have a plan. My plan was to drive all around America, talk to all the Kennedy Assassination Conspiracy theorists and researchers, find out the truth about how JFK was killed, or as near I could, then write a script and make a movie out of it. I started in New York, crossed the country, and went down to California. Along the way I met researchers—there were lots of them in those days—working away debunking the single bullet theory, or deconstructing the Warren Commission's conclusions, or doing independent ballistics tests, or any number of other arcane investigations into the case. One of the guys I found most interesting was Fred Newcomb, the author of *Murder From Within—Lyndon Johnson's Plot Against President Kennedy*. Newcomb was a photo researcher who proved that the famous photo that ended up on the cover of *Life* Magazine of Lee Harvey Oswald holding the *Daily Worker* and the Italian Carcano 91/38 murder weapon, was doctored and faked to help set up Oswald as the patsy. Newcomb and a bunch of other bright guys at UCLA gave me lots of material for my film, and I eventually carried on back east toward Dallas. Exploring the School Book Depository and

Dealey Plaza, and meeting people in Dallas like Jack Ruby's underworld associates, and Oswald's mother, Marguerite Oswald ("a mother in history", as she called herself) were highlights of the long research trip. I returned home to write it.

Once again, though—nice script, but no money, thus no movie. The film was made—by someone else. Less than a year after my grand tour, some indies in Hollywood came out with exactly the film I wanted to make. Theirs was called *Executive Action*. I thought they made a great film, but they had all kinds of problems getting it into movie theaters, and it sank, little seen. More fodder for those of us who believed then—and believe today—that there was a massive conspiracy behind the JFK murder, and the cover-up of it. Years later, the story was done again—Oliver Stone's *JFK*. Again—great film, great filmmaker. Stone is the kind of director I want to be when I grow up. When's that going to happen?

Me?

Maybe by now I got the message. These big grandiose films were awfully hard to get financed. Maybe I should try something more modest. So I found a play—great play, only four people in it, one setting—an apartment. No cars, no guns, no period costumes. *And* I found a producer—Chalmers Adams—who was a hell of a lot better at raising money than I was. Only trouble was—the original stage director wanted to make the film himself. He of course had a better inside track on it than I did. He found *him*self a producer; they hired my pal Barry Pearson to write it and my other pal Steven Markle to star in it, and they made the movie. It didn't set the world on fire, but at least they got it done, which was more than I could say.

The Wreck of the Edmund Fitzgerald

Ratch Wallace, a Producer, Writer, Actor and Senior BC Ferry Captain (a unique resumé) tried to get this one going from soon after the famous lake freighter sank in 1975 until well into the new century, with everyone in town attached to it for a while, including me. Gordon Lightfoot wrote, recorded, and released the song in a few weeks; Ratch and all of us trying to help him worked on the film for twenty-five years, and it still never happened.

Living on Plastic

Another con-man themed story, but at least this time contemporary, containable, and doable. Or so I thought. I brought in a young journalist in Vancouver named Joe Wiesenfeld and the two of us spent eight months on it. The script was good enough for Joe to use as an initial calling card to help create a great career for himself as a TV writer, but again, in the end, for me, eight months down the drain.

Bond of Fear

I became fascinated by the cinematic potential of the Stockholm Syndrome—the strange, very common phenomenon of hostages falling in love with, even becoming partners with, their captors. After three cons took hostages at the maximum-security B.C. Penitentiary, a powerful bond, maybe a love affair, developed between the leader of the cons, Andy Bruce, and the leader of the hostages, social worker Mary Steinhauser. In the melee trying to end the hostage-taking, Steinhauser was shot and killed by a prison guard's bullet.

What a story. I managed to get some development money to go out west and attend the trial of the three hostage-takers, research the details, and write a script. Allan King came aboard as the Producer, and he and I spent a summer trying to figure out a way to get the financing raised. We thought we could sell it on the casting, so I was sent off to Hollywood to try and find some movie stars. I set up shop in a bungalow suite at the Chateau Marmont Hotel—in fact the very same suite that John Belushi would die in four years later—and began trying to cast the film. A young Tommy Lee Jones expressed an interest in it. I met with one of Hollywood's classic beauties—Lauren Hutton, and with the quirky star of Robert Altman's great film, *Nashville*, Ronee Blakely. All three of them would have been wonderful in it, but it wasn't to be. Allan and I couldn't get the financing together, and both of us had to make a living, so he went off to direct a TV drama, and I cut my losses by turning the material into a long article for a big magazine of the day called *The Canadian*, and later, for *Reader's Digest*.

Stuntman!

Barry Pearson and I thought that we had a good one with a story about the behind-the-scenes shenanigans on a B action movie. We wrote it all winter (kept us off the streets, at least), then I spent a full summer trying to find a tax-shelter-financed film producer to produce it. Lots of fancy meetings in the Windsor Arms Hotel (epicenter for Hollywood North back in those high-flying days), but in the end, nothing really came of them. I did get some money to make a trailer for it—or what we'd today call a sizzle reel. I did a very bad thing, which probably gave me bad karma and cost me the movie. I wanted to shoot a high-speed car chase around an old western town. (Sounds weird, I know, but if you read the script it did make sense.) I rented the Kleinberg back lot western town, then went out and got two rental cars. Knowing that my stunt drivers might have a scrape or two, I ticked off all the insurance riders on the rental form, then handed the cars over to the pair. Sure enough, by the end of the day, a few side panels had met a few hitching posts. Sorry, Avis's insurance company. Mea culpa. Bad karma. Nice sizzle reel. No movie.

Deliver Us From Evil

Pearson and me again—this time with an underwater teen horror film with a haunted shipwreck full of poltergeists. Good idea for a little popcorn flick, don't you think? We brought in a young writer; she turned in a good script. I enjoyed reading it—trouble is, no one else seemed to. I got distracted by the need to pay the mortgage, so had to abandon it and went off to make a thirteen part series of gynecology films. Meanwhile...

F.I.S.T. and *Phobia: A Descent into Terror*

Norman Jewison asked me to work as a directing intern on his Stallone labor-organizing flick; then soon after some producers asked me to play the same role for legendary icon John Huston on his

236

psycho drama. Don't really know why I turned them both down, but I always felt I should focus on my own projects, no matter how small, rather than work on other people's, regardless of how big. So they too make the list.

Paddle to the Amazon

Amazing true story of an old coot who, with the uncertain assistance of his two sons, paddled his canoe from his home in Winnipeg to the mouth of the Amazon River in Brazil. I spent months on the phone from L.A. with Don Starkell in Manitoba, trying to get the film rights to his book. He liked me, wanted to see a film get made, but he just couldn't get his ornery mind around the idea that he would have to share any film revenues with his book publisher—so, just to spite them, he refused to sell the rights. The only outfit that made anything out of this aborted deal was Sprint. If you think cellular long distance charges are high today, try to remember what they were like in 1990.

There Is No Second

Interesting subject for a film—the byzantine politics behind America's Cup Yacht Racing. I ran around Toronto and Los Angeles trying to finance this one for a while, but finally gave up—not the first loser in the America's Cup game. Eventually, a similar story was done—as *Wind*—by Carroll Ballard, a visually brilliant director who has famously had his own struggles getting his projects underway.

Bluenose

Another racing film—this time about the famous winning schooner that graces the Canadian dime. Producers Allan Levine, Gerry Arbeid, and I hustled this one for a while, with a good script from a veteran Nova Scotian writer, but it never hit the starting line. Neither I, nor anyone else, made a dime on this one.

Juliana and the Medicine Fish

Terrific juvenile novel about a teenage girl, a broken family, and a giant muskellunge that I thought would make a great film. The novelist, Jake Macdonald adapted a good screenplay from the material and I spent a year with him and producer Gary Howsam, with Graham Greene attached to headline it, trying to make it happen. They say a fisherman should expect to make 10,000 casts before he's going to land a musky. Sometimes it feels like the same ratio applies to feature films.

I kept trying to make it for a few years, but eventually my options lapsed, and Jake found someone else—a young producer in Winnipeg—who loved the story as much as I did, and wanted to have a go at it. After a year or so of hustling, he thought he had all the money raised, hired a cast and crew, and started shooting it. Not so fast, apparently. The money dried up in the first week, and the shoot imploded. What was supposed to be a big feature film ended up a patchwork half hour of cable TV. This can be a rough business.

Swimming With Eels

This was an important one for me. For years I wanted to tell the story of Marilyn Bell's 1954 swim across Lake Ontario, and the crazy Toronto newspaper wars that surrounded the famous swim. Finally I got at it, did a lot of research, met Marilyn and all the old reporters who battled each other to cover the swim—the first ever across Lake Ontario. I raised a lot of development money to write and re-write scripts, got various producers involved, and ultimately got connected with the ubiquitous CBC to make the show. In the end, though, the producer who made it for the network elbowed me out of the project, claiming that a film with a sixteen-year-old girl at its center needed a young female director. He hired one, and they shot it in Montreal, which doesn't look like Toronto and isn't on a lake. They made a mediocre film, left out what I saw as the most entertaining parts of the story, and created what I thought were libelous portrayals of her coach, and the CNE organizers of the swim. But, hey—no sour grapes from this kid.

Cheetah

After my two years in Africa in the early nineties, I wanted to get back to the dark continent, so collaborated with a veteran Hollywood television writer with credits that went back to *Dr.*

238

Kildare on the pilot script for this series about an African eco-warrior. This one literally crashed and burned. My collaborator, Gerry Sanford, was caught in the Northridge earthquake of 1994. He survived, but the walls of his apartment collapsed, buried, and destroyed his copy of our script. I still have mine, but I may as well throw it out one of these days. It's never going to get made.

Whirlwind

The U.S. Coast Guard employs swimmers who jump out of helicopters during raging storms to help people off sinking boats—but there are some within the Coast Guard who feel it is a foolishly dangerous way to try to save lives. Good dramatic material for an action film. Researched it, got a writer to script it, tried to get it made—but hey, rest in peace, it was lost at sea.

How They Make "The Simpsons"

Wouldn't it be fun to go backstage and see how *The Simpsons* gets made? I thought so, and pitched the idea to 20th Century Fox, which owns the series. They agreed; it might be a good film, and if they ever wanted to make it, and got everyone involved to agree to doing it, they'd do it themselves. Didn't need my help, thank you very much. I did get to spend a very interesting and fun afternoon drinking beer with Tim Long, one of their senior writer/producers, listening to his very funny stories about the show, so it wasn't completely a bust.

Snakehead Passage

In the late nineties the papers were full of stories about Chinese illegal immigrants, assisted by shady agents known as "Snakeheads", making their way to Canada and the U.S., many of them crossing the Pacific on leaky overcrowded freighters. I spent over a year on this one—writing it, getting a lot of enthusiastic support from the pay television network Movie Central, shooting yet another sizzle reel, running through budget after budget, casting it, hustling it around the Cannes Film Festival, presenting it at one of these formal pitch session competitions that have become fashionable (this one at the Toronto Film Festival)—and getting

239

really close to getting it made. Close only counts in the game of horseshoes, not in the game of feature filmmaking. Another script I was once passionate about that I should probably now toss in the recycling bin.

The Biograph Girl

I abandoned or disowned most of the losers in this chapter long ago. Not this one—I still think it could be a winner. Florence Lawrence was a girl from Hamilton, Ontario who became the world's first movie star, turning out dozens of movies for DW Griffith until her star was eclipsed by another girl from just up the lakeshore, Mary Pickford. Lawrence was abandoned and forgotten, scraping by as an extra at MGM, until she eventually committed suicide in 1938 at age 52. That's the real story. American writer William J. Mann used it as back-story for an inventive novel, imagining that Lawrence had faked her death, and creating the fictional conceit that she was found, living in a Hamilton nursing home and became a star all over again at age 102.

I bought an option on his book, and three of us wrestled it into a script. Great story about the movies, fame, success, and failure. The project itself failed in its first incarnation, but I still believe in it. Wanna finance a movie? This one could (still) be a winner.

Alien Invaders!

OLN gave me a nice chunk of money to shoot the pilot for this look at invasive animal species around the world. We put out a casting call for young personable biologists with charisma and stand-up comedy experience, willing to film an audition of themselves interacting with an exotic, dangerous animal. Seemed like a tall order, but over fifty video files showed up in our Dropbox. We picked the best seven, re-auditioned those, picked the best three and went off filming with them, chasing down Burmese pythons and Nile monitor lizards in the Florida Everglades, and urban monkeys in the streets and temples of Delhi, Vrindavan, and Jaipur. Turned out great. Everyone was keen on our three hosts and our work on the pilot, but when it came time to commit to moving from pilot to series, the corporate brass decided they wanted to spend all their money on *The Bachelor Canada*, not *Alien Invaders!*. It was back to the lab for my three biologists, on to a crazy spin-off for me.

Alien Eats

If the outdoor networks weren't biting on the idea of chasing invasive critters, maybe the food networks might chew on the idea of a show about eating them. Or so I thought. Invasivore cuisine, it's called. I went out and filmed the lionfish invasion of Florida and the Bahamas, and made a couple of sample reels with two prominent chefs, but the food networks all passed. Too weird. No bites at all on this one.

Indian Ink

The Aboriginal Network liked our proposal for a series in which a native tattoo artist would explore indigenous tattooing cultures around the world. At least, they liked it on paper. Once they saw our trailer, they decided they didn't like it so much. Another one bites the dust.

Bummed out yet by all this dismal failure? I am. Enough of all these fragile buds that withered on the vine. Instead, for the final chapter, let's explore a robust filming adventure that flowered and prospered.

Chapter 8
Angry Planet

Angry Planet plays on three networks in Canada, two in the U.S., and a variety of networks in Europe, Asia, the Middle East, and South America. I think we can call it a hit. Let me tell you how we made it.

The extremes of nature were our stock in trade on the show, and to that end we explored deep caves, climbed volcanoes, sailed out into big seas, hung out with any number of dangerous animals, and investigated the coldest, hottest, wettest, and driest places on earth.

It all started, though, with tornadoes. People love looking at tornadoes (from the safety of their living room—on TV) and we loved filming them. Sound like fun to you? Here's the primer on how to do it.

Tornadoes are found all over the world, but there is only one place on earth where they occur with sufficient frequency in terrain that makes chasing and filming them possible. We tried Australia and

Canada, and considered Argentina, but in those places there is too much chasing and not enough finding. In the U.S., east of the Mississippi, there are tornadoes (sometimes really big ones), but the hilly forests make for unpredictable forecasting and impossible chasing.

The only place to go is Tornado Alley—the swath of flat American prairie running from Texas north through Oklahoma, Kansas, and Nebraska to South Dakota. More tornadoes than anyplace else on earth; flat, flat country where you can see the big supercell thunderstorms forming from miles away, a great network of straight roads and few rivers (the bane of storm chasers) to get in the way. It is also, unfortunately, just about the most boring place on earth, but you can't have everything.

We would always base ourselves out of Norman, Oklahoma, home of the National Severe Weather Centre and an epicenter of supercell thunderstorm activity, but soon would find ourselves overnighting in any one of a thousand little towns or freeway motels across the Great Plains. Early every day, the storm-chasing host of the show, George Kourounis, and the other meteorologically hip guys we were traveling with would throw their bones, review a dozen weather websites, have arcane discussions about isobars and wind shear, hook echoes, and rear-flank downdrafts, make their decision about where our best target for the most extreme weather of the day would be, and we'd climb into our small fleet of vehicles, heading for a destination that might be as much as four hundred miles away. I would always travel shotgun in the thunderbird seat of George's storm-mobile, the car's floor below me littered with cameras, rain covers, lenses, batteries, chargers, maps, and notebooks. Chasing tornadoes is a bit of a strange business, reminding me a little of the old adage that has been applied to everything from warfare to flying airplanes to ocean sailing: "Long periods of boredom punctuated by brief moments of sheer terror."

It isn't actually usually terrifying, nor, if you're traveling, as I was, with someone who knows what they're doing, is it really as dangerous as it sounds. Normally you can track the twisters well enough so that you can stay out of their path (always a good idea) but get close enough to them to film them.

Fortunately George knew more about storm formation and had bigger cojones than most of the itinerant weather geeks out on Tornado Trail, so on our third tornado-themed show we decided we would up the ante by driving right into the dense inner area of the storm that chasers call "the bear's cage" to film the big hail that these supercells can produce. Even the most daring of tornado chasers usually try to steer clear of these most dangerous parts of the storms. Most sensible people don't want to get their cars pounded by the vicious hail, but George saw it as a badge of honour, so we'd dive into the midst of them. (He can name every obscure Kansas or Oklahoma one-stop-sign town where each dent on the hood of his storm-mobile was created.) Hail hunting is not a recommended practice, unless you are willing to risk your life for a TV show. As we wore caving helmets and leather jackets, even golf ball-sized hail wouldn't likely kill us. But a heavy hailstorm can be so dense it can wrap around a tornado, making the twister invisible both to the eye and to radar. Drive into one of those and you could be in big trouble. Fortunately, we managed to avoid any, came out with a new episode we called *Highway to Hail*, and moved on, unscathed.

Hurricanes are a different matter. You can't sit on the outside with them. If you want to film hurricanes, you have to get right inside them. We tried hard to capture Hurricane Isaac, a meandering Atlantic storm that threatened to pound the south shore of Newfoundland. I flew into St. John's with George and meteorologist Mark Robinson, landing as the outer rings of the storm were blowing the Newfie fog across the runways. We got ourselves well set up on Cape Spear (easternmost tip of North America), ready for the big storm to come ashore. Unfortunately, man proposes, but God disposes. While we waited, Mark, a stringer at the time for The Weather Network, called his contacts back at the station, to learn that the big storm had taken a sharp right out to sea, and the island had dodged the bullet. We were out of luck.

Hurricane Dean in Jamaica was a much better—and much worse—experience. We were well positioned for it, as we were chasing waterspouts in our *Angry Planet* speedboat *No Fear* in the Florida Keys as it made its way across the Atlantic, through the Antilles, and on toward Jamaica. Once we determined that it was likely to make a direct hit on Jamaica, we hauled the boat out of the water. We tucked it away, not knowing if we'd ever see it again, as the storm was then forecast to eventually hit Florida, and drove north up the Keys. In Key Largo we picked up Jim Lawrence, a guy considered to be the Grand Old Man of hurricane chasing, who commands an encyclopedic knowledge of hurricanes. If you want to know exactly what wind speeds Hurricane Gilbert was clocking two days before it slammed the Yucatan in September of 1988, Jim's the man with the answer.

We drove Jim up to Miami Airport, and the three of us jumped on a plane for Montego Bay. It is, not surprisingly, remarkably easy to get on a plane heading for a town about to be clobbered by a hurricane. Nobody else wants to go there. We each had our pick of the seats on the almost-empty jet—the last one for the island before they closed the airport. The scene at the Montego Bay terminal was of course quite different, with long lineups of tourists and locals desperate to get off the island before the big storm hit.

After filming the frantic departures for a while, we headed out and found a hotel to stay in. As they dropped all their lawn chairs into their pool for safekeeping and screwed plywood covers over their windows, I went out and found us a cab driver who would drive us the following day, taking us wherever we needed to go to get into the eye of the storm. I taped "TV" in big letters on the hood of his car to avoid getting hassled by the authorities on the shut-down roads, while Jim and George analyzed the various predictions to figure out where the wildest part of the storm would likely be.

The next day we drove into it, getting almost as far as Ocho Rios (with only one gas station still open) to search for the biggest waves, the strongest winds, the people in peril, the damaged boats, and flotsam-covered beaches. Frequently, we had to stop on the near-empty roads to pull downed trees and huge branches out of the way. George managed to (just) avoid being swept out to sea by the massive waves; I managed to keep the cameras dry, and Jim was able to observe us two young 'uns, carrying on the wet nutty traditions that he had begun fifteen years earlier. By late in the evening we were back at the hotel. The hurricane-chasing gods were with us. Neither the hotel, nor any of us, nor our taxi, nor our equipment had much more than surface damage from the big Category Four hurricane. The real drama, for us, wasn't until the following evening.

The next day we filmed some flooding and clean up. By the late afternoon the winds had died right down and the sun was even starting to peek out. All the electrical power on the island, though, was still down. That evening, even though there was a 6 p.m. national curfew, we decided to head out on to the dark streets of the town to look for a restaurant. Of course, typical of Jamaica, we were immediately glommed on to by some young guys. They wanted to "help us". They want to "show us where to go." They didn't want any money; they just wanted to "be our friends."

With these two hooligans in unwanted tow, we searched the dark streets for a restaurant, only to find that all were closed. We gave up, decided to return to the hotel, and began walking back. As we got closer to our hotel, our young pests changed their tune. They wanted some money for helping us out. We resisted.

"We never wanted your help," said George.

"You never did help," added Jim.

"Bugger off," said I. "Get lost."

We resisted, but they insisted. Finally, to get rid of them, I pulled out my wallet. In the darkness, I pawed through the Jamaican bills, trying to remember the exchange rate, trying to find an appropriate sum to pay off the pair. As I fumbled and hesitated, one of the pair whipped his hand out, grabbed my wallet, and took off running down the street.

247

"Holy shit!" I exclaimed.

George took off after the kid. I followed, running as hard as I could to try to keep up. About half way down the block the kid ran across the crowded road. George followed. I continued, running parallel with them, on the other side. The kid was heading for a dark downtown scrubby beachfront park—an unlit hangout, we learned later, for thieves and low-lifes. The kid weaved in and out of the oncoming traffic. George, momentarily forgetting that the ex-colonial Jamaicans drive on the wrong side of the road, ran right into an oncoming car. Running beside him, out of the corner of my eye I saw him get tossed up on to the hood like a movie stuntman. He slid across the windshield, rolled off the roof, and...kept on running.

There was a nineteenth century stone wall running alongside the park. The speedy thief found an opening in it, deked through, and disappeared into the darkness. Close on his heels, George was about to follow him through the gate into the park, when a streetwalker, lolling by the opening, addressed him.

"I wouldn't go through there, if I were you," she warned him.

He didn't. Instead, as I caught up to him, he checked himself for broken bones, and we found, to our amazement, he was a little bruised, but uninjured. The police came by, and were sympathetic and helpful (and very glad we didn't go into the thieves' park), but I never got my money or wallet back. We did, though, make it out of Jamaica in one piece, and made an episode out of it. Saved the mugging story for the book, though. Got to give you readers a few scoops.

The following year, we found ourselves tracking not one, not two, but three hurricanes that were simultaneously crossing the Atlantic toward the Caribbean and America. We decided, as briefly described in Chapter Three, to drive down to the south to link up with the first of them, Gustav, and see how things developed from there. Gustav crossed Cuba as a Category 4 hurricane and was aimed straight for New Orleans. We were headed there too, proceeding from the opposite direction. When we arrived, the city was like a ghost town. Only three years after Katrina had reminded them of their extreme vulnerability to Mother Nature, the city was now under mandatory evacuation. It became the largest mass exodus in American history—one that we had witnessed, and filmed, driving through Mississippi and Louisiana against a massive stream of thousands of vehicles heading away from the coast.

The city was now under martial law, with military personnel on every corner and Humvees rolling through the streets. All the big networks rolled into town with their satellite trucks and the journalists, us included, took over the one downtown hotel that was staying open (though with its windows covered and doors sandbagged against the expected flood).

At the last minute Meteo Mark and the other storm trajectory experts with us decided the storm was veering well west of the city, and so late in the evening before the morning it was predicted to make landfall, we packed up everything and abandoned our safe Marriott HQ, driving out into the storm. We had got to know many of the big network crews and reporters, especially Brian Williams, the anchor of NBC's Nightly News, and they watched us head out from the hotel into the night in our wacky vehicles, the roofs covered with stormchasing gear and spare gas cans. I think many of them envied our ability to fly by the seat of our pants and go where the wind blew us. Once the big American news-reporting machinery sets down, it can't always just pull up stakes and charge off into the unknown, as we could.

We drove across the rain-whipped bayous to the spot our weather boffins predicted would be the new bull's eye for the storm—the town of Houma, Louisiana, where we found a fairly bullet-proof open three storey parking garage, which we took over, setting up tents and hammocks to wait for the storm to arrive. By morning, the town was being pounded with 105 mph winds, and we were out in it, filming nature's wrath as it tore through the streets, canals, and creeks of the largely abandoned burgh. We all split up,

249

looking for the best action. At one point, George and I left the rest and were jumping through an abandoned downtown street that was littered with fallen and falling power lines. We never found out if they were live—it obviously made little sense to test them with a toe prod. Later, I lost him too, and stood alone on a big deserted street, filming a big hanging advertising sign in front of me, swaying violently in the wind. As I rolled the camera, on cue, the sign blew off its hinges, and crashed to the street below, shattering into pieces.

With Gustav captured, we returned to New Orleans to see what the National Hurricane Center had to say about the next piece of natural theater, which was, in traditional alphabetic order, Hurricane Hanna. Hanna had a unique path to it, making a complete circular loop just north of the Dominican Republic, killing more than 500 people in Haiti, and then heading for the US. It looked like it would make its American landfall somewhere in North Carolina, so we jumped in the storm-mobile and headed off to meet it. It was of course a long drive, this time heading in the opposite direction of a massive convoy of emergency vehicles heading into Louisiana for the mop-up of Gustav.

We met up with Hanna way up in Myrtle Beach. It was another remarkable and exciting storm, kicking up big waves, rattling windows, clogging drains with a massive dump of rain, and culminating at about three in the morning in a massive power failure that finally put an end to our filming.

The next in line, Hurricane Ike, biggest storm of the three by far, was still out at sea, gathering strength for a major hit—first on Cuba, then on the Texas Gulf Coast. We headed back south to meet it, wherever it decided to land. En route, I got on the phone with the U.S. Air Force. The Hurricane Hunters are a special wing of the USAF, based at Keesler Air Force Base in Biloxi, Mississippi, that fly directly into major hurricanes in specially equipped Lockheed WC-130J aircraft. It is pretty impressive aviation, thought completely impossible until American Colonel Joe Duckworth (egged on by some British trainee flyers) successfully flew a single-engine trainer aircraft through a Texan hurricane in the summer of 1943. It is still considered a dangerous thing to do. Five aircrews have died flying into the storms since the practice began, following Duckworth's flight.

We'd been trying to get a ride to photograph the Hurricane Hunters since we started the series. It was always difficult to arrange. They only confirm that a mission is a go at the last minute, and so they'll take you only if you're right there in Biloxi, ready to climb aboard. There had been missed opportunities, cancellations, and false alarms in the past. This time looked more promising. Ike was rapidly turning into a very big storm, and as it was approaching the Gulf Coast, from the Atlantic, so were we, from northern Georgia. As George drove south, I kept the telephone pressure on the media liaison lieutenant at Keesler. Keep bugging someone long enough and they'll finally say yes just because it will mean you'll stop phoning them. My guy finally said yes when we were somewhere north of Jacksonville. They were definitely headed out tomorrow, he told me. If we could be at the base by seven in the morning, we could get a ride—into Cuban airspace.

After exchanging high fives over our success, George put his foot to the floor and we booted across the Florida panhandle to Mississippi. When we boarded the next day we discovered we almost had the run of the massive plane. Along from the six-person crew, there were only four guests on the plane—a local print reporter, a visiting General, and the two of us. We rumbled down the runway in the big plane and took off into the Gulf. Within two hours we were entering the hurricane. To make things even more interesting, we were entering Cuban airspace—in a USAF plane. We didn't drop any bombs, but we did drop lots of weather reconnaissance dropsondes out of the belly of the plane, then received data from them about the gathering storm as they fell toward Cuba or the Caribbean.

Every time we made another pass through the inner bands of the storm into the eye we were shaken up and buffeted around. It's the second best roller-coaster ride in the world. (The best is the zero-

251

gravity parabolic space-training jet, the so-called "Vomit Comet" which we also flew on, for the show.)

Finally, with sufficient information gleaned from all the dropsondes, we packed it in and headed back to Mississippi. Once we landed, we learned that the storm had finally left Cuba, and was back over the hot Caribbean, picking up energy and wind speed as it plowed forward toward Texas. We bid our new Air Force buds goodbye, jumped in the storm-mobile, and booted it westward, looking for the optimum spot to meet it.

We set out for Galveston Island, which looked like it was going to be the bull's eye, but, again, the city was under mandatory evacuation orders, so we had great trouble finding a base to work from. Finally, with the storm only twelve hours away, we found the last available rooms in a chain beachfront hotel—one of the few that were remaining open. At least, it was until the lawyers at the hotel chain's corporate headquarters heard the latest NOAA forecast for the storm.

As we rose on the day Ike was going to hit, we heard it too:

"NOAA Weather Radio *Extreme Weather Alert* for Category Five Hurricane Ike. A mandatory evacuation order is in effect for the Texas Gulf Coast from Corpus Christi to the Louisiana border. Persons who have not evacuated may face certain death. Many residences of average construction directly on the coast will be destroyed. Widespread and devastating damage is likely elsewhere. Vehicles left behind will likely be swept away. NOAA urges absolute precaution; Ike is an extremely dangerous and life-threatening hurricane."

Yikes. And we're going to hang around and film it, all for your TV-viewing pleasure. Couldn't I have just dreamed up an idea for a nice little studio cooking show, instead of this?

No sooner had we heard NOAA's reassuring forecast than the room phones all began to ring. It was the desk clerk, telling us they had been told by head office they had to kick us out. We had to

252

leave within half an hour. They were closing the hotel, and evacuating.

Great. Now we're not just trying to film this thing, but trying to film it without a bunker to retreat to.

We hit the streets, driving down the beachfront boulevard with seventeen-foot waves crashing against the seawall, and sloshing across the road. The seawater would sometimes pick up the entire vehicle and slew it across the road.

By now, power lines were coming down, sparking fires across the city. The flooded roads meant fire trucks could not get to some of them, so the firefighters just watched, and the fires were just left to burn, sending black smoke billowing across the sky. Not so good for the owners watching their buildings and boats going up in flames, but, to be self-serving about it, dramatic footage for me.

Finally, we found a big, bulletproof hotel on the sea front that was remaining open as a base for the mayor, city officials, police, firefighters, and news crews. Mayor Lyda Ann Thomas, Anderson Cooper, and the rest had booked every room, so we just camped out in the parking garage and big lobby. Fortunately, our gang was smart enough to park their vehicles on the third floor of the garage. The cops filled up the first floor with theirs, and by the end of the storm every one of their cruisers was filled to the door locks with seawater.

The storm was at full velocity by midnight. The hotel staff had screwed wooden covers on all the first floor windows, and secured extra covers over the doors. Nonetheless, with all the firemen and police tromping in and out in their wet clothes, and the horizontal rain and sea spray squeezing through every crack, the fine carpets of the spacious lobby were soon soaked. An eerie, howling wind shrieked through the hotel. CNN had chained down some big klieg lights in front of the hotel, which was convenient for me. I was equipped with a Spintec Rain Deflector (a spinning glass device mounted in front of the lens, made in dry Israel, of all places), so with their lights and my rain protection, I was able to get out and get some footage of the storm. It was tough to go far though. Not one hundred feet in front of the hotel was a maelstrom of waves and flying debris. The previous night we had eaten in a Hooters on one of Galveston's piers. By now it had been completely destroyed, the roof and walls broken in pieces and hurled across the island, the fryers and fridges now in the ocean. At its peak, this ferocious storm made the winds we had experienced over the previous weeks with Gustav and Hanna look tame and pathetic.

At about 3 a.m., I had an interesting encounter with a survivor of the storm's fury. Once I heard the beginning of his story I turned the camera on him, cranked up the audio in order to hear him over the wailing wind. He was a commercial shrimp fisherman named Steven Rushing.

"Yeah, I was burnt by too many past warnings of storms that never amounted to anything," he told me, "so I decided not to leave my house. Then, when it hit, my relatives were begging me to evacuate, but it was too late. By midnight the water was pouring into the house, under the door and through the electrical outlets until I was in waist-deep water."

He decided they had to leave, and so, once the eye came over and the winds temporarily calmed down, he smashed through a window, climbed out and into the garage, where he had a ski boat, now floating in the deep water. He pushed it around to a doorway, pushed it open, picked up his wife, pregnant daughter and younger kids, and motored though the flooded Galveston streets.

"Finally it ran aground and we waded the last two blocks here. Heard this hotel was still open. Now I've probably lost the boat. Lost my house, probably lost my shrimp boat, too. Everybody's safe here, except for five puppies we had to leave behind. But we'll have to start all over."

After filming the terrible destruction the next morning, we determined to try to get off the island. We came close to a little disaster ourselves. Travelling in a convoy of three vehicles, we started

254

slowly making our way through the flooded streets. You never know in a flood whether you are going uphill or down, whether the water is getting shallower or deeper. Suddenly, it began to get deeper and deeper, and then, just as the vehicles ahead emerged on to dry ground, ours, not equipped with a snorkel on the air intake, stalled and came to a grinding halt. My driver got pretty mad. In four years of filming high-tension adventures, it was the first time I saw George lose it.

Our adventure came to an ignominious end as one of our storm chasing colleagues tied our vehicle to his with a piece of rope, and towed us out of Galveston. But our troubles were nothing compared to some of the sights we saw on the way out of town. The causeway was littered with big fifty-foot yachts and fishing boats (one of them, bizarrely, with the engine still running) that had been ripped from their marina moorings and hurled up on to the highway. The social order was starting to disintegrate as well, with the first signs of looting and arrests. Time to split.

Once we finally got off the island, we regrouped and began thinking about how to solve the car problem. There wasn't a gas station or store open for sixty miles in any direction, let alone a mechanic at work, so we were on our own. We came up with the crazy idea of disconnecting the hose to the windshield washers, unscrewing the sparkplugs, and then sucking the dirty seawater from the cylinders with the tube. I don't remember who got to do the sucking, but it wasn't me. I as usual had the excuse that I had to film the operation, so I avoided the dirty job. To our great relief (and surprise), it worked. We got rid of the water, sprayed a little WD-40 onto the pistons, put it back together and presto, it started. Good ol' Honda. We raced the remnants of the hurricane up the Mississippi valley, and headed home. Another episode in the can—one of my favorites, and an award-winner. It was the first of two that won CSC Awards for my cinematography. And George still drives his storm-mobile, now with 400,000 kilometers on it.

We specialized in covering the wettest weather places on

earth, but also went to some of the driest. We started with the most interesting and photogenic desert anywhere—the sculpted arches and buttes of Utah and Arizona. We moved on, as described earlier, to film an ultra-marathon running across Death Valley in the hottest week of the year. We later filmed in the brief storm season that hits the Great Australian Desert in early December, filming the water that almost instantly evaporated from flash flooding in one of the most drought-ridden parts of the planet. If you still don't believe in climate change, go check out the scorched Australian interior (or the melting glaciers of Argentina) and see what's happening there.

We crossed the Arabian Desert from Abu Dhabi almost to the Saudi border, travelling across the empty sand dunes in a small convoy of three 4WD trucks. There is a good reason they call this corner of the world the Rub' al Khali, or Empty Quarter. There is almost nothing there but sand. No towns, no people, no sounds, no bugs, no birds, not even any planes overhead. A few camels wandering around. Other than them, nothing. We learned how to drive (and how not to drive) in the soft sand, getting stuck and having to pull ourselves out, or dig ourselves out, dozens of times. If ever all of our vehicles had got stuck, our bones might be still there today. Fortunately, we had two pro German rally drivers with us, and they managed to always keep at least one vehicle operational to tow the others free.

Wanting to do an episode about the birthplace of hurricanes, we headed for the biggest and hottest desert on earth, the Sahara. Many of the windstorms spinning out of the hot sands are blown from the desert out in the Atlantic, some of them crossing all the way to the Caribbean and developing into tropical storms or hurricanes, given names like "Adeline" and "Beatrice". We flew into Bamako, the capital of Mali, then drove out through the intriguing Dogon Country and along the meandering Niger River, then north toward Timbuktu. There was no air conditioning in the Land Cruiser, and the heat was intense. I eventually ended up with heat exhaustion lying across the back seat, wearing nothing but my turban, wrapped around my midsection like a sarong, occasionally waking from my delirium to pour water on myself from my (now hot) water bottle, to try to cool off.

Eventually, as we did so many times in the Arab Emirates, we got badly stuck in the soft sand. This time, though, we had no associates to pull us out. Fortunately there was a tiny village of mud huts in the distance, and the men and boys came out in their djellabas to try to help. I was too far gone to participate, so I just moronically shouted impatient heat-crazed commands from the back seat. Eventually I dragged myself from the vehicle, and emerged to supervise. Some of these young kids living in the middle of nowhere had probably almost never seen strangers close up before. When they saw me, sweaty, wild-eyed, half naked, with blue dye from the wet turban streaking down my back and legs, they probably wondered if this was the "Great Satan" they had been warned about.

I recovered quickly in Timbuktu, and we spent several days there filming the fabled desert city. We knew there were U.S. and Canadian State Department warnings about travelling to Timbuktu, and recognized we were a bit conspicuous there with our white skin (actually, still blue, in my case) and big cameras. After a few days, our Malian guide started hearing street rumors, and got a bit nervous for our safety. There was concern that we might be the victims of kidnapping or at least banditry as we headed out of town and back south across the vast tracks of the Sahara. He decided to put out the word that we would be leaving the next day late in the afternoon, then instead, we rose very early and sneaked out of town via back alleys at 5 a.m. Either our ruse worked—or it was a false alarm. We had no issues and crossed safely back across the southern Sahara, eventually getting back to Bamako and home. It was a great experience, a good film, and there was a nice spin-off from it. Our fixer on the shoot, Ross Velton, had such a great time working on the film (his first) with us, that he completely changed his life plans, went off to London for some journalism training, and now follows our footsteps as a freelance reporter and videographer in Haiti and Latin America.

Being Canadians we were, of course, well positioned to take on the extremes of cold weather. We also knew how to dress for it. (When people complain of being cold, I quote the old maxim, which is that there is no such thing as bad weather, just bad clothing.) As has already been described, we took on -50° temperatures both in the Yukon and for many days and nights dog sledding and tenting on Baffin Island. We also tented in Antarctica—and, most memorably, kayaked there with a pod of fifty-foot humpback whales one stormy afternoon.

In order to film what they claim is "the world's worst weather", we bunkered in with the meteorologists at the top of Mount Washington, New Hampshire, for a cold and windy January week. The odd confluence of weather systems at the mountain peak create winds so extreme (231 miles per hour is their record) that some of the buildings at the met site are actually chained to the rock, to prevent them from being blown away.

The most entertaining winter filming we did was triggering avalanches in the Canadian Rockies. At one point we were with the Canadian military when they shut down the Trans-Canada Highway for a few hours at Rogers Pass in order to knock off some threatening cornices. While dozens and dozens of eighteen-wheelers and RVs idled at the roadblocks, we trundled out to the danger spots with the soldiers. They aimed their big howitzer up at the snowpack, and handed George the trigger.

It got even better when we crossed the border from Alberta into BC. There, their preferred method is to fly over the mountain, and drop bombs on the menacing snow. (Below, front-end loaders stand by, ready to push the results of the avalanches off the highways.) They took us up in their JetRanger, and as I filmed, George was given the delightful job of tossing the dynamite sticks out the open door of the helicopter. I'm not sure if women really get this, but men truly dig throwing bombs out of helicopters, especially when they aren't throwing them at other people, and aren't being shot at.

258

Well, it's all fun and games until you get to Calgary airport in order to fly home. We of course had been through dozens of airport security scanners for the series, and I'd had my fair share of hold-ups and hand inspections of all the photographic and audio gizmos I travel with. This, though, was the first time that the buzzers all went off and the entire security area went into red alert. Seems all that bomb throwing had left some nitro-glycerin residue on our star's fingers. For once I got to gloat. It wasn't the usual—him waiting for me to have all my crap pawed through, but rather me waiting as he got the full shake-down by Calgary security, who at the end of it all told him he'd made their day; it was the first time ever any of them had got to participate in a full-scale high-alert search.

Deserts and avalanches make great pictures—caves perhaps even better ones. I had filmed in three caves before *Angry Planet*— the spectacular Škocjan Caves of Slovenia, an abandoned cave/diamond mine in South Africa, and the undersea coal mines of Cape Breton Island, Nova Scotia. I knew them to be difficult but fascinating places to film in. On the new series we explored much deeper into more exotic and complicated cave systems. We started with a small cave in eastern Ontario, but upped the ante on it by swimming and kayaking into it in the dead of winter, with frigid temperatures rising to more reasonable ones as we descended deeper into the cave.

After the show had been on the air for a year, we were contacted by an experienced caver named Tony Morley who thought we should come with him and some fellow speleologists to explore the little known wet caves of northern Vancouver Island. We started by getting some training with them on rappelling underground by entering the Rat's Nest Cave in the Rocky Mountains. The Rat's Nest is closed off by a locked grate, but Tony had the key, so we hiked in to it, and entered, locking ourselves in once we were all inside so no one else could enter. If you are prone to claustrophobia, it is a bit of a strange feeling, locking yourself into a hole in the ground. Don't lose that key, Tony! I actually am prone to claustrophobia, but after flying in a jet fighter, being strapped into a Mach Three centrifuge, and scuba diving through dark underwater tunnels, I've just learned to control it with will power. The Rat's Nest had additional auditory charm—it was underneath a working mine, so as you crawled through it you frequently could hear dynamite explosions above you. Our training session included squishing ourselves through exceedingly narrow chimneys that are part of the labyrinth. One of them had been appropriately named the "Psyche Squeeze". Once Tony determined that we were not going to freak out underground, we all headed out to the Vancouver Island caves for the main event.

The Vancouver Island caves are far off the beaten path, and very difficult to find. We travelled down forgotten dirt logging roads, once spending nearly four hours tramping through the rainforest looking for an overgrown cave entrance. On a previous trip Tony and his pals had had a very bad car crash on one of the roads, and had to wait *three days* before anyone else came along to give them help.

One of my favorite caves there was called the "Vanishing River" where a reasonably large river just disappears into a hole in the rock, reappearing over a mile away. Are you an adventurous sort, disappointed that Everest has been climbed, Machu Picchu found and the whole world has been explored? The Vanishing River hasn't. Figure out a way to travel through that and you'll be the first person ever to do it. We didn't try. We did, though, enter the "Eternal Fountain" cave, a hidden picturesque beauty that you enter by going through a waterfall.

I promised you much earlier in the book to tell you of the dangers of over-heating. Here it is. The deepest cave our team entered required us to set up a long rope from an overhang down through wide, deep, open space into the cave. The four strongest cavers of the expedition—Tony, George, and two others—first descended the rope, then began exploring the wet cave from there. I situated myself on a ledge about a third of the way down, filming their descent and then their ascent. After an hour or so, Tony, the first one to start back up the rope, began "jugging" up using an ascender on the line. The trouble was, he was wearing a seven-mm.

wetsuit under heavy caving overalls to protect against the cold water of the cave. As he got midway up the rope, he began to realize that he was now very overdressed, and he began sweating profusely, overheating and weakening as he tried to pull himself up the rope.

It was a bit of an awful thing to film, as there was nothing we could do to help, as we watched him slowly struggle to haul himself up. I'm sure that he was beginning to see his life flash before his eyes, and think the end might be near, as he hung exhausted and baking eighty feet above the cave floor, with another fifty feet to go to the top. We shouted encouragement to him, but how much does that really help? He did finally make it, pulling himself over the final rocky lip with, I'm sure, profound, exhausted relief. George and the others, having witnessed this wicked slog from the bottom, wisely stripped off their wetsuits before ascending, and thus had a much easier time of it.

While in B.C., Tony told us of a cave that had just been discovered in Mexico—an extraordinary hot cave filled with the world's largest crystals—some of them weighing as much as thirty tons, one of them sixty feet long. It took me two years of negotiating to get permission to enter and film the Naica Crystal Cave in Chihuahua, Mexico, but the difficulties were well worth it. Only about sixty people have been fully inside the cave—most of them scientists and a few other photographers and filmmakers. The authorities there wanted to charge me several thousand dollars to enter the cave, and told me they would only allow a team of two people to explore it. I pleaded for three, and when they agreed I invited Nik Halik, a very successful Australian financial wizard and adventurer to join the expedition with us. Nik had already descended to the Titanic aboard the Mir submersible, managed to convince the Egyptians to allow him to sleep overnight inside one of the tombs of the Pyramids, and spent a million dollars training with the Russians to fly to the space station (though they reneged on the deal, and bumped him from his flight for the Cirque du Soleil's Guy Laliberté, who paid $40 million for the privilege.) He had also travelled to Antarctica and through Tornado Alley with us. We knew Nik to be a great travelling companion—and he was willing to share the high costs of this new adventure.

The Crystal Cave is 1000 feet below ground and very close to a magma chamber (an underground pool of liquid rock), and thus has temperatures of over 120° F (49° C), and 90 to 99% humidity. I decided I'd better go into training for this one. At the time I had a sauna in my house, so I sat in it daily, cranking the heat higher and higher, lowering my sensitivity to extreme heat, and also testing out the cameras and microphones to see how they would perform in the extreme environment.

We decided to apply to the Explorers Club to do the trip as an authorized flag expedition, and so once we were approved, we began by flying to Manhattan to pick up the flag, then flew down to Dallas and Chihuahua. The Mexicans were well organized for us, providing us with full refrigerated suits and respirators that would blow cool air into our lungs and onto our eyes, preventing them from burning up. They also had a paramedic on site for us, who took our blood pressure before and after entry of the cave, and would have stopped us from returning to the deadly chamber had we exhibited any signs of stress. They allowed us twelve fifteen-minute entries from the cool (100° F) antechamber, into the Crystal Cave, over the period of one long day.

It was amazing how taxing the cave was on your body. After each entry, you would return to the antechamber, doff all their refrigeration and respiration equipment, drink a full two-liter bottle of water, then collapse in front of a fan. After zonking out for twenty minutes of recovery, you'd get up to prepare the gear to go back in.

It really is the most spectacular environment on earth, with thousands of massive perfect selenite crystals hanging from the ceiling and walls, formed over millions of years while the cave was filled with hot, still water. It was only because of the mining activities that the water table was lowered sufficiently to drain the cavern and reveal the crystals, first to a pair of miners who broke through the wall in 2000, searching for lead, zinc, and silver, and instead found a

262

natural cathedral of selenite. One of these days, perhaps soon, the mine will close down, turn off their pumps, and the hot water will return, filling the cave up so that it can never again be seen by human eyes.

You'll recall at the end of Chapter One I learned of Kenya's Elephant Cave, and determined to go there one day for the series. I tried to get things going a couple of times, but Kenya, especially the western area around Mount Elgon, where the cave is, was in violent turmoil for well over a year because of the national elections. Finally, the political conditions improved, and the timing seemed right, so we set out on an elaborate travel itinerary that would take us not just to Kenya but on to Russia, Uzbekistan, Ukraine, and Turkey, and one where the dangers were invisible but deadly—rabies, Marburg virus disease, anthrax, plague, and radioactivity.

In Nairobi, we linked up with a Kenyan film production company, who looked after the local logistics, and we set out to cross the country by Land Cruiser. I timed our expedition for October, as that is one of two times of the year when it is possible to witness one of the most spectacular (and angry) sights of nature—the massive migration of millions of wildebeests and zebras from the Maasai Mara National Reserve south toward Tanzania. The climactic moment of the migration is the crossing of the Mara River, where hundreds of crocodiles lie in wait for the ungulates, and dozens of vultures circle above preparing to dine on the remains.

The worst phrase you can hear as a nature, adventure, or extreme-weather filmmaker is, "You should have been here last week." We had heard it before—most memorably while trying to film forest fires in the Yukon, when we apparently had just missed that most elusive and awesome of angry natural phenomena—the fire tornado. Now, we heard it again, in Nairobi, where local knowledge had it that we were too late—the animals had likely all crossed the river by now. Local knowledge is usually right, but this time, fortunately, my long-distance research was right, and they were wrong. When we arrived in the Maasai Mara, our local guides there got us out to a spot on the Mara where we found thousands of wildebeests and zebras, pawing at the banks of the river, nervous, agitated, quite obviously aware that swimming across the fast moving, croc-filled river was extremely dangerous, but driven by some intense evolutionary need to cross it and head to the grasslands in the south.

The lighting was right, our vantage point was right, both the protagonists and antagonists of the drama were assembled, and finally, one brave zebra bolted into the river and began swimming. The rest watched for ten or twenty seconds, then, as he seemed to be making it, followed, en masse. The river was soon filled with animals, swimming and wading for their lives. The great majority made it, but as I rolled camera one unlucky wildebeest was taken down by a croc, drowned, and eventually eaten. Many more had been captured by the giant sixteen-foot crocs, though not on camera. We later found a bone yard on a curve of the river, where I filmed George talking to camera while surrounded by the bones and carcasses of hundreds of animals who had come to an unfortunate end in the dangerous waters.

We moved on to Mount Elgon, and climbed (first by Land Cruiser, then on foot) to the unique Elephant Cave high on its flanks. It is, as far as is known, unique in the world—a cave carved out of the rock by elephants. It is a beautiful cave, with a waterfall pouring across part of its mouth, a giant open cavern leading into a complex cave system consisting of passages and chambers littered by large pieces of rock that have fallen down from the roof. While researching it I discovered it had been mapped, by a California biologist and bat expert named Don McFarlane. I contacted him, and in the end brought him with us to help us explore the cave. Don had the same interest in the cave that we did—the extraordinary, unusual creation of the cave, carved by elephants, and the strongly suspected, but unproven allegation that the cave was possibly the home of the deadly Marburg virus disease, a hemorrhagic fever nearly indistinguishable from Ebola virus. Two of the very first human victims of the gruesome pathogen had both been in the cave shortly before exhibiting symptoms of the disease.

On the hour-long hike up from the dirt road, Don told us of three more potential dangers in the cave. Not only did elephants enter the cave searching for salt, but also other animals—including hyenas. The back galleries were absolutely teeming with bats. Were they rabid? Did they carry the Marburg virus? No one wanted to use personal experience to find out—though one of us soon would find out whether at least one of the flying mice was carrying deadly pathogens.

As well as the hyenas, elephants, and bats, the entrance to the cave was also home to a large population of hyrax. These rotund furry little mammals look harmless, but they carry a parasitic flea on them that transmits leishmaniasis—another gruesome tropical disease, not quite so deadly as Marburg, but still one you don't want to catch. Oh, yes, and I forgot—one more danger Don warned us of—breathing in the dust kicked up by walking through bat poop can be extremely bad for your lungs—and there was about 10,000 years worth of bat poop on the cave floor we'd be walking on.

Taking note of these various dangers, we set up shop inside and got to work exploring and filming the cave and its residents and visitors. To protect us from these miscellaneous hazards, I brought along gas masks, goggles, and full protective suits. Truthfully, while they did look a bit like the very official white hazmat suits you see guys wearing in movies with names like *Virus* and *Contagion*, they were actually disposable house painters overalls that I picked up at Home Depot. With luck, the germs wouldn't notice the difference and would be scared off by them.

The lads brought their own gloves. In Don's case—padded leather gloves. In George's, two pairs—one leather, the other thin medical rubber gloves. Confusion over which pair to wear almost led to disaster.

As for lighting up the dark remote cave, I came up with a novel solution. I had purchased a big truck battery and a charger for it in Nairobi, and now we suspended the heavy battery from the middle of a long bamboo pole, and two of our porters carried it up the mountain to the cave. From there it was up to us—they weren't going in. I just dragged the battery, an inverter, and a big Chimera soft light behind me on a makeshift toboggan, with George and Don helping yank it through the more convoluted passages.

How the elephants had made their way deep into the pitch-black depths of the cave I don't know. After all, they can't see in the dark any better than we can. But the evidence was there—deep inside we could plainly see where the big pachyderms had tusked away at the walls of the cave, gouging it in their quest for salt. We did come upon the skeleton of a buffalo that had presumably slipped off the path in the dark, broken its leg, and died there. There are also crevasses where young elephants have sometimes lost their footing and ended their lives in the depths of the cave.

Every day, we explored deeper and deeper into the cave as well. Finally, at the back of it, we found a gallery roof covered with thousands of sleeping bats. As I shone the light on them, they began to wake up, and hundreds of them started flying around us. Don decided this was a perfect opportunity to try to capture one of the beasts for his research. He went running up the slope into the sea of flying bats, arms outstretched, trying to grab one from the air. After a short beat, George, in his usual fashion, tried to help. He too went running into the bats, trying to catch one for Don's research lab, and, of course, for our film. Naturally I rolled camera on all this action.

Don was the first to catch a bat. A minute later, George snatched one from the air, too. Only trouble was, George had forgotten that he was not wearing his thick leather gloves, but only his thin surgical ones. As the captured bat squirmed around in his hand, it twisted around—and bit him right through the thin latex into his thumb.

Oh, gawd. Now we had a major crisis. Don took the nippy little bat, and George peeled off the glove. Sure enough, just like in vampire movies, there were the bite marks, a little blood dripping from them. He was scared—but he was still working. I continued to roll video on him; he continued to do his TV host thing, breathily describing to camera what had just happened. I pulled out my first aid kit, but, hey, I think I bought it at Home Depot along with the overalls. It was designed more for junior's camping boo-boos than for curing obscure tropical diseases. There was no rabies serum, nor any Marburg virus antidotes in it. So, we slapped some Polysporin on, bandaged him up, and waited to see if there were any symptoms. We also discussed what we were going to do next. Were we headed home, to the land of Canada's famous skilled doctors and universal health care? No—we were headed for Uzbekistan, which is not so well known for its advanced medical clinics. Specifically, we were headed for the dusty desert that was once the Aral Sea—one of the worst centers for tuberculosis in the world. Even more specifically, we were headed within a few miles of Vozrozhdeniya Island, one of the most disgusting charnel houses on earth, still infected by thirty years of Soviet testing of anthrax, smallpox and bubonic plague bio-weapons.

However…George didn't exhibit any symptoms at all of any problems from the bat bite. Good ol' Polysporin. So we continued our filming, wrapped our shoot, headed back to Nairobi, bid Don farewell in London, and set off for Moscow, then to Tashkent, then, at four in the morning, right across Uzbekistan to the dusty city of Nukus. Following thirty-four hours of driving and flying after leaving the cave, we recuperated briefly in the desert town on the Turkmenistan border. Soon, we were linking up with our guide for the new adventure, Octyabr Dospanov (named for the celebrated month of the 1917 revolution), and we were off on another long Land Cruiser expedition into the wilderness. This time our goal was not to see natural disaster, but instead manmade disaster, specifically the eco-disasters created under the former Soviet Union.

We started by driving out for a couple of days to the town of Mo'ynoq. Mo'ynoq was probably first built in the Middle Ages, peaked in the 1970s, and is now rapidly declining back into its medieval past. For thirty years it was a center of the USSR's fishing industry, but today it is perhaps the only fishing town in the world that is over seventy miles from the nearest water. The Soviets, and to a degree, the Tsars before them, thought they could turn the deserts of Uzbekistan into fertile ground for growing cotton, so over the years they diverted all the rivers that ran into the Aral Sea—once the fourth biggest lake in the world (so big, they called it a "sea", though it was then fresh water). The sea has now shrunk—to less than *one tenth* of its previous size—in less than thirty years. What is left (far from Mo'ynoq) is now polluted, and salty. The fish have all but disappeared.

In Mo'ynoq, we explored the huge fish packing plants (abandoned), the airport (awash with broken glass and yellowing, discarded waybills and boarding passes), and the fishing port. The sea is now dried up. Camels roam across the old seabed, and numerous rusting, eighty-foot fishing trawlers lie derelict on the sand. From Mo'ynoq, our little convoy headed north, off-road (actually, on-sea). It took us a day of driving before we finally saw water, and when we finally got there Octyabr was shocked to see that it had retreated much further from the last time he had visited—only a month previous. We camped out on the cold desert wilderness, and pushed north, almost to the Kazakhstan border.

We wanted to get as close as we could to Vozrozhdeniya Island, the evil island that was home to a Soviet biological weapons research center from the fifties to the nineties. Hey, George wasn't infected by Marburg virus in Africa. Let's see if he's susceptible to anthrax or bubonic plague here.

The Aral Sea has dried up so much that the island is now a peninsula, joined to the mainland. This has environmentalists alarmed, as they fear that rodents and small animals may now be able to get to the island, become infected by the remnants of the research station pathogens, and then wander out into the countryside. We got close, but weren't able to quite get on to it, which was perhaps a good thing. Eventually, we headed back, exploring northern Uzbekistan and then returning to Tashkent. We travelled around the big old Silk

Road city on the elegant subway system, replete with chandeliers hanging in the stations, built very deep with long, long escalators, to double as nuclear bomb shelters during the Cold War. While travelling on the subway we were accosted by secret police guards, demanding to see our passports and seeming to suspect us of being spies. I suppose, in a way, we were.

We flew on to Ukraine, to film the remnants of a notorious disaster far more dangerous than Vozrozhdeniya. En route, we explored a recently uncovered Soviet bunker straight out of James Bond—or Austin Powers. In Balaklava (home of the famous headwear worn by skiers—and bank robbers), the Russians carved out a mountain, turning it into a giant secret submarine pen. Gates in the mountain opened to allow the subs to enter underwater, and surface inside in underground canals. To muffle the sounds and provide an excuse for all the traffic at the site, the Soviets built a fake quarry on the side of the mountain. They claim the Americans never cottoned on to their big *SMERSH*-like lair, although whether the CIA's U-2's and satellites and real spies all missed the mountain sub nest is something only they know for sure. It all made for a cool little sidebar part of the show, but it wasn't life-threatening enough for *Angry Planet*, so we headed off to...Chernobyl.

The Chernobyl disaster was the worst nuclear accident ever—a massive explosion and fire that released a dangerously huge cloud of radioactivity into the atmosphere. The accident, on April 26, 1986, was kept secret by the Soviets, until a Swedish nuclear plant, nearly 800 miles away, began detecting such high levels of radioactivity in the air that they thought their own plant was having a meltdown. There was a huge evacuation in the Ukraine, though in many cases it was too late. An independent Russian report claims there were over a million premature cancer deaths from the disaster between 1986 and 2004. Officially, Russia disputes this number, but not the quarter of a trillion dollar cost expected to be the final bill for the clean up—an amount that virtually bankrupted the USSR. "Clean up" is not the right expression, for the "Zone of Alienation"— nineteen miles in all directions from the reactor—will not be habitable, it is predicted, for 20,000 years.

A perfect story for *Angry Planet*. But how to do it? The area is closed to journalists and to the public—though we heard that in 2008 things were loosening a bit and it might be possible. The Ukrainian Falun Gong movement (remember Falun Gong—from Chapter Five?) caught wind that I wanted to film their country's most notorious landmark. They thought of me as a hero, for having made *Beyond the Red Wall*, and they wanted me to come to Ukraine— mostly so they could do interviews with me for their own films and magazines. They pulled a few levers and talked to the right people, and suddenly it was arranged. George and I could get in to the closed Zone of Alienation, the abandoned "Atomic City" of Pripyat, and Chernobyl. In fact, if we wanted to, we could stay right inside the Zone of Alienation, for two nights. (More, they thought, might be dangerous.) Well, why not? In for a penny, in for a pound. I'd already sired two lovely children, and George didn't want any, so we were good.

We drove in from Kiev, through many checkpoints and guard gates, to a compound close to the central dead zone, where they provided us with rooms in a barracks-like building (where we and our translator Anna were—surprise!—the only guests), then proceeded to offer us vast quantities of inedible food. And, uh, just asking, but where did the animal that provided us with this mystery meat live, exactly? Wasn't one of those pigs we saw on the drive in from the gates, was it? I asked Anna, but she just smiled, and didn't bother passing on my query to the cook.

From there we moved on to see Pripyat. Amazing, awful place. Life just ended there the day they rounded up all 49,000 inhabitants, put them on buses, and drove them away. Pencils are still on school desks, lying beside picture books about Lenin and Marx. Hospital beds still have blankets on them, cupboards still stocked full of drugs, bandages and syringes. The paint is peeling off the walls, but there is no vandalism, since no one can get in to vandalize. Our guides warned us against walking on the moss that

270

grows on sidewalk cracks, as it is a sponge, sucking up high levels of radioactivity that might contaminate our boots. But apart from that, we had free rein, and could go wherever we wanted. We explored the hospitals, the schools, the stores, and apartments. I photographed dolls, left behind in the grass, now weathered by the severe winters and the summer sun, but unmoved, since little Sonia dropped them there in April of 1986. Our favorite photo-op was an elaborate travelling carnival, set up in a park, ready to open the day of the disaster. Weeds now grow through the bumper cars. The rusting seats of the abandoned Ferris wheel squeak as they sway gently in the wind.

After more fine dining, and another night's stay at the Chernobyl Hilton, the next day we visited the ponds and rivers where firemen had sucked water to fight the blaze, and where contaminated heavy water from the reactors had been dumped. From there we moved on to the main show—the ruined reactor itself. As we approached it, I held a Geiger counter out the car window, and filmed it. All the labels and instructions were in Cyrillic, so I didn't know what the numbers exactly meant, but I did know they were rising, and the pace of the clicking increasing, as we approached the big site.

When we got to Reactor Numbers Three and Four (the really bad ones), Sergei gave us our marching orders. We could move to within about 300 feet of the site, and we had exactly fifteen minutes to stay there, if we wanted to keep living. Anna translated for us. He pulled out his little cell phone, and set the timer. It was a bit like Andy Warhol's famous "Fifteen minutes of fame", except this time it was "fifteen minutes and you flame".

Filmmakers are notorious for pushing the time constraints and wearing out their welcome. Not in this case. If Sergei thought fifteen minutes was the limit, we didn't argue with him. He punched the button on his phone, and we began moving at high speed, getting it done. Between us, over the years, George and I had referred to a lot of our seat-of-the-pants cinematography on the series as "Shake 'n

Bake" shooting. This time, we were really flying. Er—frying. By the time his phone timer hit 14:59, we had got what we got (or not—whatever), jumped into Sergei's Lada and I gave him that familiar phrase, "That's a wrap. Let's get out of here." He didn't require a translation to know what to do.

Nothing like a beeping Geiger counter, a countdown timer, and the threat of sterility to focus the task at hand. Fifteen minutes was enough time for me to get what I needed. Although you haven't had anyone timing you, I'm sure the few hours or days or whatever it has taken you to read this are all you really need (and want) to learn about my life, and my adventures in filmmaking. Thanks, dear reader, for sticking with me to the finish line. I'll end the story here, with the sun setting behind us as we drive away from the abandoned shell of the destroyed, ruinous nuclear plant, heading out to the fresh air and green grasses of Ukraine, and then, on home.

Thanks

Filmmaking adventures cost money. My first thanks go to all the producers, networks, agencies, investors and supporters who made the financial commitments that made these film projects happen.

The biggest and longest-running production described in the book, *Angry Planet*, would not have happened without the support of our Production Executive at OLN, Patrice Baillargeon. He was an extremely supportive and creative network executive. Without him this book would be considerably shorter and less interesting.

George Kourounis was an extraordinary collaborator on most of the 21st Century adventures described in the book.

A special thanks to my editor Marjorie Lamb. Marjorie is a skilled writer and editor, whose enthusiasm for the book meant a lot to me, and whose skillful editing has made it a better read for you. She can be found at <http://tinyurl.com/writerinres>.

Many thanks also to my team of beta readers, who made invaluable suggestions while I was finishing the manuscript. They included Jeff Willner, Michaele-Sue Goldblatt, Barry Pearson, Ashley Rowe, Nancy McLeod, Allan Levine, Lesley Rowe, Jason Schoonover, Patricia Murphy, and Stephen Broomer.

Finally, and most importantly, I would not have been able to spin around the world making films for the last twenty years without the support from my wife Carolyn and our two daughters, Ashley and Brianna. Carolyn's uncomplaining endorsement of my travels and encouragement of my work simply meant the show could go on.

19606694R00151

Made in the USA
Charleston, SC
02 June 2013